Contemporary Accounting and the Computer

Dickenson Series on Contemporary Thought in Accounting
John W. Buckley, Editor

*Contemporary Studies in the Evolution
of Accounting Thought* — Michael Chatfield

*Contemporary Thought on Federal
Income Taxation* — Charles J. Gaa

*Contemporary Accounting and Its
Environment* — John W. Buckley

*Contemporary Accounting and the
Computer* — Leonard W. Hein

forthcoming:
*Contemporary Cost Accounting and
Control* — George J. Benston

Contemporary Auditing — Wayne S. Boutell

*Contemporary Studies of Behavioral
Science in Accounting* — G. H. Clawson

*Contemporary Studies in International
Accounting* — Paul Kircher

*Contemporary Accounting
Theory* — Eldon S. Hendriksen

*Contemporary Accounting
and Management
Information Systems* — Norman H. Carter

Contemporary Accounting and the Computer

Leonard W. Hein

California State College, Los Angeles

Dickenson Publishing Company, Inc.
Belmont, California

Library of Congress Catalog Card No.: 79-90785
Printed in the United States of America

To my wife, Mildred

Contents

Foreword

Advances in accounting thought and practice occur with such rapidity that the traditional textbook is often out of date before it reaches the student. Furthermore, new contributions to accounting are distributed among numerous technical journals, and neither the teacher nor the student can cope efficiently with this immense and scattered mass of knowledge. . . .

In accounting instruction there is a tendency to concentrate on techniques while neglecting to relate these techniques to the empirical world. For example, elementary accounting texts often focus on bookkeeping mechanics and fail to give the student an awareness of the social environment within which accounting operates, or of the interaction of accounting with its environment. Similarly, introductory tax courses may emphasize rote learning of the internal revenue code, while important topics in taxation theory, legislation, and administration are left unattended. Of course, a textbook orientation is justified by the abundance of technical skill and knowledge required of an accounting student, but it is increasingly important to update textbook material, introduce students to the cultural dimension of accounting, and relate the technical textbook material to contemporary accounting practice. . . .

The paperback volumes in the DICKENSON SERIES ON CONTEMPORARY THOUGHT IN ACCOUNTING, therefore, are designed to serve two main functions: (1) to bring together in one volume the best contemporary thought in each subject area, and (2) to extend the student's understanding of the subject matter beyond the textbook's necessary limitations. Important savings in faculty and student time may be realized by giving the student, in a single volume, the reading materials that the instructor would most likely wish to assign if he exhausted the journal literature on a particular subject and selected the most appropriate articles. Also, by providing a broad exposure to the subject area and its environment, the instructor may perform a better service for his students than he would by relying solely on instruction in the technical skills of accountancy.

Although there is a relationship between the books in the series and conventional accounting courses, teacher experimentation with these materials may suggest their appropriateness to new courses.

The editors hope that their selections will stimulate teachers' and students' awareness of the new advances in accounting thought and practice.

John W. Buckley
Series Editor

Preface

The electronic computer was born in 1946. The popular press immediately christened the newborn infant *giant brain* and then proceeded to prophesy that the electronic monster would some day (perhaps) rule man. The more conservative of these prognosticators predicted that the new marvel at least would extend the power of man's mind as much as prior mechanical developments had extended the power of man's body.

Accountants are by nature conservative. During the period immediately following the above noteworthy event, they generally were unmindful of its potential impact on their profession. Even the much-vaunted daring and farsightedness of the American businessman appeared to be lacking during the early days of computer development. For it was the United States government, so frequently categorized as sluggish and unimaginative, which saw the data processing potential of the electronic computer. The first large-scale, general-purpose, electronic computer (the UNIVAC I) was installed in the Bureau of the Census in 1951.

Three years passed before business attempted a similar installation. In 1954, General Electric placed into operation a similar UNIVAC I. Thus the use of the large-scale electronic computer in processing accounting data became a reality.

Did accountants then respond actively to the challenge? No, indeed. Many felt and some still feel (perhaps rightly so) that accounting theory is independent of the means of bookkeeping. But accounting theory is just one segment of the discipline of accounting. Two other areas, auditing and systems design, are far from being independent of the means of processing data. So the accountant is finding that the electronic computer is obtruding more and more upon his thoughts and upon his practice. Even that most conservative of organizations, the American Institute of Certified Public Accountants, was forced belatedly to recognize the impact of the computer upon the practice of its members. This august body in 1965 (a long nineteen years after the computer was born) cited as one of its major objectives research into the present and future effects of the computer on the profession.

Clearly, then, the contemporary student of accounting must also consider and study these effects. There is no longer a dearth of articles on computers in the accounting literature. The pendulum has swung, so that now the number of articles is so great that some selectivity is required. Rare, indeed, is the student who would be willing or could find the time to wade through this voluminous literature.

The literature appears to be classifiable into twelve generally distinct categories. Nevertheless, some articles are sufficiently broad so as to extend beyond the bounds of one or more of these artificial topic areas. This volume comprises thirty-one articles which make, I believe, a significant contribution to each of the twelve areas. The selection was not an easy task because of space limitations, and many significant articles had to be omitted. Except for the historical category, and because of the rapid advances of computer technology and resultant application utility, preference has been given to the more recently published material.

The utility of this collection of articles in the accounting curriculum is limited only by the ingenuity of accounting professors. Its primary use is as an adjunct to the first course in principles of accounting. Here appears to be the best place to appeal to the imagination of young accounting students. But it can also support many other courses in accounting, for example, intermediate, auditing, systems, cost or managerial accounting, as well as a basic course in data processing.

The first area (Part 1) covers the relationship of the accountant to EDP (electronic data processing). Just what this relationship should be is far from settled. Accounting opinion ranges from "no knowledge of EDP required," to the other extreme, that "the EDP system should be designed and controlled by the accountant."

Part 2 presents some of the basic computer concepts necessary for the understanding of items covered in the other articles.

Three important historical events are presented in Part 3. While the accounting world generally ignored the advent and early development of the computer, one farsighted accountant was an exception. His recognition of the importance of computers to accountants is contained in his article "Electronics in Accounting." Although many other important historical events could be cited, two of the most important from the viewpoint of the accountant were the first installation of a large-scale business computer, and the development of the third-generation computer.

Parts 4, 5, and 6 cover three important areas of the accountant's practice, namely, auditing, internal control, and information systems.

The question of whether or not to install an electronic computer, and if so, which one, is of prime importance to business managers. But is this a task for the accountant? The accountant's role is explored in Part 7.

Will the computer have any significant effects upon management practices and upon the organization structure? What the accountant should know about these important areas is discussed in Parts 8 and 9.

For what actual accounting applications are electronic computers being used? Can the small business profitably utilize such applications? The list of potential applications is long and varied. Some sample applications are presented in Part 10 with further suggested readings listed in the bibliography at the back of the book. The use of the service bureau by the small business is covered in Part 11.

One of the most powerful uses of electronic computers is in the area of business simulation. Three important articles on this topic are presented in Part 12.

I wish to express my sincere appreciation to the authors and publishers who so generously granted permission to reprint the articles used.

Los Angeles, California   Leonard W. Hein

Contemporary Accounting and the Computer

1 EDP AND THE ACCOUNTANT

Information Technology and the Professional Accountant

Gordon L. Murray

Historians of our profession will inevitably have to conclude that the accountant of our times was afforded unique opportunities, for it was in the early 1950s that the business world first attempted to apply computers to its operations, and since then, in a brief span of years, production of computer equipment has proliferated, a broad body of data processing techniques has developed, and now information technology is emerging that is concerned not only with generating and processing data but also with more effectively communicating and utilizing the output of such computer systems as may feasibly be built.

That the accountant is affected by these developments is clear, for data and information are at the very core of his professional interest. The nature and degree of these effects remain to be clarified. Some accountants may be merely witnesses to developments and may only adapt traditional approaches and techniques to new situations as best they can. Others will not only participate in shaping these events but will assert active leadership. Much remains to be done, and so far our profession has done precious little in relation to both the magnitude of the problems that require solution and

Reprinted by permission of the author and the publisher from *Management Services*, Vol. IV, No. 6 (November–December, 1967), pp. 15–21.

the dimensions of the opportunity to establish a position as leaders in the field.

Whether historians ultimately report a gain or loss in the stature and role of the accountant during the remainder of this century will depend largely on the effectiveness of our current response to these opportunities.

This article, therefore, proposes to explore in broad terms what is going on in this field and then to focus on a few of the more fundamental questions the imaginative accountant will be seeking to answer.

We hear elaborate predictions of a computerized society. These, and the strange technical language associated with computer systems, tend to obscure some fundamental facts.

Data Processing Not New

Data processing has been an inherent activity of man since he first recognized that reliance on memory provided an insecure basis for action. His response was to record the information he acquired, and once it was recorded he saw the possibilities in manipulating and analyzing it and the advantages of recording the results for future reference. The essential procedures of data processing—classifying, sorting, calculating, summarizing, recording, communicating—have not changed. They continue to be the basic operations performed in all data processing irrespective of the equipment or techniques applied.

The changes that have occurred lie in man's newfound ability to perform basic data processing operations more efficiently—matters of equipment and technique—and to better define his information needs—a matter of analysis and understanding. Progress has, of course, been made on both of these aspects. Historically, however, major attention has been first on equipment capability and processing techniques; only in recent years has the priority of emphasis shifted to delineation of information needs. This is not to say that advances over the years in the degree of sophistication of business information have not been significant. They have been. But it seems to me that in this field we usually invent a better machine and then seek a use for it, rather than the other way around. Perhaps we have traditionally developed better engineers and mechanics than we have people who have the interest and ability to analyze the complexities of the business organism and then to identify all of its relevant informational requirements.

The existence of this order of priority of attention between equipment/techniques and information requirements is especially clear with regard to the present state of the art—data processing by electronics through use of the computer—because the computer was not invented to process business data but rather was borrowed from more scientific fields. Having been borrowed, it has been subjected to modification and adaptation to fit the business applications at hand. Essentially it has been applied to do what was already being done, but in greater volume, at faster speeds, and hopefully, but elusively, at lower cost.

New Computers Keyed to Business

Now, however, the third "generation" of computers has appeared and the first installations are being made. This new equipment represents far more than modification and adaptation. Now for the first time we have equipment and related programing and operational techniques designed especially for business data systems to meet business information requirements so far as they have been visualized up to this time.

A wide range of system characteristics is now available. Some equipment has very high input and output speeds, tremendous calculating rates, massive data storage capacities and random access capability. Other equipment is more modest and therefore costs less, permitting its use by much smaller business organizations. All these systems continue merely to sort, calculate, summarize, record, and communicate—but with great flexibility and capacity.

Classification—the initial coding of data—is a basic data processing operation but was not included above among functions of electronic data processing equipment because it must be done before entry of data into the system. This operation also is subject to new techniques. The applicable code for any entry into a system is determined through human judgment. Once noted, either manually or mechanically, on a form or record, however, it may be entered into the system through optical scanning or magnetic devices that read the codes electronically. Further, some installations dispense with the form or record altogether and provide for input by a mechanical keyboard at the source of the transaction: for example, at the machine, if it be a labor time or job record in the factory, or at a cashier's window, or at a receiving dock.

Output, too, has undergone changes in techniques: the results of processing and storing data can be displayed on television-like devices or other visual media that may provide no reference documents at all.

Significance of Networks

Probably the most significant developments of the moment, and for some time to come, lie in the area of "networks"—systems by which multiple locations, where decisions are made and transactions occur, are linked into a central computer installation. Such networks may encompass all or the more significant plants, warehouses, and sales offices of a company. Through input and output devices at the various locations, the company serves the entire complex. Information received is sorted, calculated, summarized, and recorded, and reports are prepared for management and other purposes. Outlying locations may interrogate the system to obtain the information they need. Or the network may require that a remote location transmit data to the central unit where it will be processed immediately and the result read back to complete the transaction.

This concept may be extended to networks within a company, where various departments share the capability of a single computer to receive information at random, to process a number of transactions at one time, and to transmit results as processing is completed. Such time-sharing networks need not be confined to a single company. Unrestricted access to a computer may be extended to several companies by the owner company on payment of a fee.

Another type of network link may be established between the computers of two or more companies with mutual transactions—the purchases of one company are, for example, the sales of another. The output of one company's system—a purchase order—is the input to the system of the other; the shipping documents and the invoices of the seller activate the accounts payable system of the buyer. With a network link, instead of exchanging paper forms, direct inputs and outputs are made between computers. Punched cards are already being exchanged between some companies for such purposes, and direct data communication links are being established between buyers' offices and sellers' warehouses. This speeds the flow of goods and helps reduce the inventories of both parties.

Consideration is now being given to establishment of computer service centers, linked to various companies that have interrelated transactions. For example, airlines selling tickets covering flight segments on more than one airline, railroads interchanging traffic, or retailers selling to the same customers.

It appears, at this point in time, that we can expect refinements but no startling new developments in the central electronic data processors. Nor is there any compelling need for such developments at the moment, as our ability to design applications has not nearly reached a point that fully utilizes present equipment capabilities and capacities. What we can expect are considerable improvements in the techniques for building network systems—in communications input and output devices, transmission, and the message switching areas. All the predictions for national and international communications traffic indicate that substantial increases in data transmission are expected and at a rate of increase substantially in excess of that of voice transmission. This applies to all types of communications systems—wire, microwave, cable, and communications satellites.

The foregoing paragraphs show that electronic systems have immense capabilities for processing data, but information technology takes us beyond mere quantity and requires an answer to the key question: "What data for what purpose?"

What Is Management?

The art of management was once defined as "making irrevocable decisions based on incomplete, inaccurate, and obsolete information." The purpose of business information is to narrow the areas of uncertainty in decision making. Information technology comprehends the determination of that information pertinent and relevant to management of an enterprise and then provides it more completely, accurately, and currently.

In the past, the scope of management's view of its informational needs was conditioned by limitations in the data processing techniques available. Now that these techniques have so expanded, prior limitations no longer apply and emphasis is shifting to a more careful identification and definition of requirements for operating a business: What are the decisions that must be made? How will they affect overall results? What information is pertinent to these decisions? What are the critical time factors? Today, given a broad capacity for processing data, those who define requirements for business information can proceed with fewer inhibitions and consider a higher degree of quantification, establish mathematical relationships, and in most cases can confidently adopt a more scientific approach to their operations. This emphasis on business information requirements places the computer and the associated techniques in a proper perspective—as the means to an end, rather than the end itself.

Effect on Business

Before discussing information technology's impact on the professional accountant we should consider its impact on business. The two situations are closely related. Obviously there are many ramifications of this subject and only a few of the more important ones can be discussed here. Obviously, too, all of the effects have by no means been identified.

The approach in developing systems effectively today must necessarily be broad—far broader than in the past. The appropriate scope is companywide both functionally and geographically—with all functions and organization units and both planning and control practices and the underlying day-to-day operating procedures covered. Thus many areas—and many people—are to be subjected to change. A willingness to challenge traditional practices and then accept the consequent changes are prerequisites to success.

A properly stated objective of such a program refers to three aspects—planning and control, operating systems, and then data processing and communications systems.

Planning and Control

Planning and control are broader than merely an accounting system. They concern planning information as well as historical information, all other types of data as well as dollar data, and communication of results and actions. The purpose is control of operations by establishing accountability at the various levels of the organization. The basic questions are—

What needs to be controlled to properly manage the company (control areas and factors)?

How should each area and factor be planned (predetermination of results)?

What needs to be accounted for or measured (disclosure of results)?

What needs to be reported (to whom and for what purpose)?

Operating systems are defined as the procedures and records used in day-to-day decision making and conduct of the business. They are included in the overall system because planning and control data are derived from operating systems; control data essentially are used to measure the effectiveness of operating systems; and modern data processing methods depend for maximum effectiveness on a fully integrated approach—one data system for all purposes.

When the planning and control system and the operating systems are implemented through use of electronic data processing and its related communication components, a "total system" is the result.

Organization for this level of systems development effort requires the involvement of senior executives, including the chief executive officer. Top management often does not have sufficient understanding of the intricacies of electronic data processing systems techniques. Systems technicians, on the other hand, usually do not understand the management art. Unless the top officers directly participate in defining requirements for the system, the result may satisfy the technician but fail to make the potential contribution to management effectiveness.

Past experience clearly shows that the degree of success in operation of electronic data processing systems is directly related to the degree of management participation in their development. In the future this factor will be even more critical.

Participation by senior executives obviously requires significant amounts of their time. But more significant are shifts in their perspectives that are likely to result from introspective analysis of their own and their subordinates' jobs and the job relationships within the structure. It should be expected that no matter how the system ultimately develops, executives will apply different priorities and standards of relevance to the various elements of their responsibility and authority.

Centralizing Decision Making

Information technology at this level can be expected to affect not only the quality of decision making but the place in the organization structure where various decisions are made. Management decision making today is for the most part significantly fragmented. Separate decisions are made throughout the organization structure on specific subjects that in the aggregate have their effects on broader matters. Each individual decision maker seeks the information necessary to make his limited decision. Organization structures are built on the theory of the specialization of individuals and compartmentation of functions. Information systems have been built in response to this type of structure.

However, now that it is practicable to provide one person in one position with total information on a broader question—information that is accurate, timely, and carefully selected for relevancy—we may have fewer decision makers and better decisions. Consider for a moment a fundamental problem: How much of what to manufacture, and when? This involves a complex of decisions by persons with interests in sales, procurement, personnel, production, warehousing, traffic, and probably other functions. Under today's highly compartmented organization structure and fragmented decision making, there is no guarantee that the myriad separate decisions will in the aggregate produce the best final decision on the broader question.

Flattening the Organization

Centralized data processing does not necessarily require a centralization of decision making and does not necessarily result in it. But, if the total information to make a broad decision is all together at one place, it seems illogical to communicate it, in segments, to several persons for purposes of making only limited decisions. The organizational implications of centralized data processing point to a broadening of the span of control assigned to any one position and fewer echelons overall.

The initiative for developing and applying this more sophisticated level of information technology may come from the chief executive officer, the head of a functional group such as marketing or production, or the financial officer. In the past, when systems were of limited scope, it was the financial officer who most frequently took the initiative, and the first application usually served accounting needs. Production, marketing, and personnel applications would then be added to some degree in due course.

Shift in Responsibilities

In the days when punched card tabulating systems represented the top degree of sophistication, the foregoing was almost universally accepted as a normal course of events. As the first and second generations of computer systems came on the scene we saw in a few companies a shift in the assigned responsibility for such systems to production, marketing, or to newly established functions. Some observers who have been assessing the achievements attained through computer systems conclude that where the potential has not been realized, it is because the system was oriented too much toward accounting, because the computer was misused as a large-scale bookkeeping device, and because the financial officer frequently had too narrow an outlook. There is little question that this has been so in many instances, but whether it is valid to conclude that financial officers should generally not have jurisdiction over such systems is a question still unresolved.

Traditionally, it has been the financial officer, in addition to the chief executive, whose position had an overview of corporate affairs. His position epitomized the concept of functional control because it required him to exercise authority over the policy and procedural aspects of accounting-related records wherever they were maintained in the company, and this extended to an internal audit responsibility over such records.

Information Function Emerges

Nowadays with increasing frequency we observe a new function emerging —the information function. We see vice presidents for information systems, vice presidents for administration, directors of planning, and a proliferation of titles applied to positions concerned with matters of an accounting nature, yet established separate and apart from the financial function. These positions vary in scope and may cover systems development and maintenance or extend to actual operation of the information system including the equipment, and inevitably this function extends to interpretation of results. An integrated information system, of course, includes all the accounting records as well as other data, yet such positions are seldom headed by accountants. Frequently these executives are computer specialists with backgrounds in any one of a variety of disciplines—engineering, mathematics, or the behavioral sciences. The growing tendency is to identify them all as information specialists.

This trend has been taking shape for some time and its pace is accelerating. The more this new breed of information technicians becomes established, the more the financial officer's traditional role will be eroded. Some financial executives seem scarcely aware of what is happening, others accept the trend as inevitable or perhaps feel inadequate to cope with it, and others offer strong and sometimes successful resistance. In any event, the financial officer has much at risk and while he may assert his "right" to this function, "right" has little to do with it. Where the finanicial officer ultimately ends up is going to depend primarily on the individual: Does he take the initiative, hold a broad view, and demonstrate that the company's total interest will be served by putting him in charge of the information function?

Limitations as to length of this article have permitted only a few of the more important aspects of information technology's impact on business to be identified. Similarly, only a few aspects of the impact on professional accountants can be mentioned here. The primary intent, in any event, is to indicate something of the scope of a development whose total dimensions have not yet been defined.

Challenge—and Opportunity

Information technology offers both a challenge and an opportunity to our profession. A challenge, to our ability to adapt traditional approaches and procedures to these new conditions; an opportunity, to increase the effectiveness of our auditing and tax services through the application of these new techniques. A further opportunity, to extend our management services by performing as consultants in supplementing client efforts to bring these techniques to bear on their operations.

Generally accepted auditing standards and procedures (within their meaning in the United States) covers such matters as evaluation of internal control, planning and timing of work, and evidential matter. Advent of the computer and of information technology may cause no alteration of present standards, but considerable ingenuity will doubtless be required in the procedural aspects.

Internal accounting control is of primary interest to the independent auditor. There appears to be no reason why control should not be at least as effective in an electronic data processing system as in any other. Yet, it cannot be assumed that good internal control automatically carries over into an EDP system or that such controls are necessarily improved. The independent auditor must still establish the degree to which he may rely on the system of internal control in discharging his responsibility. New and revised auditing techniques and procedures are required in this phase of the work when basic changes occur in the assignment and segregation of duties associated with the system, the quantity and type of documentation, the form of the records, and in other aspects.

The auditor must proceed on notice that these new systems are generally devised by nonaccountants, both on the client and equipment manufacturers' staffs. These people often have a low sensitivity to internal controls as the auditor views them and may even resist additions or modifications in the overall electronic data processing system that to them, at least, do not serve the primary purpose of the system. To our knowledge we have not yet had a major catastrophe attributable to internal control deficiencies in such a system. But this will surely come, either through errors in system design or, as more and more people become sufficiently expert in such systems to visualize their potentialities as instruments of fraud, through deliberate falsification.

Considerable work is being done on the subject of internal controls in electronic data processing systems in the United States and no doubt in other countries. But, as a profession we have not arrived at conclusions and formalized a position on this vital subject.

The planning and timing of our work and our review of evidential matter must also be considered. The new system may not practicably provide the type of continuous records of transactions that we are accustomed to; records may be updated by "erasing" an entry on magnetic tape and superimposing new data; input to the system may be made directly without documentary evidence; and other features may be found that facilitate operation of the system but require basic modifications in the auditor's planning and timing of his work. Auditing may have to become more continuous and current, rather than consisting essentially of a post-audit of the past.

Many of the auditing problems associated with these systems may be avoided when the auditor asserts his interest and arranges to participate in design of the system. In this way he can assure that proper internal controls and other features are incorporated in the system; it may be wholly impracticable to provide them later.

The Accountant's Stake

In any event, the professional accountant has much at stake in these new system developments, even if he decides merely to pursue a defensive role regarding his traditional function.

Considerable opportunity exists for the professional accountant to increase the level of effectiveness of his accounting, auditing, and tax services by applying the newly available techniques.

In accounting, for example, when we have a question we frequently search our literature and files to find precedentary evidence as one aspect to be considered in our resolution of an appropriate course of action. Present equipment capability exists for developing massive information retrieval systems. The fundamental difficulty is in finding ways to classify and code relevant information. Think of the possibilities afforded by being able to summon instantly all the evidence of past practices pertinent in developing an answer to an immediate question.

To some degree accountants are already applying the new techniques in their auditing work—but they have only begun to tap the potential. They are using their computer programs on clients' or service centers' equipment to process data needed to make their audit tests. Computers are being used to test inventory computations, to stratify inventory and accounts receivable balances in the application of statistical sampling procedures, to run ratio analyses that may detect fluctuations worthy of investigation.

Tax returns are now being prepared by computer—and it should be added, parenthetically, that government tax authorities in the United States are using computer systems to keep track of taxpayers and to audit tax returns.

As the professional accountant learns more about electronic data processing and information technology he will find many other applications to his own function. This must be so, not only because of his own needs to increase the effectiveness of his work but also because he has an obligation to keep the cost of professional accounting service commensurate with its economic value.

Management Services Area

The broadest impact of the new information technology on the professional accountant—if he aggressively asserts his interest—is in the management services area of his practice. Accountants, particularly in recent years, have greatly extended their consultive services to assist client management in attaining more effective operations. The subject matter of these services has grown to the point where some accounting firms will assist in almost any problem in all functional areas of the business. There is significant debate within the profession in the United States as to how far these services should extend, but there is general agreement that information systems are and should be at the core of the accountant's interest.

The scope, importance, and uniqueness of information technology have conditioned management to seek and accept outside counsel on these matters. Management, not having faced these problems before, recognizes that its staff may not be fully qualified to achieve effective results. The advice of equipment manufacturers, while readily available, is subject to their self-interest. There is, therefore, the essential requirement for someone with a thorough understanding of the business aspects of the problem coupled with a fundamental understanding of the possibilities and limitations of information technology who can function in an objective consulting capacity. Through the assumption of this role, the professional accountant exercises a unique opportunity for leadership.

Ties with Management

The professional accountant, no matter how broad a role he elects to play or how well he performs it, is not likely to control the effect of information technology on the position of particular financial officers in their companies. As pointed out earlier in this paper, the financial officer's role in the future is likely to vary widely, depending on the ability and outlook of the individual involved.

It is apparent then, that the professional accountant may find his own position eroded if he identifies himself largely with the financial officer. In the past the financial officer had custody over the books and records with which the independent accountant was concerned. To the extent this no longer is so, the accountant will need a broader and closer relationship with general management than heretofore, not only to perform his traditional role but also in the capacity of consultant to management on information technology.

Ours is an era of rapid and fundamental change. The impact of electronic data processing and information technology strikes first at management. Its subsequent effect on the professional accountant is inevitable. For those with a narrow view "change" is synonymous with "problem." For those with a broad view and enterprising attitude, "change" is synonymous with "opportunity."

EDP in the Accounting Curriculum

Leonard W. Hein

The accounting curriculum does not ordinarily exist as a separate entity, but in most cases it is an integral part of the curriculum of the school of business. It would appear, therefore, that a discussion of EDP in the accounting curriculum would be more meaningful if it were based upon a consideration of EDP in the general business curriculum. With this concept in mind, I would like to cover four general areas:

1. The present and future impact of EDP on the business, political and social environment.
2. EDP instruction in the general business curriculum.
3. The possibility of the introduction of an EDP or information processing major.
4. EDP in the accounting curriculum itself.

I shall consider two aspects here: my personal recommendations, and the recommendations of the American Accounting Association Committee on Courses and Curricula—Electronic Data Processing.

First, let us consider the present and future impact of EDP on the business, political and social environment. I am hoping that this discussion will leave the reader with a feeling for the role that the EDP specialist, particularly the systems analyst-programer, is now playing and is likely to play in the future.

Reprinted by permission of the author and the publisher from *The Journal of Accountancy*, Vol. 120, No. 2 (August, 1965), pp. 78–84.

I regard this as being important because the attitude of the schools of business has been that programing as a subject is not of senior college level and should be relegated to the terminal programs of the junior colleges. I presented the following facts to the deans' meeting in San Diego last November. Perhaps readers will find them as significant as the deans appeared to.

The history of computers on the business scene is relatively short. The first electronic computer was developed in 1946; the first data processing installation as we conceive it today was that of a Univac I in the U.S. Bureau of the Census in 1951. The first business data processing installation was that of a similar computer at General Electric's Appliance Park in Louisville, Ky., in 1954. Just prior to the Census Bureau's application, the greater computer pundits were of the opinion that six of the giant brains would be adequate for the computational requirements of the United States. It took three more years to realize the potentialities of business data processing, and we are this year celebrating the eleventh anniversary of the first business installation. Instead of the six computers originally projected as meeting the country's needs, we now have in excess of twenty thousand.

And what about the future? There is no one alive today who can completely envision the potentialities, but many prognostications are being made. One group is looking toward the millennium, when the perfect life will exist on earth; that is, an abundance of physical goods and the leisure to enjoy them. There are others who are crying "Doom! Doom!" at the top of their lungs. Of these latter, Donald N. Michael, in his pamphlet "Cybernation: The Silent Conquest," may be cited as a prime example.[1] I shall have occasion to quote Mr. Michael in a moment. Nevertheless, whichever road we travel—to earthly paradise or to hell on earth—we can be certain that the computer programmer is going to play a significant role.

While the schools of business in their pronouncements tend to talk about education for top management, as a practical matter much of their energy is expended in preparing people for positions in middle management. But the conclusion of a number of people who have studied the matter, including our friend Mr. Michael, is that middle management as such will disappear and its place will be taken by computers. To do this, of course, the computers must be programmed, and who is to program them? Not graduates of business schools, for we have relegated this instruction to the junior colleges.

According to Mr. Michael, middle management represents the elite of our present society; if it is to disappear, will any group take its place? He says, "It is possible that the new middle elite, the engineers, operations researchers and systems analysts, will absorb the standards of the group that they have replaced."[2] If our main product, middle management, is to disappear,

---

[1] Donald N. Michael, "Cybernation: The Silent Conquest," a report to the Center for the Study of Democratic Institutions, Santa Barbara, Calif.

[2] Ibid., p. 20.

one might expect that schools of business would be educating for the successors to those obsolete positions. Of the three occupations mentioned by Mr. Michael, it would appear that the training of engineers might be outside the scope of schools of business. Such computer-oriented areas as operations research and systems analysis, however, pertain directly to business management; yet the schools of business have made only feeble gestures in these directions, permitting the important programs to exist in schools of engineering and in mathematics departments.

Shift in Recruiting

But you may say, education for top management was our original goal and the disappearance of middle management will have no effect upon this. Turning once again to Mr. Michael, he says, "In business and industry the shift has already begun toward recruiting top management from the cadre of engineering and laboratory administration, for these are the people who understand the possibilities of and are sympathetic to computer-based thinking."[3] And yet we relegate the teaching of computers and computer programing to the junior colleges. It could be argued that those who are sympathetic to computer-based thinking need have had no training in computer programing. Yet casual observation reveals that those who do not thoroughly understand computers tend not to trust them and try to do their thinking around rather than through the computers. And in the final analysis, no matter what other controls are imposed, the computer programer will determine what information the top management receives, for the computer programs will be far too complex for a noncomputer man to understand and evaluate.

Even the government will be dominated by computer people. According to Mr. Michael:

> The government must turn to computers to handle many of its major problems simply because the data involved are so massive and the factors so complex that only machines can handle the material fast enough to allow timely action based on understanding of the facts.[4]

He goes on to describe the confidential nature of the information so programed and says that it would be unlikely that the information would be shared with competing political parties. But even if the information were so shared, Mr. Michael says:

> . . . let us assume that somehow the operation of the government has been reorganized so that procedures are enforced to permit competing political parties and other private organizations to have access to the government's raw data, to have parallel systems for the processing

[3] Ibid., p. 36.
[4] Ibid., p. 33.

of data as well as to have access to the government's computer programs. Even then, most people will be incapable of judging the validity of one contending computer program compared to another, or whether the policies based on them are appropriate.

This condition exists today about military postures. These are derived in good part from computer analyses and computer-based games that produce probabilities based on programed assumptions about weapon systems and our and the enemy's behavior.[5]

We have considered how the computer will take over the duties of middle management. In a number of situations today, and in many more tomorrow, it will take over the entire production process. There exist today oil refineries in which there are no production people other than those engaged in maintenance. Economic data such as raw material prices and market prices of the products which the refinery is capable of producing are fed into the computer. The computer then plans the optimum product mix and proceeds, without human intervention, to achieve that mix.

The optimists, looking at the world through rose-colored glasses, will retort—and they base their beliefs on past experience—that new developments, such as the computer, merely cause temporary dislocations and that completely new industries re-employ the dislocated people. They could cite, for example, the computer industry which resulted from this new development.

In the application phase of the product of the computer industry, vast numbers of bookkeeping machine, billing machine and calculating machine operators have been displaced. The optimist will observe that many of these people were retrained as key-punch operators, computer programers and computer operators. If we may remove the rose-colored glasses for the moment, we will see that the key-punch operator is now being phased out. She is being replaced by automatic recorders, by optical readers and by other input devices. Even the junior programer—the type we so generously relegated to the junior colleges to train—will eventually be and to some extent is now being replaced by the computer.

But the computer factories, of course, are quite another situation. Just visualize the thousands upon thousands of people required to build all those computers. Since 1958 it has been my practice to take my students on a field trip to a certain computer factory in Pasadena. The guide would first take us into the design section where we would see desk after desk occupied by design engineers busily engaged in making wiring diagrams for the computers. We would then go through the factory. The students thought they had been transported into paradise, for there were row upon row of curvaceous lovelies, as far as the eye could see, soldering irons flashing, constructing these marvelous giant brains. I am not sure whether the students learned much about the construction of computers, but they certainly enjoyed the trip!

[5] Ibid., p. 34.

On one of our more recent trips we were ushered into the design room. The desks and the design engineers were gone. Instead there was a computer spewing out wiring diagrams at the rate of six hundred to a thousand lines per minute. Naturally, I felt a twinge of pity for the poor design engineers and wondered momentarily whether they were enjoying their weekly unemployment checks. We then went out into the factory. Horror of horrors! Gone were the rows of curvaceous lovelies. Gone even were the flashing soldering irons. I presume that you have guessed it! There stood three computers stolidly but swiftly and accurately wiring complex computer panels.

Ever since the advent of the computer and its early appellation of "giant brain," there has been a running fight as to whether or not computers can think. First the pros were on top, then the cons took over. As time has progressed, however, the pros have been regaining position. In fact, the cons have their backs to the wall. As a dying effort, the cons might claim in hollow triumph that, even though the computers may be able to think like human beings, at least they do not have the ability to biologically reproduce themselves. My previous discussions should tend to refute even this claim. In fact, in this area the computer has the definite advantage. The human being produces only a small image of itself; it takes several decades for the image to develop into the real thing, and the result rarely is any marked improvement over its progenitor. The computer, on the other hand, is capable of producing a second generation which is far superior to the parent.

There can be little doubt of the tremendous effect that computers will have on business and on government. A little reflection should prove that the people who control the computers may well control the entire operation. Should you be unwilling to accept this concept, you should at least agree that the computer will play an important role. And whatever a computer does, a programer has had to teach it.

For those who remain skeptical, let me give one more "way out" example. With existing technology, it is possible for a design engineer to draw a rough sketch with an electronic wand on the surface of a cathode-ray tube, and to give the computer the dimensions and other specifications. The computer will then produce a finished scale-drawing of the part designed. But does this tale end here? Indeed no! The computer will then prepare instructions for fabricating the part on a machine tool, submit the instructions to the tool, and the tool will then proceed to fabricate the part. But remember! It took a programer to teach the computer.

EDP Instruction in the General Business Curriculum

If, as seems virtually certain, the computer will be a central force in businesses of the future, taking over many of the duties of management and practically all the duties of production, can schools of business safely continue to allocate an almost insignificant segment of the curriculums to computer study? The answer appears to me to require such a resounding "no" that I am tempted to go way out in my recommendations. I shall restrain myself, however, and confine my recommendations to what I regard as being a very conservative position.

I can detect at least four levels of instruction in programing which the schools of business should consider. The first is a course in computer technology and programing for the general manager of today. I am not so naive, however, as to believe that such a course will provide the business manager with the knowledge to cope with the extreme complexities of the computerized business information systems of the future. Rather I would regard such a course as part of the general education segment of the curriculum and would recommend it as a required course for all curriculums. If computers are going to have an impact on our environment that even the least visionary among us predict, then everyone should have some familiarity with them, just as they should have some familiarity with astronomy, physics, chemistry, psychology, etc.

The next level of education required for students of the schools of business would be that of preparing the quantitative people to solve their fairly complex problems on the computer. I am thinking here of the statisticians, operations researchers, etc. While their problems are fairly complex, the programing required to solve them is relatively simple (that is, relative to the next group to be considered). If the above course is offered at a fairly rigorous level, including the writing and debugging of several nontrivial programs, it will also be adequate for this second group.

Introduction of an EDP or Information Processing Major[6]

It has been traditional in schools of business to educate for positions in such functional areas as accounting, finance, marketing and management; typically, in functionally organized businesses, the heads of these groups are at the vice-presidential level, reporting directly to the president. If it can be established that there is in fact an information processing function with an importance at least equal to the traditional ones, then there is an adequate precedent for the inclusion of an information processing major in the business curriculum.

Traditionally there has not been a single data processing function in business but rather a group of relatively unconnected functions. The term

---

[6] Much of the material in this section is taken from an article by the author, "Isolating the EDP Curriculum," published in the *Journal of Data Management*, April 1965, pp. 46–50, and is reproduced here by permission.

was most commonly applied to the processing of accounting data. Even here, however, separate departments were frequently set up to handle general financial accounting and the cost and inventory accounting, the latter in many cases being more closely allied to the manufacturing department. There are, nevertheless, many areas of business other than accounting which require the processing of data. Some examples:

1. The marketing department requires extensive sales analyses and market research analyses. In the first case the help of the accounting department may be used and in the second case the help of the statistics department may be sought, but frequently such data processing has been effected entirely within the marketing department itself.

2. The statistical department prepares various statistical reports and performs correlation studies for such uses as forecasting.

3. The production department processes data for production scheduling and production control.

4. The research and development department processes data required for its design and experimental work.

5. The operations research department (a new department) ingests data from all sources and spews out hopefully useful results.

This list is not intended to be exhaustive but merely illustrative of the several classes of data requiring processing.

Prior to the advent of the electronic computer, each of these departments tended to process its own data, using its own personnel and equipment. Severe limitations were placed on the amount of data which could be processed both by the cost per unit of processing and by the time required for processing; frequently the results were produced too late for effective use.

The electronic computer reduced both the cost and the time per unit of processing. It had, however, three important drawbacks: (1) It required a very large capital investment; (2) it required specialists to program and operate it; and (3) it had the capacity to handle the data processing of all the various departments. These factors have changed the data processing picture in a number of ways: (1) The demand for the processing of data shot upward as it became feasible to process enormous quantities of data within acceptable time periods and at economic costs; (2) the high capital costs of computers prevented each department from acquiring its own; and (3) the scarcity of trained EDP personnel similarly mitigated the tendency of the several departments to hire their own programers and operators and then to use the central computer, although this method has been used to some extent.

Thus the high cost of electronic data processing equipment is forcing a movement toward the creating of data processing centers within each business and to a lesser extent toward the creating of a centralized data processing function within that center.

Location of the Computer

The electronic computer was originally conceived as being a processor of mathematical data, and hence its early applications to business problems were largely in the research, development and engineering fields. Thus the computer and the computer personnel tended to be attached to the research or engineering departments. The computer specialists were almost exclusively mathematicians, scientists and engineers.

It soon became apparent that the computer could be used to process accounting data. Where computers had been installed in Research and Development or in Engineering, the accounting department would "buy time" on the computer, with the computer facility remaining under the control of the original "owner." In other cases the accounting department was the first to see the efficacy of computer operation, and hence the computer resided in that place in the organizations.

The location of the computer facility, then, was largely a matter of accident. As more and more departments began to realize that their data could be advantageously processed on the computer, the owning department began to "sell" more time, and the computer center moved in the direction of so-called open-shop operation. This tendency was checked, however, by the scarcity of skilled specialists such as programers and operators. As a result, the computer center moved toward a closed-shop operation, whereby the service purchaser received the entire data processing package, including the planning and programing and the operation of the computer. In this case the receiving department needed merely to submit the raw data to be processed.

The playing of the role of general data processor has caused the functionaries of the computer centers to become restive in their positions as subsidiaries to the originating departments. Since their duties encompass the entire business, they reason, the data processing department should be at the vice-presidential level, reporting directly to the president. Such an organizational position has been achieved in a number of cases. The dreams of grandeur do not stop even at this point. I have been told informally of one large company which has placed the data processing function, united with systems and procedures, under a committee of the board of directors equal in stature to the executive committee.

It is therefore apparent that a distinct data processing function is developing in business organizations and that it is gradually establishing itself on a high rung of the organizational ladder.

If, then, you would grant that there is an information processing function in business, and that therefore we in the schools of business should educate specifically for this role, what would be the proper curriculum? The following suggestion is admittedly one man's opinion—my own—and I offer it for consideration.

No educational curriculum can encompass all that everyone thinks should be included. A maximum number of semester hours, usually about 120, is ordinarily placed upon an undergraduate curriculum. What is considered to be an optimum is therefore necessarily a series of compromises, including only those areas of study deemed to be the most important.

The American Accounting Association has for a number of years advocated that the accounting curriculum be split into three segments, with the percentage weights allotted as follows:

General education	50%
Business	25%
Accounting	25%

In the suggested EDP curriculum the 50 per cent general education component is retained. The remaining 50 per cent is to be divided approximately equally among:

Accounting	12½%
Business	12½%
Mathematics	12½%
Data processing	12½%

This would permit about fifteen semester hours to be devoted to each of the fundamental areas. Since in each area there are many more courses available than the allotted fifteen units, exactly which to include and which to exclude can give rise to extended controversy. The following choices represent, as I said, one man's opinion.

Choices for Accounting

For the accounting area, the courses are:

	Units
Introductory	6
Intermediate	3
Cost	3
Controllership	3
	15

The rationale behind the selection of the above courses deserves some consideration. Since much of the data processing of a business involves accounting data or closely related data, and since the results must be summarized in ways that are useful to management for internal decision-making and (perhaps summarized in a different manner) for external reporting, the importance of a thorough grounding in accounting theory can hardly be overemphasized. This grounding is provided by the nine units in introductory and intermediate accounting. The cost course was selected to familiarize the student with cost accounting systems, which will usually be an important segment of the total information system. The course in controllership is intended to demonstrate the contribution that the controller can make to the management team. The selection, design, production, and distribution of managerial reports is to be thoroughly considered. The selection and installation of proper controls to insure the integrity of the reports and the safety of the company's assets are to be emphasized.

The courses for the business segment are:

	Units
Principles of management	3
Production management	3
Marketing management	3
Financial management	3
Statistics	3
	15

NOTE: It is expected that six units of economics would be part of the general education segment.

The suggested curriculum is for *management* in information processing. The managerial aspects of the program are highly significant. The manager of information processing is moving rapidly up the organizational ladder. To perform effectively in this position he must be well educated in the principles of business management. The first course, principles of management, is designed to familiarize the student with the principles of organization, planning and control. The next three courses are concerned with the problems of management in each of the functional areas of production, marketing and finance. The final course is contemplated as being statistics applied to business and economics problems. It could, perhaps, be argued that this course should be mathematical statistics, in which case it would be transferred from the business component to the mathematics component.

The courses for the mathematics area are:

	Units
Analytic geometry and calculus	6
Differential equations	3
Probability and set theory	3
Matrix algebra and linear programing	3
	15

NOTE: It is expected that college algebra will be part of the general education segment.

There can be little doubt that a large segment of business data processing involves the processing of mathematical or scientific data. For this segment of his work the professional information processor requires a thorough understanding of basic mathematics. Unquestionably, the mathematics program suggested is a bare minimum. For example, if unit limits would permit it, a course in numerical analysis would be very useful. Nevertheless, the program suggested would provide the solid background that the information processor would require. If the course in statistics were moved from the business segment to the mathematics segment, the suggested program would closely parallel (insofar as the use of standard mathematics courses permits) the recommendation of the Committee on the Undergraduate Program in Mathematics.[7]

The courses for the data processing segment are:

	Units
Accounting systems	3
EDP-I, principles and practices	3
EDP-II, business applications, systems and controls	3
EDP-III, advanced programing systems	3
Operations research	3
	15

Except for those in the data processing segment, all the above courses are currently being offered in most colleges and universities; hence their utilization in the suggested curriculum would probably involve little, if any, controversy. In the data processing segment the course in accounting systems and, more recently, the course in operations research have been similarly accepted. The EDP courses occupy a less secure position. Many colleges and university schools of business offer at least one computer-oriented course. Very few have a comprehensive program leading to a degree in information processing. My personal opinion is that such a degree program *should* be offered and *will* be increasingly offered if business and industry evidence a demand for it. The rationale behind the data processing segment is that of advanced professional work in business systems, with the primary emphasis being placed upon EDP systems. The accounting systems course would acquaint the student with non-EDP systems and should ideally contain an introduction to EDP. The three-course EDP sequence would provide the student with a thorough professional com-

---

[7] Committee on the Undergraduate Program in Mathematics, "Tentative Recommendations for the Undergraduate Mathematics Program 'of Students in the Biological, Management and Social Sciences," Mathematics Association of America, January 1964.

petency such as to permit him to enter the information processing profession. The segment would be capped by a course in operations research techniques as applied to business situations.

EDP Education for the
Professional Accountant

I have spelled out the curriculum for the information processing major with such detail because, first, I wish to emphasize the significance of this new department since it is now taking over many of the functions of the industrial accountant and will continue to do so at an ever-increasing pace. And, more serious from the viewpoint of accountants, the information processing departments tend to be staffed with people who received their education in the fields of mathematics, engineering and sciences. Second, I wish to use the above curriculum as a basis for my recommendations for education for the accounting profession.

What EDP education is required for accountants is by no means a settled issue, least of all among the accountants themselves. There are discernible at least two schools of thought. One is that the theory and practice of accounting is independent of the method of bookkeeping, and therefore the accountant need not be a computer expert. If the attest function of the accountant were to be ignored, this position might be tenable. However, the public accountant and the internal auditor must audit computer-based accounting systems. Members of the first school of thought, however, have devised a technique called "auditing around" the computer. This group of accountants, of course, consists primarily of those who have not become and probably do not intend to become computer experts.

A second school of thought holds that the audit of a computer-based accounting system should be made, at least in part, by a process known as "auditing through" the computer. Just what degree of computer sophistication this requires on the part of the accountant is again an unsettled question. In my own mind I question whether any complex computer-based accounting system, other than one leaving an audit trail similar to that of a traditional accounting system, has ever been truly or adequately audited. Much remains to be done in the development of effective audit procedures. I am convinced, however, that if the accountant is to retain his professional position, he must develop a high degree of computer sophistication. In fact, the above-suggested EDP curriculum, with the exception of the accounting segment, represents the type of education needed by the professional accountant. The curriculum as suggested consists of 120 semester hours. If we add three courses—one in advanced accounting, one in auditing and one in taxes—the curriculum becomes a fairly reasonable 129 units. All that is now lacking is a course in the foundation of business law, which could be included as a part of the general education. If required, one or more of the mathematics courses could similarly be classified as general education.

The "Figure Specialist"

What does this curriculum do for the accountant? The accountant likes to present himself as the figure specialist on the management team, yet he is notoriously lacking in the mathematical discipline which is required for the more complex manipulation of figures. The accountant is increasingly utilizing the tools of the statistician, and again sophistication in this area requires a better mathematical background. The industrial accountant is rapidly losing ground to the EDP specialist, who tends to set up information systems which ignore the traditional accounting requirements. The suggested curriculum would materially reduce both the mathematical and the EDP gaps now so glaringly apparent. But notice that it does not damage the traditional accounting curriculum of which most accountants are justifiably proud.

My recommendations, I am afraid, contrast sharply with those of the American Accounting Association Committee on Courses and Curricula— Electronic Data Processing. I admit rather reluctantly that I put my signature to the Committee Report. The reluctance is due to second thoughts that I have had since the completion of the report. While I agree that what the report recommends is good, I believe that it commits the error of being too little too late—the sin of which we are all too often guilty.

At the undergraduate level, the Committee's recommendations are:

At the undergraduate level accounting students should be exposed to electronic data processing in three stages:

(a) Concurrent with or prior to the introductory accounting course, students should receive instruction in a basic programing language, and should be able to write simple computer problems in that language.

(b) Accounting instruction in a variety of subject-matter courses should incorporate some computer-oriented problems where subject matter is conducive to formulation; but such instruction should convey the principles basic to an understanding of the profounder, nontechnical issues to which computer solutions are being applied.

(c) The traditional systems course should continue to include a coverage of electronic data processing as one of the aids to accounting.

Added emphasis should be placed in this course on logical information flows and on multidimensional information requirements rather than on the form and content of specific accounting records. The systems course must also look more toward principles applicable to *all* information systems, and less toward description of hardwares and computer languages.

By this three-stage approach the accounting student will be enabled to make use of the computer as a problem-solving tool, as an element in accounting information systems, and as a basis for a more logical approach to analysis of enterprise transactions. Computer technology then becomes a natural part of an accountant's education without distracting his attention from the essence of his subject matter.[8]

I fully agree with these objectives as far as they go, but I am increasingly convinced that they do not go nearly far enough. The complete report of the committee was published in the April 1965 issue of *The Accounting Review*.[9]

The question then arises: Can my recommendations be implemented? The answer is, of course, a flat "no." Why? Because we do not have and are unlikely to have available in the foreseeable future the faculty for such a program. There are extremely few academicians who would have the knowledge and training required for the suggested department of information processing. Most of the qualified people are out in business and industry. They are unavailable to us on two counts: (1) they are academically unacceptable because few have Ph.D.s, and the possession of a master's degree is almost equally rare; and (2) even if we would accept academically unqualified people, our relative salary structure is such that the positions we could offer would probably be unattractive to them.

Two potential sources appear to be available: (1) educate new professors for information processing in our Ph.D. programs, and (2) retrain existing professors. Both of these avenues present such almost insurmountable difficulties that without extreme motivation on the part of the administrators of schools of business their potentialities can be almost completely discounted. Consider, first Ph.D. programs as a possible source. Two major barriers exist: (1) the faculties lack almost completely the motivation to educate Ph.D.s in the field of information processing (I am referring here to schools of business. Other faculties, such as engineering and mathematics, are moving in with highly potent programs); (2) even should the faculties desire to produce such Ph.D.s, the instructional staff for the Ph.D. program is virtually nonexistent.

Can existing faculties be retrained? I presume there is agreement that a professor should have more knowledge than is contained in the subject matter of his course. That is, the professor teaching the general education

---

[8] Leonard W. Hein, Richard Mattessich, Elzy V. McCullough, Robert E. Seiler and Gardner Jones, "Electronic Data Processing in Accounting Education," *The Accounting Review*, April 1965. p. 422.

[9] *Ibid.*, pp. 422–428.

and quantitative specialists course in computers should have more knowledge of computers and computer programing than he could get in taking a similar three-unit course. In my opinion, it would require several years of intensive part-time training and education to produce an adequate instructor. But why should any professor engage in such a pursuit? I have found little if any motivation on the academic scene. He would be preparing himself, with little hope of reward, for a discipline which is currently looked down upon by his colleagues—a discipline that they have already relegated to the junior colleges. The motivational problem is one to be solved by school administrators. Perhaps the solution could be increased pay, decreased work, opportunities for advancement in rank, prestige, or a combination of these.

The competency of a professor in the department of information processing is a different matter. He must be an expert in information processing systems, systems analysis and design, computer programing including compilers, generators, simulators, monitors, etc., and many other areas. To attain this competency requires many years of education and experience. To retrain existing professors along these lines is almost inconceivable, for an extreme motivational force would be required.

The above presents a rather pessimistic view of the future of schools of business in the field of computer-based information processing, and the outlook is bleak indeed. However, this does not mean surrender. I say begin, even though unprepared. Preparedness will come with experience. Set up the program and put it into operation. It will, admittedly, function very poorly in the beginning. If we resolve, however, that each succeeding semester will be better than the preceding, we will soon have adequate computer instruction in our schools of business. As the late President Kennedy so eloquently said, "Let us begin."

Management Information Systems: Who'll Be in Charge?

Robert Beyer

The subject of management information systems raises some healthy, controversial questions, including when and how such systems will be universally adopted. There is no doubt, however, that they will become increasingly significant in the process of achieving more effective management planning and control. For those of us who believe that the fragmented information systems in general operation today are inadequate in coping with growing pressures on management for faster, more complete, and more fully integrated information, the need for truly management-oriented, unified systems has become increasingly urgent.

There is already a definite trend toward more integrated and more dynamic systems. Actually, with improved management techniques and more sophisticated uses of the computer, we have a present ability to apply a "total systems" approach to information. It is an approach which uses the latest developments in accounting, mathematical techniques, and the social sciences. It uses high-speed, high-volume electronic devices to extract, assimilate and correlate all pertinent internal and external data from subsidiary systems.

A systems approach thus provides a single, centralized source of consistent information upon which management can draw—in a real-time mode—

Reprinted by permission of the author and the publisher from *Management Accounting*, Vol. XLVIII, No. 10, Sec. 1 (June, 1967), pp. 3–8.

for better decision-making. It can also provide the means to examine the anticipated effects of alternative decisions.

The final degree of totality and integration of management information systems will be determined by the need, skills and imagination applied to their design and implementation. At present, any question about totality of integration—any question as to how fully integrated the systems can or should become—is purely academic.

Our first concern, therefore, should be with the first logical step toward more unified systems rather than with ultimate development. That step is the greater consistency of all key control data, and it is now being taken.

The Information Specialists

The developing concepts of more centralized systems at the management level should be of major interest and concern to controllers and management accountants because they can and should be among the candidates chosen to design, apply and control the systems.

The future director of management information could emerge as one of the most influential posts in the corporate hierarchy. Some say it may become the most powerful position in the future corporation, second only to the chief executive officer. It is a goal to which a number of administrators of computer-oriented disciplines within, and on the periphery of, the corporate structure can realistically aspire.

Where the function has been formalized at all, its responsibilities currently are incorporated under various titles and at various levels. Its ultimate place in the upper echelon, however, is casting larger shadows as the trend toward unified systems gathers momentum.

John L. Carey, executive director of the American Institute of Certified Public Accountants, envisions a whole new profession of information specialists vying for this position. Among the creative information specialists Mr. Carey sees emerging are "engineers who have acquired supplemental accounting training, economists who have learned some accounting and engineering, and operations research men who have studied systems and computer technology."[1]

Therefore there is a formidable competition for the role of director of management information. Formidable—but not insuperable to those management accountants who are willing to appraise objectively their present qualifications and the new capabilities and attitudes they must acquire to be regarded as serious contenders.

The significant challenge to management accountants, however, is the

[1] John L. Carey, *The CPA Plans for the Future*, pp. 244–245.

fact that though some have been involved in varying degrees in the *planning* of the newer systems, they have not been generally *responsible* for them, nor have they been generally regarded as the logical designers and directors.

The reason for this lack of unanimity is as much attitudinal as technical on the part of management—perhaps with some justification. In many cases, top managements suspect that accountants lack the over-all corporate point of view—that they concentrate too much on the functional specialty of accounting and give too little attention to user-information needs. They also suspect accountants of being dragged into change instead of anticipating it, and reacting appropriately and effectively to it. Moreover, many business leaders believe that management technique will change so fast, as a result of the new computer capabilities, that the relative importance of many features of the purely accounting function is already receding in the corporation.

The function is not likely to become extinct; undoubtedly there will be a continuing need for accountants to handle external reporting, tax returns, S.E.C. work, and the financial inputs to the over-all management information system. Computers will play an increasingly greater part of this type of work, too. But the management accountant's role, however, will be a distinctly minor one in the future as compared with that of the director of management information.

Challenge to Accountants

The combination of lack of recognition for responsibility in the new systems and the fact that the role of the management accountant will surely lessen in importance, represents a double-edged challenge. To put it plainly, management accountants must become part of the evolution of information systems or cease to be significant figures in the corporate structure.

With this sobering thought in mind, let us examine what management accountants have going for them in a positive way, and what they must do to identify themselves with information systems development.

The accounting report traditionally has been the most significant management control tool. Management accountants have been responsible for many of the manual, even if financially-oriented, information systems of the past. While they offer no "open sesame" to modern information systems control, they are *foundations* on which to build and project competence in the newer systems.

It is significant that competence in at least the principles of accounting is one of the prime prerequisites of an information systems director. Therefore, other-type candidates must develop at least as much competence in accounting as accountants must develop in the other specialties. This is not to say that the various kinds of candidates must achieve equal proficiency in all of the desirable qualifications. It does mean that the successful candidates will have demonstrated the predominant value of his own specialty to the responsibility, all other qualifications being equal.

In addition to their traditional roles, management accountants have participated in many of the special-purpose (ad hoc) information systems that have been developed over the years to meet particular information needs. In the process, the profession has developed a number of management techniques that are being applied to today's problems.

The most significant of these user-oriented techniques has been the expansion of the basic concept of accounting from purely historical, financial reporting to encompass management planning, decision-making and control. This was the genesis of Profitability Accounting—one of the principal features of which provides the means for more systematic and effective profit planning. Through the integration of all the modern techniques of accounting, it focuses on management's ultimate objective: profitability.

From the concept of Profitability Accounting have come improvements in other user-oriented control reports. Among them have been: the summarizing and reporting of key data in trend format which gives management a fast overview of financial results; budgeting and reporting by responsibility to enable management to trace variances to specific events or individuals; and the integration of financial information so that accounting is compatible for all its intended uses.

While these applications to management's current needs are not entirely new, they are indicative of the movement of the profession—within its own field—into the area of better management information.

The New Techniques

At the same time, other disciplines have been developing additional management techniques with which we must become familiar and even adept.

Mathematical Techniques

Mathematical techniques have become particularly prominent in their accelerating growth in recent years. The science of statistics has enabled management to make better forecasts of events by probability estimates, correlation and sampling. Accountants can participate in this by establishing control limits on an exception basis to enable management to exercise better control.

Operations Research

Operations Research has given us "model building" which provides the expression of interrelationships in mathematical form. It helps to develop a better framework for forecasting and decision-making.

Some of the mystery can be taken out of the term "model building" if flexible budgets are regarded as a fairly simple form of forecast model which depicts the impact of varying volumes on costs.

Operations research has also furnished management with linear programming and other techniques for determining optimum solutions to problems with numerous interacting variables.

Market Research

In addition to its own particular techniques of test marketing and in-depth customer interviewing, market research now uses the tools of statistical sampling and model building which, combined, provide more complete information to management.

Social Sciences

We cannot afford to overlook the contributions of the social sciences. Although the effects of studies in economics, psychology and sociology may seem indirect, we can appreciate that the information we need and its communication will be affected by increased knowledge about:

How business responds to its economic environment.

How people are motivated.

How to use formal and informal channels of communications in the receipt and dissemination of information.

How decisions are reached and implemented.

How to improve the company's organization of responsibility and authority.

How to structure the manager's function.

Computer

Finally, there is the computer which has had a greater impact in a shorter time than any other development in the business environment. While it has little in concept to do with the establishment of more integrated information systems, it is obviously essential to the functional effectiveness of such systems.

The computer has only four fundamental advantages relative to management information systems with which the management accountant need concern himself:

It is faster and more accurate than any combination of management accountants. If its use is effectively planned, more and better work can be completed sooner.

It has the capacity to handle almost any volume of information required of it. Major advances in mass storage with random access to such storage have changed nearly all earlier predictions of the extent of the computer's usefulness to management.

Its costs are now acceptable and almost any reasonable volume of information can be manipulated in almost any way that will best serve the purpose.

And, despite the earlier hyperbole, it is brainless. It can do only what intelligent, creative human beings tell it to do and how to do it.

These fundamental aspects of the computer are rather simple. From the practical point of view, however, the more knowledge the management accountant has about how the computer does its work and how it can be creatively applied, the more effective will be his use of its powers.

Essential Attitudes

In assessing his qualifications for the future role of director of management information, the management accountant has some attitudinal adjustments of his own to make. These adjustments will determine the degree of his participation in the steps the company must take in planning its systems organization. They will also effect the steps which he, personally, must take to identify himself significantly with it.

One essential attitude is recognition that accelerating change is the dominant characteristic of our time. Management cannot afford to delay more effective systems design if it is to anticipate and "manage" change instead of merely reacting to it.

Another essential attitude is that of recognizing the need to develop a total corporate viewpoint. The management accountant must develop an instinctive ability to view the corporate organization as an entity rather than a collection of separate functions. This is the ability to think in terms of the interaction of the parts to the over-all corporate objective.

The attitude with which the management accountant approaches the information he is capable of providing will often determine its ultimate usefulness. This attitude focuses on user needs—the use that is or can be made of information. High-speed printers can produce data faster than any human can read, much less comprehend. The real need is for intelligent selection of information and a sensitivity to how it can be presented most usefully.

Finally, there is the attitude of acceptance of the new management techniques—whether developed within the profession or elsewhere. Some of these techniques may turn out to be fads, but others will produce genuine long-term benefits. Openmindedness and creative imagination are valuable assets in a period of dynamic change.

Management Steps in Systems Planning

The most useful contributions to systems planning in the organization obviously will be made by those who know what must be done and, beyond that, how to do it or have it done.

Since there is no universal definition of the purpose and objectives of management information systems, the first logical step is the creation of a formal plan. The company must determine what it needs from its system, and how it will commit its people and other resources to achieve it. If the plan is to be viable, it must include considerations about the direction in which systems development as a whole is headed.

Each company must determine its approach to system planning in terms of its own special circumstances. The reference to a planning group suggests the preference for a task force approach which provides for the participation of both line and staff personnel—the users of information as well as the providers. Even if it originates at the highest level of management, greater cooperation will be gained through the task force approach than from the words of wisdom handed down from Mount Olympus in the form of a plan that is a *fait accompli*.

One of the first problems likely to be encountered in systems planning is the most common. It has to do with the organizational gaps in the various specialized talents needed for systems design and implementation. The various advanced management techniques have grown so rapidly that we have virtually outstripped the supply of available technicians. Identification of these talent gaps must be followed by answers to a series of questions as to how and when they can be filled. For example: Do future plans call for a full-time operations research mathematician, or can that specialty be filled by a multipurpose systems man? Is a full-time computer hardware specialist needed? How much market research will be conducted?

The answers to some questions may lie in the employment of part-time help or the retention of a consulting firm. On the other hand, many of the specialties will require a full-time person or even a staff. These talents will have to be recruited from the outside or be developed internally through formalized training programs.

Another point that must be considered is the impact of new management information systems on the organizational structure. There may well be shifts in functional responsibilities. Some companies, for example, have considered establishing a director of materials whose responsibility would be the physical flow of products through the plant from raw material to finished goods. It is similar to the marketing concept of product manager.

Our concern in the present instance, however, is with the assignment of the responsibility for management of information systems. The problem is:

How can the management accountant identify himself more fully and significantly with the design and management of these new systems?

Steps for the Management Accountant

During this period of dynamic change, every craft, business and profession can take heed of the slogan, "You can't get tomorrow's job with yesterday's skills." Those of us who can use our present skills, however, as a springboard to the future are indeed fortunate.

The skills, knowledge and experience of the management accountant are far from obsolete, but they do need to be expanded and adapted to new needs and new techniques and technologies. The accountant has always been an information-oriented person, an assembler and analyst of data, and a skillful presenter of facts. These are the abilities, given new dimensions to achieve broader objectives, which will serve the more dynamic information systems of the future.

But, as we have seen, accounting will be only one of the disciplines required in these systems. There will be a critical need for people who have the ability to coordinate and supervise all component disciplines. If the management accountant is to aspire realistically to their direction, he faces a regimen of personal and professional development which will equip him to understand the capabilities—and the limitations—of all the information disciplines participating in a functioning system.

He can achieve identification with systems development through the assumption of a leadership position within his own organization by taking the initiative in the establishment of informational programs which will promote interest in, and demonstrate the advantages of, better systems design and implementation.

Conclusion

Management information systems is a highly competitive league with many eminently qualified candidates contending for the responsibility. Management accountants have in their favor the traditional identification with the essential management controls and the information systems of the past. It is not enough to ensure their role in the new systems, but it is a solid base from which to project broader corporate vision and competence in the developing techniques of modern management.

2 BASIC COMPUTER CONCEPTS

Electronic Computers and Managerial Decisions

Leonard W. Hein

The Computer as a Decision Maker

The trend in business management is to reduce all aspects of the business to arithmetical quantities and then to analyze these factors mathematically in the attempt to develop and maintain optimum business conditions. Although many business aspects still defy adequate quantification, much progress has been made. Since business operations are exceedingly complex, any adequate analysis of even presently available information requires the processing of unending quantities of data.

Mathematicians and other scientists have recently done much research on the development of mathematical models representing certain business conditions. Probably the major impetus for this development was the introduction of the high-speed, electronic computer. Many of the mathematical models developed would have been of small use if the computations had to be made by hand, for the results would have been obtained too late to be used for decision making; in fact, in many cases, hand processing could not have been accomplished at all.

Some idea of the speed of modern electronic computers may be obtained

Reprinted by permission of the author and the publisher from *The Quantitative Approach to Managerial Decisions* (Englewood Cliffs, N.J.: Prentice-Hall, Inc., 1967), pp. 8–17.

from the following comparisons: The first electronic computer, the ENIAC, was developed in 1947. One of its tasks was to compute the trajectory of projectiles, which it could do in 30 seconds, half the time required for the flight of the projectile. It would take 2400 girls operating desk calculators to make the same calculations![1]

The first general-purpose, large-scale electronic computer was the UNIVAC I, developed in 1951. It astounded the American public in 1952 by analyzing the trends in the Eisenhower election and early correctly predicting the results. The UNIVAC I had a capacity many times greater than the ENIAC. (Computer capacity may be measured with respect to many factors, such as input-output capability, internal operating speeds, repertoire of available commands or operating codes, and so forth. UNIVAC I represented a great advance in most of these aspects.) Yet the super-scale computer, IBM STRETCH, had announced internal speeds so fast that, in 24 hours, it could make the same computations as UNIVAC I computing 24 hours a day, 365 days per year for the eight years following the Eisenhower election (1952 to 1960).[2] Such performance could not in practice be achieved because of input-output limitations. Present internal speeds permit approximately one and one-half *million* additions per second.

Many of the mathematical models so far developed are not intended to make managerial decisions directly, but to analyze the probable results of alternative decisions so that managers may select that result most nearly meeting their objectives. Other models are designed to obtain the optimum results under existing conditions.

A very useful managerial principle is that of management by exception. The manager first lays down guidelines which specify limits or norms. Then clerks investigate each detailed situation and compare it to the guidelines. Only the exceptional cases—those outside the limits—are submitted to management for consideration. This, of course, is decision making, but of a lower order. It is a type of decision making to which electronic computers can be easily adapted, and here computers found early use in business data processing. The role of computers in decision making is being rapidly expanded. Entire refining plants have been placed under the supervision of computers, with product mix being varied as supply and demand factors change. The future of computers as decision makers is indeed bright; so bright, in fact, that many observers view the future role of computers with alarm, fearing lest their use go too far in replacing human beings.

Although it is sometimes necessary to employ electronic computers when utilizing many of the mathematical tools discussed in this book, understanding electronic computers is not a prerequisite to understanding the tools.

[1] Eugene M. Grabbe (ed.), *Automation in Business and Industry* (New York: John Wiley & Sons, Inc., 1957), p. 217.

[2] Graham Jones, "Trends in Computer Hardware," *Datamation*, 7 (January, 1961), 11.

Illustrative problems can readily be solved with paper and pencil methods. In fact, many of the smaller practical problems can be solved this way. Nevertheless, some familiarity with electronic computers is desirable as a basis for understanding how the tools may be applied to solve problems too complex for hand solution.

Electronic Computer Hardware

The mechanical and electronic components of an electronic computer are referred to as the electronic computer *hardware*. So-called electronic computer software will be discussed shortly. The hardware may be divided into five major components or types of components, namely, input unit, storage unit, arithmetic unit, control unit, and output unit. Individual computers can come equipped with one or several of each of these units, with the possible exception of the control unit, and some computers have several types of control units.

The relationship between these major components is shown in Figure 1. The solid lines show the major flows of information within the computer; the dotted lines extending from the control unit to each of the other units are control lines showing that all other units are under the direction of the control unit.

Information to be entered into the computer is usually on punched cards

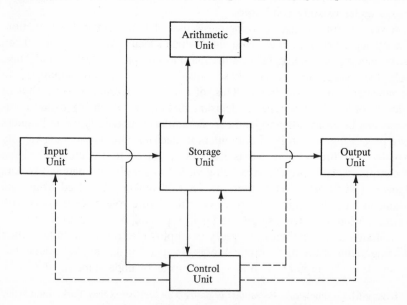

**Figure 1. The major components of an
electronic computer.**

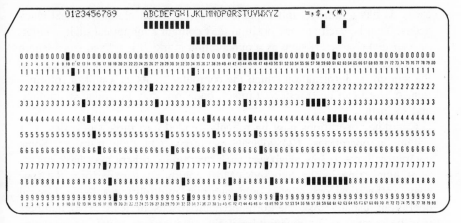

Figure 2. Typical punched card.

(Figure 2), punched paper tape, or magnetic tape. The latter is very similar to the magnetic tape of a home tape recorder. Input units that can read printed material are now available but are not yet in widespread use for typical data processing operations.

All information is normally entered into the computer through the input unit and placed directly in the storage unit. While in the storage unit, the information to be processed as data is indistinguishable in form from the information which is to instruct the computer in its operations. That is, both data and computer instructions are stored in the storage unit. Information to be used as data goes into the arithmetic unit to be processed. After processing, the data are usually returned to the storage unit. Information to be used as instructions for the computer goes into the control unit. Instructions usually tell the computer (1) to perform some arithmetic function, such as add, subtract, and so forth; (2) to make a logical decision, such as do one thing if A is greater than B, otherwise do something else; (3) to bring information into or out of the computer. Notice that information can go from the arithmetic unit into the control unit to become an instruction. This is possible because data and instructions are both stored in the same general form and can therefore to some extent be used interchangeably. Information being brought out of the computer goes from the storage unit to the output unit.

How the Computer Processes Data

In order to discuss how the computer processes data, a somewhat simplified hypothetical computer will be considered. This computer reads information from punched cards and as an output punches information into cards. It has a storage unit capable of storing 9000 alphanumerical characters. That is, each storage position may contain a numerical digit, a letter, or a special character, such as a punctuation mark. It is a fixed word-length computer with a nine-character word. A *computer word* may be defined as the amount of information which the computer treats as a unit of information. A word can be transferred intact; one word may be added to another, and so forth.

Computer operations may be roughly divided into three categories: (1) arithmetic operations, (2) logical operations, (3) data transfers. Some computers have as few as sixteen such operations, others may have operations numbering in the hundreds. Most computers can perform the four basic arithmetical operations—add, subtract, multiply, and divide. Logical operations usually take the form of comparisons or tests. Two numbers may be compared for magnitude: if the numbers are equal, perform one operation; if unequal, perform another. Data transfers involve the transfer of information into or out of the computer, from one place in storage to another, into or out of the arithmetic unit, and so forth.

Since the hypothetical computer has 9000 storage positions and a nine-character word length, it is capable of storing 1000 words. Each word location is identified by an address of three digits. The first address is 000 and the last is 999. Remember that either data or instructions can be stored at any of the 1000 addressable locations.

Assume that two numbers, 15 and 25, are to be added. Further assume that the 15 is stored in memory location 808 in the form 000000015 and the 25 is stored in location 926 in the form 000000025. The following computer program will cause the addition to be performed and the sum to be stored in location 758:

Location	Operation	Address	Instruction Address
000	RAD	808	001
001	ADD	926	002
002	STO	758	003
003	HLT	000	000

The location column merely indicates where in memory each instruction is located. Four instructions are needed, and they are stored in locations 000–003. Each instruction consists of nine characters (hence a computer word) and therefore can be stored at an addressable location.

To start the computer, the operator tells it to go to location 000 for its first instruction. Since the operator designated location 000 as containing an instruction, the computer transfers the nine characters, RAD808001, to the control unit. The control unit separates the instruction into three parts:

(1) the operation code, (2) the data address, (3) the instruction address, thus:

Operation	Data Address	Instruction Address
RAD	808	001

It analyzes the operation code as to which operation to perform. The RAD tells the computer to reset the arithmetic unit to zeros and to then add into the arithmetic unit the number stored at the data address, location 808. The number 15 is stored at location 808, therefore the arithmetic unit now contains 000000015.

The first operation is completed, and the last three characters of the first instruction, 001, indicate the location of the next instruction. The nine characters at location 001, ADD926002, are automatically transferred to the control unit and are analyzed. The ADD indicates that a straight addition is to be performed (without resetting the arithmetic unit to zeros). Thus the contents of location 926 (the number 25) are added to the number in the arithmetic unit, which now contains 000000040. The next instruction in location 002 says to store the contents of the arithmetic unit in location 758. Location 758 now contains the desired sum, 000000040. The last instruction in location 003 stops the computer. Since every location must contain nine characters, the remaining six characters of this instruction were filled with zeros.

An Illustrative Computer Problem

A more complex, but still very simple, computer problem will help to clarify many of these concepts. A company has 10,000 sets of three unequal, positive numbers. It wishes to list the smallest number in each set of three. That is, each set of three numbers is to be examined, the smallest number is then to be selected and listed.

Very complex data-processing problems are generally handled in three phases, namely, process analysis, detail flow charting, and computer coding. Although the simple problem selected for illustration could be coded directly into a computer program without such extensive analysis, the three phases will be presented.

The process flow chart is illustrated in Figure 3. It shows the flow of the work through the system as it passes from person to person or machine to machine. The first task is to key punch each set of three numbers on a card. There will then be 10,000 cards in the input deck. The task of the computer is to select the smallest number of each set and punch it on a card. The output deck will also have 10,000 cards, but each card will now contain

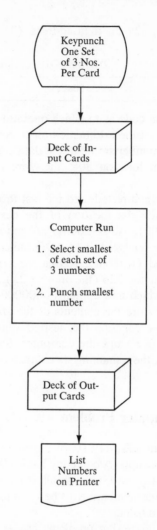

Figure 3. Process flow chart.

only one number. The information in the output deck is then listed on the printer.

The three numbers on the input deck may be referred to as *A*, *B*, and *C*, respectively. They will be punched into the card as follows (see Figure 2 for the available 80 columns of a punched card):

Number	Card Columns
A	1–10
B	11–20
C	21–30

The next step is to analyze the detailed operations to be carried on within the computer. This is most easily done by means of a detailed flow chart (Figure 4). No standardized symbols have been developed for detail flow charting. Each computer manufacturer has developed its own set of symbols. Those illustrated were developed by the UNIVAC Division of Sperry Rand Corporation.

The first symbol (Start) designates the entrance point into the analysis.

The next symbol ① is a connector to which a return in the flow of information will occur. The [Read] indicates that the information from one card

is to be placed in storage. The next box (A: B) is a logical decision box and

has two paths leading from it. If *A* is greater than (>) *B,* the flow goes to the right; if *A* is less than (<) *B,* the flow goes downward. If the flow goes to the right, then *B* is compared to *C.* Again two possible paths are available. If *B* is greater than (>) *C, C* is the smallest number. It is sent to output and punched on a card. The flow then goes back to connector 1, and the information on the next card is read in. This cycle is repeated until all 10,000 sets of numbers have been analyzed. A typical speed at which this process could be performed is about 250 sets of numbers (cards) per minute. The limiting factor would be the speed of card punching, which is a mechanical (not electronic) process. (Trace each of the possible flow paths in Figure 4. A thorough understanding of this simple flow chart is highly desirable).

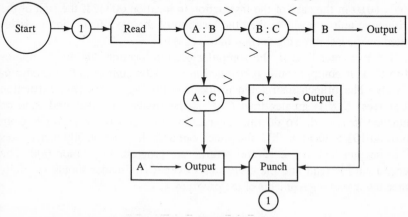

Figure 4. Detailed flow chart.

The final step is to code the computer program, that is, to write the instructions for the computer. In writing the instructions, the detailed flow chart is carefully followed:

Loca-tion	Opera-tion	Data Address	Instruction Address	Remarks
000	RDC	100	001	Read one set of numbers
001	RAD	100	002	
002	SUB	101	003	Compare A to B: if A < B, go to 010;
003	BMI	010	004	if A > B, go to 004
004	RAD	101	005	
005	SUB	102	006	Compare B to C: if B < C, go to 013;
006	BMI	013	007	If B > C, go to 007
007	RAD	101	008	C smallest
008	STO	200	009	Store in output area
009	PCH	200	000	Punch and return to 000
010	RAD	100	011	
011	SUB	102	012	Compare A to C: if A < C, go to 014;
012	BMI	014	007	If A > C, go to 007
013	RAD	101	008	B smallest
014	RAD	100	008	A smallest

Fourteen instructions are required for the program (in comparison to most practical programs, this is a very small number). The instruction in location 000 causes the computer to read (RDC) the information from the first card in the deck. The three numbers are placed in storage, A in 100, B in 101, and C in 102. The next three instructions compare A to B. This is done by subtracting (SUB) B from A and then testing the algebraic sign of the arithmetic unit. If the sign is positive, A is greater than B; if negative, B is greater than A.

The instruction in location 003 requires some explanation. It is called a *branch* or *logical instruction*. Notice that all the other instructions have a data address portion and an instruction address portion. The branch instruction has two instruction address portions. In this case, if the sign of the arithmetic unit is negative, the next instruction location is designated by the center three digits (010 in the case of the instruction in location 003). If the sign of the arithmetic unit is positive, then the location of the next instruction is designated by the last three digits (004 in this case).

If A is greater than B, the computer goes to location 004 and compares B to C. This comparison is performed in a fashion similar to that used previously. The branch instruction in location 006 again has two instruction addresses. If B is greater than C, C is the smallest number and is to be punched in a card. To do this, instructions 007 and 008 transfer C from location 101 to location 200, the punch-out area. Instruction 009 then causes C to be punched in a card and returns the program to location 000. The second card is read and the cycle starts over. (The reader should carefully trace the remaining segments of the program.)

Electronic Computer Software

The computer programs so far discussed were coded in machine language. *Machine language* is a language intelligible to the computer. It is, however, difficult for the computer programmer to work in machine language. To help overcome this difficulty, a large number of programming aids, frequently referred to as *electronic computer software,* have been developed. These aids usually take the form of symbolic assembly programs, interpretive routines, compilers, and generators.

Symbolic assembly programs are designed primarily to permit the programmer to write in English language symbols rather than in machine language. The computer then converts the symbols into a machine language program. The program just discussed, if written in a typical symbolic language, might appear as follows:

Location	Operation	Data Address	Instruction Address
START	RDC	A	
	RAD	A	
	SUB	B	
	BMI	BBIGA	ABIGB
ABIGB	RAD	B	
	SUB	C	
	BMI	CBIGB	BBIGC
BBIGC	RAD	C	STORE
STORE	STO	PUNCH	
	PCH	PUNCH	START
BBIGA	RAD	A	
	SUB	C	
	BMI	CBIGA	BBIGC
CBIGB	RAD	B	STORE
CBIGA	RAD	A	STORE

Notice how closely the symbols used follow normal English usage. Most symbolic assembly programs permit great latitude in selecting symbols. The usual restriction is in the maximum length permitted. Location and instruction addresses need be used only when the flow does not follow in sequence. Assembly programs may also perform other services for the programmer. Where some form of assembly program is available (and almost every computer has one or more assembly programs), few programmers code in machine language.

A more complex form of assembly program is known as a *compiler.* A compiler utilizes *macroinstructions.* One macroinstruction written by the programmer is converted into several (frequently many) machine language instructions by the compiler. Compilers may be machine oriented or problem oriented. A compiler is said to be *machine oriented* if the programmer must follow closely the pattern of the computer logic and machine language. It is said to be *problem oriented* if the programmer is permitted to write in the language and logic of the problem.

The output of an assembly program or a compiler is a machine language program. The programmer writes his program according to the rules of the assembler or compiler. His work is then processed on the computer under the supervision of the assembler or compiler, which then produces the machine language program. An *interpretive routine* permits the programmer to write in a nonmachine language, but it does not produce a machine language program as an intermediate product. Instead, the output of the interpretive routine is the results sought by the programmer—the problem solution. Interpretive routines are useful for one-shot programs. Because they are slow and inefficient, they are not suited to repetitive business data processing.

Generators produce specialized programs to fit the needs of the programmer. Examples of generators are sort generators and report generators. When the programmer desires to have the computer produce a certain type of report, he merely specifies the description of the report to the report generator, the number of columns required, the headings, and so forth. The report generator then produces a machine language program which will in turn produce the desired type of report.

The foregoing are a few examples of computer software. There are many other kinds, and much research is being done in producing better and more varied kinds of programming aids.

Standards for Computers and Information Processing

Gordon B. Davis

In the United States, there are over 40,000 computers. These were supplied by some 30 American manufacturers and a similar number of foreign computer manufacturers. These manufacturers are supplemented by hundreds of suppliers of computer components and computer operating supplies.

Each manufacturer's equipment has unique characteristics but each has some connection with equipment and supplies provided by others. There is frequently a need to exchange data between different systems. Not everyone uses the same words to mean the same things. These and other considerations make it desirable to develop industry-wide standards. This article is a report on the current status of standards for computers and information processing and their relevance to the CPA.

The United States of America Standards Institute (USASI)

Formerly called the American Standards Association (ASA), the United States of America Standards Institute is a private, voluntary federation of about 150 trade associations and professional societies plus over 2,000 member companies interested in developing standards.

Reprinted by permission of the author and the publisher from *The Journal of Accountancy*, Vol. 124, No. 3 (September, 1967), pp. 52–57.

USASI acts as a facilitating and co-ordinating agency in the development of voluntary standards. A standard is approved only if it is supported by consensus of all national groups substantially concerned with its scope and provisions. Standards prepared under USASI auspices typically have wide acceptance. More than 2,000 standards in the fields of engineering, industry, safety and consumer goods have been developed and approved under its procedures. In short, a "USA standard" is a voluntary, national standard arrived at by common consent and available for voluntary use.

Through USASI, the United States is represented in the International Organization for Standardization (ISO), The International Electrotechnical Commission (IEC) and in the Pan American Standards Committee (PASC). USASI thus is the focus for both United States standards and U.S. participation in international standards.

USA standards are proposed through two basic methods:

1. *Existing standards.* An existing standard which originated within a technical society or group may be submitted for approval as a USA standard. Approximately one-third of the standards have come through this channel.

2. *Developed standards.* A technical society or group may develop a proposed standard on assignment by the USASI. This is typically performed by a sectional committee. A sectional committee is composed of representatives of all groups or organizations substantially concerned with the scope of the standards project. The sectional committee is the method used most frequently for computers and data processing.

The X3 Sectional Committee on Computers and Information Processing

The sectional committee for computers is designated as X3, "Computers and Information Processing." Each sectional committee has one or more organizations which are designated as sponsors to give administrative support and direction to the committee. The sponsor is responsible for the administration and direction of the standards project. The sponsor organization for the X3 sectional committee is the Business Equipment Manufacturers Association (BEMA). X3 operates under the following scope: "Standardization related to systems, computers, equipments, devices and media for information processing." The ISO counterpart is Technical Committee 97, Computers and Standardization.

Membership in X3 is by national association, society or organization and is divided equally into three groups of members: general interest, consumers and producers. Each member is entitled to one vote. The American Institute of Certified Public Accountants is a general interest member. The committee has eight subcommittees responsible for the technical work of considering standardization (Figure 1). In general, membership on these subcommittees is by individual rather than by organization.

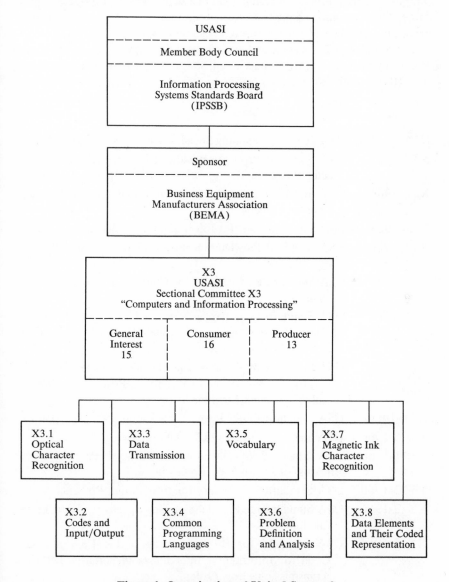

Figure 1. Organization of United States of America Standards Institute X3 Committee.

The representative of the AICPA on the X3 committee is the Manager, Computer Technical Services of the AICPA staff. Two alternates have been appointed from the computer advisory staffs of CPA firms, currently Vico Henriques of Arthur Young and Company, Washington, D.C., and Dennis Mulvihill of Touche, Ross, Bailey and Smart, New York. These three computer experts prepare recommendations with respect to proposed standards. These recommendations are submitted to the AICPA data processing committee which decides how the AICPA should vote.

The following USA standards have received final approval and are available in published form from the United States of America Standards Institute, 10 East 40th Street, New York, N.Y. 10016.

Number	Title
X3.1-1962	USA Standard Signaling Speeds for Data Transmission
X3.2-1963	USA Standard Print Specifications for Magnetic Ink Character Recognition
X3.3-1963	USA Standard Bank Check Specifications for Magnetic Ink Character Recognition
X3.4-1963	USA Standard Code for Information Interchange
X3.5-1966	USA Standard Flowchart Symbols for Information Processing
X3.6-1965	USA Standard Perforated Tape Code for Information Interchange
X3.7-1965	USA Standard Interchange Perforated Tape Variable Block Format for Positioning and Straight Cut Numerically Controlled Machine Tools
X3.8-1965	USA Standard Interchangeable Perforated Tape Block Format for Contouring and Contouring/Positioning Numerically Controlled Machine Tools
X3.9-1966	USA Standard FORTRAN
X3.10-1966	USA Standard Basic FORTRAN
X3.11-1966	USA Standard Specification for General Purpose Paper Cards for Information Processing
X3.12-1966	USA Standard Vocabulary for Information Processing
X3.13-1966	USA Standard for Parallel Signaling Speeds for Data Transmission
X3.15-1966	USA Standard for Bit Sequencing of the USA Standard Code for Information Interchange in Serial-by-Bit Data Transmission (Low Order)
X3.16-1966	USA Standard for Character Structure and Character Parity

Sense in Serial-by-Bit Data Communication in the USA
Standard Code for Information Interchange

X3.17-1966   USA Standard Character Set for Optical Character Recognition

An Example—Flowchart Standards

The standard which is currently the most important for the CPA is the standard for flowchart symbols. This example was chosen not only to illustrate the activities of the USASI but also to inform accountants about this standard.

Flowcharting symbols are useful because they give a visual picture of the activities being described. As the computer industry developed, each manufacturer produced a separate set of symbols and separate flow chart templates to implement them. This caused confusion especially for persons—such as certified public accountants—who deal with many clients.

A preliminary set of flowchart symbols was prepared by the USASI committee. These were widely adopted in the industry. Prior to their publication as a standard, a conflict developed between the ISO international proposals and the USA proposals. The compromise is reflected in the revised standards published in June 1966.

It will take time for the revised standards to be implemented by all users but the advantages of the standards are such that the CPA should encourage their use. All manufacturers are expected to adopt the USASI symbols; some have done so immediately and the others have indicated they will do so. The new AICPA professional development courses on EDP documentation, "Systems Flowcharting" and "Program Flowcharting and Decision Tables," use the USA standard symbols.

The USASI standard flowchart symbols for information processing are summarized here. Additional flowcharting symbols currently under consideration by the International Standards Organization are also presented since these, when approved, will be proposed as additions to the USA standard.

Expected Developments

The following standards of special interest to CPAs are now being balloted:

Proposed USA Standard Use of Flowchart Symbols in Flowcharting for Information Processing.

Proposed USA Standard COBOL.

Basic Symbols   Specialized Input/Output and File Symbols

Input/Output

Represents an input/output function. It may be replaced by a specialized input/output symbol.

Punched Card

Punched Tape

Process

Any kind of processing function. May be replaced
by a specialized processing symbol.

Document

—————— Flowline

Flowline to show sequence of operations and information. An arrowhead may be used to indicate
direction if it is not the normal left to right and top
to bottom.

Magnetic Tape

Input/output functions using a specialized medium.

- - - - Annotation

Manual Input

A means of adding descriptive comments. Connected by the broken line to the point where comment is
meaningful.

Information is entered manually at the time of processing by means of an online keyboard, switch
setting, etc.

**Summary of USASI standard flowchart sym-
bols.** The complete flowchart standard is
contained in United States Standard Flowchart Symbols for Information Processing,
USASI X3.5-1966 [revised].

Processing

Input/Output and Files

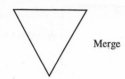

Merge

Combining of two or more sets of items into one set.

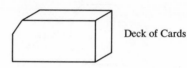

Deck of Cards

Collection of punched cards.

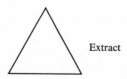

Extract

Removal of one or more sets of items from a set.

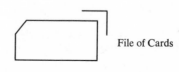

File of Cards

A file of related punched cards.

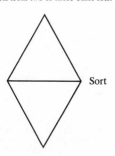

Collate

Merging combiner with extraction — forming two or more sets from two or more other sets.

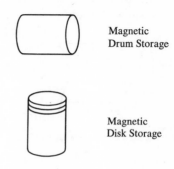

Magnetic
Drum Storage

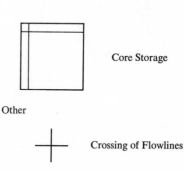

Magnetic
Disk Storage

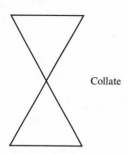

Sort

Arrangement into a particular sequence.

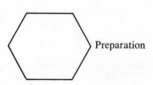

Core Storage

Other

Crossing of Flowlines

Junction of Flowlines

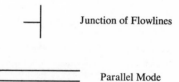

Preparation

Preparation procedures prior to processing.

Parallel Mode

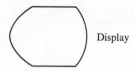 Display

Information is displayed for human use at the time of processing by means of online indicators, video devices, console printers, etc.

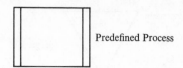 Predefined Process

Names a process specified elsewhere; e.g., a sub-routine.

 Communication Link

Information is transmitted automatically from one location to another. An open arrowhead may be used to indicate direction of flow.

 Manual Operation

Offline process geared to the speed of a human being.

 Online Storage

Storage of information that can be accessed direct-ly by the computer; e.g., drum, disk, strips, etc.

 Auxiliary Operation

Offline process performed on equipment (such as sorter, collator, card to tape converter) not under the direct control of the central processing unit.

 Offline Storage

Offline storage of information, regardless of medium on which recorded.

Additional Symbols

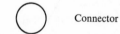 Connector

Connector used at the junction of several flowlines or to represent a continued flow when the flow is broken by the physical limitations of the flowchart.

Specialized Processing Symbols

 Decision

Decision operation in processing which determines which of two or more alternate paths will be taken.

 Terminal

A terminal point in a system at which information can enter or leave; e.g., start, stop, halt, delay or interrupt.

**Additional flowchart symbols proposed
by ISO.**

The proposed standard for use of flowchart symbols supplements the USA standard for flowchart symbols with standard conventions for symbol identification, connector referencing, symbol stripping, etc. The proposed USA standard COBOL defines standard modules in the common business-oriented language. This should reduce confusion as to the COBOL features implemented on a particular computer by providing standard specifications for different levels of implementation.

The standards effort in computers and information processing will probably become increasingly important to the CPA, both because of the CPA's increasing involvement in computers and because of the changing emphasis of USASI to standards of special interest to the CPA, such as standards for software and data elements. The American Institute of CPAs can therefore be expected to provide continued support for USASI and continued participation in X3.

3 HISTORY

Electronics in Accounting

Adolph Matz

While cost determination was the chief task of the accountant during the war years, and while the reconversion job was tackled and completed more quickly and more efficiently than many expected, the task of waging a successful battle in competitive enterprise is about to begin.* Sales forces, production men, design and equipment engineers, personnel and public relations officers have been marshaled to the aid of management. But cost- and profit-minded executives cannot overlook the assistance of the accounting division. The comptroller and his staff compose an integral unit of business management. The preparation of monthly or annual statements has long been recognized as the quintessence of the accountant's task. Weekly payrolls, inventory records, billing methods, etc., fall within his realm. But the execution of these tasks cannot and should not retain his sole interest. Today as never before the industrial accountant faces the great and ever-challenging responsibility of providing top management with a prospective cost and profit picture that will enable executives to appraise future policies regarding prices, production, employment and profits. Many premises and preconceptions must be taken into consideration by the industrial accountant.

Reprinted by permission of the author and the publisher from *The Accounting Review*, Vol. XXI, No. 4 (October, 1946), pp. 371–379.

* The author wishes to express his gratitude to Mr. John H. Davis, Research Engineer, Institute of Advanced Study, Princeton, N.J., formerly with the Moore School of Electrical Engineering, University of Pennsylvania, for the technical assistance rendered in the preparation of this article.

Again, it is not the mere preparation of such management aids that is important; more valuable still is their timeliness and the possibility of preparing them quickly and efficiently. Much criticism has been heaped upon the accountant in the past because of his delay and slowness in preparing daily, weekly, monthly or annual reports or forecasts. But the fault does not always rest with the accountant. Often in spite of all manual and/or mechanical help, he is unable either to complete the job or even to present all the multiple possibilities that could be computed and should be presented by changing the premises. The solution of the problem of "normal capacity" has perplexed many executives and accountants. But the problem still remains and must be brought to management's attention in the light of its true influence upon the future picture of the company.

The execution and solution of the many tasks ascribed to the accounting division has been aided by machines, such as adding, computing and calculating machines, bookkeeping and billing machines, punch card and other tabulating, analysis and accounting machines. Most machines, together with other office equipment, have been purchased and installed in order to increase the efficiency of department and staff and also to reduce operating costs. The selection of the equipment has always been closely related to the designing of forms and records, and to improvements in routine and procedure. Yet the majority of these machines, whether hand-operated, electrically-driven computing machines or electro-mechanically-operated tabulating equipment, have been assigned to jobs such as preparation of payrolls, printing of checks, payroll distribution, inventory records, material distribution, billing methods, accounts payable methods, etc. Their use in executing these essential tasks has been so great that very little time remained in an otherwise busy schedule to serve the industrial accountant in the solution of the many problems before him. Is there a possibility that the future offers a ray of hope in his dilemma? Have scientific and engineering developments come to a point where these and many other business problems can be solved more quickly, more efficiently, and even more accurately? It can be stated that this possibility exists.

Computing Devices in Retrospect

Man's desire to create some mechanical means for aiding him in carrying out simple arithmetic processes dates back to very early times. Computing machines are not a product of this century. One of the earliest computing machines on record was constructed by Pascal (1623–1662), a Frenchman. The German philosopher Leibnitz (1646–1716) is credited with having built one of the first machines capable of performing the four operations of arithmetic. Most modern mechanical calculating machines have really nothing basic in them that was not in Leibnitz's machine. Of course, many refinements have been introduced but the fundamental idea was never changed. However, these machines were not used and known very widely as it was still impossible to duplicate parts and still achieve reliable results as is now done by modern processes of fabrication. When the modern tabulating machine with its punch card was introduced, it had a tremendous influence upon business and financial procedure. If, today, reliance still had to be placed on longhand methods, the scope and complexity of present-day business problems would be practically impossible. This new arithmetical technique has been so widely adopted that over 10,000 tons of punch cards are used each year in this country. Refinements in the punched-card method have included use of electrical contacts through the holes instead of mechanical connections; use of photocells; use of continuation of holes to give a greater amount of information carried by each card. While these inventions and developments constituted invaluable aids in some fields of human endeavor, complex problems arose in other fields, such as the physical sciences, that made specialized devices necessary. Just as higher mathematical systems had to be invented to deal with theories which could no longer be handled through ordinary arithmetic, so new devices had to be designed to make these theories of practical value. The construction of large-scale, continuous variable machines, such as the differential analyzer, and electric circuit analogy devices like the algebraic "Root Extractor," permitted the solution of certain types of differential and algebraic equations.

At the start of World War II, air attack brought the application of these techniques into the forefront in the design of antiaircraft fire control equipment. Not only was it necessary to track the plane and quickly compute its future position so that the guns could lead the plane by the right amount to insure a hit, but enormous amounts of calculations were required to provide advance data to the antiaircraft fire control director about the path of the shell fired by the gun at various elevations under various climatic conditions. The immediate solution of these problems meant the creation of large computing groups at computing machine centers such as the Moore School of the University of Pennsylvania, the Massachusetts Institute of Technology, the Ballistic Laboratory of the Aberdeen Proving Grounds, and other places. Great attention was sharply focused upon the need of adequate computing facilities to speed engineering design by mathematical solution rather than by experimental techniques, for the war-vital ballistic problems could not be solved experimentally.[1]

Somewhat in anticipation of this future need, a differential analyzer was invented and constructed in 1931 by Dr. Vannevar Bush at Massachusetts Institute of Technology, followed in 1935 by an improved model at the Moore School of the University of Pennsylvania and another one later at

---

[1] The present state of development of radar presents the possibility of solving ballistic problems experimentally.

the Ballistic Laboratory at Aberdeen. The work in this development created the Differential Analyzer No. 2 at MIT and the IBM Automatic Sequence Controlled Calculator at Harvard University in 1943. Yet the pressing need for more and faster computing devices led to an entirely new and revolutionary attack on the problem in the spring of 1943 at the Moore School of Electrical Engineering of the University of Pennsylvania, ending in December, 1945, with the invention of a purely electronic device, known as ENIAC.

The ENIAC

The successful completion of the first all-electronic general-purpose computing machine, representing the pioneering electric mechanism in its field, opens the future to the development of business machines heretofore undreamed of and may revolutionize the use of mathematics in engineering, thereby changing many of our present industrial design methods.[2] This mathematical robot, known as ENIAC (Electronic Numerical Integrator and Computer) was designed and constructed for the Ordnance Department at the Moore School of Electrical Engineering at the University of Pennsylvania in Philadelphia. This machine is capable of solving many technical and scientific problems so complex and difficult that all previous methods of solution were considered impractical. The ENIAC is capable of computing a thousand times faster than the most advanced general-purpose calculating machines previously built. The electronic methods of computing used in this new invention make it possible to solve in hours problems which would take years on a mechanical machine—a time so long as to make such an undertaking impractical.

However, the ENIAC was constructed to do not only this job but to be an all-purpose machine, that is, it could carry out the elementary arithmetic processes of addition, subtraction, multiplication, division, storing of number, and calling upon the functional value of a function for some value of its argument. With these simple processes and sufficient speed it is possible to carry out more advanced computations, such as differentiation and integration, in a practical and highly accurate way.[3]

Of course, a hydrodynamical problem in ballistic research could be solved by simple desk-type computing machines and competent help, but the time involved would be so enormous that it would not even be attempted. Tabu-

[2] See *New York Times*, February 15, 1946, "Electronic Computer Flashes Answers, May Speed Engineering."
[3] See "Project PX—The ENIAC" by J. G. Brainerd in the *Pennsylvania Gazette*, University of Pennsylvania, March, 1946, p. 17.

lating equipment or the newer types of digital machines could do the work, but it might well take a year or so to do it. On the ENIAC, however, the job could be done in about one week. The difference between the electronic speed of the new computer and any other machine means the difference between the possibility of obtaining a practical solution and leaving the problem in the category of those that are formulated but never analyzed, or perhaps of those that are formulated and finally tested by multitudinous experiments over a long and costly period of time and effort. For it must be remembered that the basic time to carry out any addition (or subtraction) in ENIAC is 200 microseconds (i.e. 1/5,000th of a second). At the dedication exercises one simple demonstration was given to the guests by adding a number to itself 5,000 times. The answer appeared in one second, and no one present could more than blink between the start and finish of the problem.

Industrial Implications

In considering the undertaking of a problem mathematically susceptible of solution by conventional computing methods, the practical aspects of time and manual labor cannot be overlooked. Leaders of our scientific world have been aware of many problems which have gone begging for want of practical means of solution. The development of new mathematical techniques has been stalled by the lack of mechanical aids to test new theories.[4] Indeed, the present computational methods are still based on systems advanced by Karl F. Gauss (1777–1855).

In the fields of industry the first practical application of this new high-speed computing device was to a mathematical problem in nuclear physics. The possibility of finding a solution without the necessity of innumerable experimental stages conducted over many years will close the technological gap between theory and practice. The development from the discovery of chain reactions to industrial application of nuclear physics is comparable to the development from the discovery of fire to the invention and manufacture of steam engines and turbines.[5] High-speed computers will indeed hasten the development of new design in transformers, rectifiers, generators, motors, gas turbines, Diesel and jet-propelled engines, aircraft and other industrial machinery. Their greatest influential contribution, however, lies in the release of the scientist's thinking from the drudgery of the multitude of minute and painstaking computations, correlations, collations, differen-

[4] See such discussion in *Theory of Games and Economic Behavior* by John von Neumann and Oskar Morgenstern, Princeton University Press, 1944, Chapter 1.

[5] See Chapter 2 on "Statement of Problem" in the official text on *Atomic Energy* prepared by Henry D. Smyth, Princeton University Press, 1945.

tiations, integrations and transformations. This freedom for thought can also be given to industrial management.

Accounting Significance

The commercial side of our modern society has never been slow in adopting the latest design in computing machines. The public has been aware of the necessity of their use in modern business institutions, such as banks, life insurance companies, large-scale manufacturing companies, accounting and engineering firms and domestic and foreign trading houses. In such establishments these machines are the life blood of their transactions. The businessman has long made use of mechanical aids in reasoning. Because of the accelerated tempo of modern business affairs, machines of higher speed remain a continuing necessity. Let us see in what way the advent of the ENIAC can mean not only entirely new types of business machines but may well also revolutionize methods and systems of dealing with everyday business transactions.

Nearly everyone has seen or used electronic tubes at one time or another. These are the tubes in home radio sets, the transmitters at broadcasting stations. The fluorescent lights in factories, stores and homes, the X-ray tubes used by doctors and dentists, the picture tubes in television receivers, and a host of other devices operate on electronic tubes. In recent years electronic tubes have won a place in industry and help countless tasks to be performed more efficiently and accurately than ever before. High-frequency radio waves used to heat-treat steel for gears and tools are produced by electronic tubes; the bonding of layers of plywood in the manufacture of plywood airplane propellers uses them. The speed of electric motors under varying load conditions is controlled by them. In resistance welding, in various highly specialized instruments, in distinguishing shades of color, the electronic tube has been called upon to measure and control chemical and physical qualities. A large variety of electron tubes have been developed that literally "hear," "see," "feel," "taste," "smell," "calculate" and "talk."

This electronic tube can be pictured as a valve that controls the flow of electric current through a circuit much as a valve controls the flow of water through a pipe.[6] An electronic tube does not generate an electric current any more than a kitchen faucet manufactures a stream of water. Unlike the valve, the electronic tube has no moving parts and very little mechanical inertia to overcome. Its action is completely electrical; therefore it operates with nearly the speed of light, and that is one of its most valuable features. Another valuable feature is that only a tiny amount of energy is required to control a large amount of current flowing through the tube. The speed

[6] *How Electronic Tubes Work*, issued by General Electric Co., 1943, p.4.

of the electronic tube is and must be the prime factor of this new, as well as of any future, computing device. As the basic principle of any computer, such as an adding machine or a comptometer, is the breaking up of complex operations into simpler component operations, so any new invention must likewise break the operations into a combination of additions, subtractions and the like. The principle of serializing or arranging in sequence would greatly lengthen the time required to solve complex problems. But it is obvious that only one method can achieve the desired result: the device must be electronic and use electronic tubes. Electro-mechanical devices as mentioned above would be too slow when vacuum tube circuits can be created that are from 10,000 to 100,000 times faster. However, the speed of the electronic tube will be of little value unless it is possible to feed the information to the machine in such a way that speedy results can be obtained.

In-Put

Many of our present-day business machines store the information gathered on cards by means of holes punched in places desired. The machine itself is controlled chiefly by a plugboard or wiring unit with additional control from the cards themselves in certain cases. As the cards are fed into the machine, one detail of a calculation can be carried out time after time. If, of course, additional different operations should be performed a modification of the plugboard or wiring unit is necessary. Therefore, it seems apparent that much work is done by the operator in taking the cards from one machine to another, in arranging or sorting them in sequence and in changing the boards. In place of paper cards the Harvard Calculator uses a paper tape in which holes are punched to feed the problem to the machine. As long as these computing devices utilize mechanical elements and relays as their essential components, the speed at which paper cards or paper tape may be put in, read or punched is generally adequate. Yet paper, either as a card or as a tape, is not the only material available. Various types of film, such as moving picture film and special cellulose tapes, are possibilities. The most suitable material, however, seems to be a tape or wire of magnetic material on which the information is recorded in the form of small magnetized regions. The recording on the wire should be performed by a typewriter similar to the ones used in offices. In order to check the information that is recorded magnetically, a paper tape would be printed at the same time. The wire can store information much more compactly than it can be stored on punched cards or paper tapes. This wire can run at high speeds, is not easily damaged by handling or repeated use, will be naturally rustproof and can be used over and over again through erasure of the magnetic impulses. The cards or tapes constitute that operational characteristic of any computing device generally classified as the external memory element.

But after the external memory element places the information in the machine, the so-called internal memory element must be called upon to solve the problem. The internal memory may be thought of as falling into several categories. There is first the problem of gathering the empirical data that are known before the machine is started. Such data can be remembered by the setting of switches on the so-called function tables or by pre-setting a number of circuits. Then there is the problem of instructing the device so that transfers between the various memory units take place, causing the arithmetic units to perform desired operations on the numbers. And finally, the problem exists of storing the numerical data which are calculated in the course of the computation and which must be available for other portions of the computation. Although for the devices using electrical components the existing methods of internal memory processes seem sufficient, it is obvious that particular attention has to be paid to this problem for an all-electronic computing machine. But the creation of a memory element that not only stores the empirical data known before, as well as the instructions required to specify and carry out the calculation, but also serves for the storage of all numerical data that have been calculated in the course of the computation of any problem, no matter how complex, will present itself as one of the greatest achievements in the construction of modern high-speed computing devices.[7]

The internal storage facilities might be looked upon as units consisting of a number of vacuum tubes that will be able to retain many digit sequences in a very definite time relationship. As a matter of fact, the development of electronic tubes points to an internal high-speed memory capacity of about 2,000 ten-digit decimal numbers. Yet, the storage of the computation is not the only advantage of this memory element. At present, the changing of plugboards, the setting of switches, and the plugging in of many interconnecting cables is necessary to change from one type of problem to another; the future computer, however, will store such operating instructions in the same manner as the computation itself is stored. By such a method the total storage capacity is utilized and at the disposal of the operator who can allocate part of it to operating instructions, part to function tables, part to the numbers that enter into and come out of the calculation.

Emphasis has been placed above upon the need of an external memory device that would read and record the information in line with the speed of the tube. As a medium a magnetic wire was considered. This suggested medium is also of importance in connection with the collating and sorting of the data. These operations are commonly handled outside the regular computing machines. Sorters with card-matching or collating devices attached constitute the generally accepted method. It is generally believed that card-

---

[7] See editorial page in *Electronic Industries*, August, 1945, page 73, in which Dr. V. Bush proposes an Electronic Desk Library.

sorting machines lend themselves better to this type of operation. Yet if, in computing a problem, sets of numbers are held in the electronic tube it seems quite logical to complete the sorting and collating within the machine itself. It is true that the sorting and collating of cards amounts to arranging or rearranging them in a definite order. When paper tape is used this arrangement is not feasible, as the old tape cannot be used any more. Not only can the magnetic wire be used again as stated above, but the speed of the electronic tube allows also a reading and recording of the information in a new sequence or new order on a new magnetic wire at something like at least 5,000 pulses per second. If it is desirable to collate the data no great difficulties will be encountered. The machine would be instructed to select the numbers or words that are to be placed on the new wire. Again working at the speed mentioned, the magnetic wire collator will be much faster than the card collator.

Out-Put

Just as the information is fed into the machine by means of a magnetic wire, so the information can be recorded on this medium upon completion of the computation. It is, of course, desirable to have the results available in some printed, photographic or graphic form. The printing of the data from a magnetic wire should offer no difficulty. A typewriter or printer type of machine is now being used with other computing devices. When, however, several reports or tabulations must be prepared which must be distributed to many parties interested, photographic reproductions of the tabulations by the automatic printer may be used. Such photographic reproductions can be issued in their final and most convenient form, since all sorting, collating and interpolating has been carried out by the computer. Even more useful will be the possibility of presenting the final answer graphically. Although today tabulations are prepared "on time," considerable time is spent and lost in "plotting" the tabular results and in drawing the curves. But in the future it will prove easier to let a high-speed computer solve the problems and simultaneously "plot" the results on the screen of a cathode ray tube. The graph can then be run off whenever desired. Such a visual output immediately available can lead the way for investigating unfavorable trends quickly and efficiently.

The question must have come to the mind of the reader: Just how large a machine must be constructed to do all this work and what will it cost to run such a piece of equipment? It must be admitted that the existing laboratory type of high-speed computing machine, mechanical or electronic, is of tremendous size and was built at considerable expense. But the development of electronic equipment will lead to the construction of computers which (if one may speculate) should be somewhat larger than the present electric bookkeeping and accounting machine known as the printer. Floor space of tabulating departments will be reduced considerably, yet this will not be the only saving. As it has been suggested that a magnetic wire instead of a paper card is to be chosen as the external memory medium, space and material-cost savings will be considerable. If we assume that an 80-column tabulating card is equivalent to about 300 pulses on about 3 inches of wire, then a commercial spool of about 12,000 feet in length can roughly fill the equivalent of 50,000 completely filled cards. The wire would weigh about one-half pound and could be stored in a small metal box. 50,000 cards would fill 25 tabulating card boxes.

With regard to personnel, training would have to be given in the future just as the operator is now being trained to handle tabulating equipment. As the new device is improved and perfected, the operator's task will be more systematic and mechanical. A few dollars' additional first cost in equipment will be repaid many times in lower cost of tube maintenance as well as greater freedom from service interruptions. The personnel will become free to watch the results, make adjustments, and serve fully and competently in the solution of the problems.

The Task Ahead

It was stated in the introduction that with the restoration of competitive enterprise, management will need a progressive accounting organization to present the facts upon which broad and decisive policies can be based. With the construction of the all-electronic computing device, the field and the future of the industrial accountant has been expanded tremendously. The field of general accounting seems to have taken the lead in these modern inventions, when we learn that "the electronic art is making inroads into many manual methods in the business operations of telephone and telegraph systems. There new applications include dialing equipment, automatic time recording and bill computing facilities, sorting of vouchers, etc."[8]

The installation of the first automatic ticketing of telephone calls system at Culver City, adjoining Los Angeles, points to the future application of mechanical methods to the accounting processes. A possible method is to arrange the ticketer so that, in addition to the digits which it now prints, it will print also their equivalents in code marks which can be recognized by photoelectric scanning. Other forms of record produced by different types of recording mechanisms may be found advantageous, and the equipment for use at the accounting center may

See editorial in the January, 1946, issue of *Electronic Industries*, p. 47.

be designed to mechanize the accounting processes to any degree found economical.[9]

How much more valuable for the individual concern, as well as for society as a whole, will the work of the industrial accountant become when the problems facing him can be thought about, solved, and presented in the shortest possible time. For the important fact should be remembered that the creation of these new machines does not replace creative thinking. On the contrary, it will encourage further thought, since it will free the accountant from the time-consuming burden of routine calculation. His time can be devoted more than ever to the solution of manifold problems such as inventory valuation at average costs instead of current purchase price, unit costs of increasing production beyond present levels, the incremental or differential cost of added output compared with selling prices, the minimum sales price in case of a shutdown to avoid too drastic losses, the abandonment of part of the output of a plant, the additional cost incurred when a "sideline" is introduced to utilize spare time and machinery and even out the production schedules, determination of costs connected with a change-over in production methods, the old problem of interest as a cost, and a host of others.[10] But these special cost problems too often must take a back seat only to be assigned later to other departments having a statistical or engineering function; and this leads to antagonism and misunderstanding among the personnel. While these problems rightfully and naturally fall in the realm of the industrial accountant, his time, efforts and abilities have been taken up with the problems of daily, weekly and monthly cost determination. In the future, however, his interest must be centered upon the dynamic features of cost analysis and cost control for recognizing, evaluating and presenting new and alternate strategies to be pursued because of greater output, greater turnover, greater employment. His accurate and intelligent appraisal of the perplexing problems connected with differential costs, burden allocation under varying conditions, distribution cost analysis, development costs, etc., will influence considerably the price- and policy-making decisions of the company's top executives. In this task the new electronic aids will prove themselves to be of outstanding value.

If the accountant by his own initiative, together with this modern mechanical assistance, can furnish management with the leads necessary for doing a better job, he will also, in the last analysis, serve society and his country. It has been stated that "Accounting questions have ceased to be wholly domestic and internal problems of the individual businessman or corpora-

---

[9] See "Automatic Ticketing of Telephone Calls" by O. A. Friend in *Electrical Engineering*, March, 1944, pp. 81–88.

[10] See "Costs for Special Purposes" by Edward T. Hanley, *NACA Bulletin*, November 1, 1945, pp. 171–177.

tion. In various ways they have become 'affected with a public interest,' as the phrase goes."[11] When, however, in the near future, high-speed computing devices will bring to light the many still untouched and untried factors of costs and production, and when these new premises and preconceptions can be presented speedily and accurately, then these up-to-date results will influence not only action by governmental bodies, decisions in the field of economics and juridical decisions, but also the most disputed areas of labor-management relations. Should the accountant be able to present facts and figures that are so valuable in this often highly controversial field in a manner which will create a better understanding of the company's position, then the work of the industrial accountant might well prove to be of inestimable importance.

[11] See "Accounting as a Means of Social and Economic Control" by T. H. Sanders, *NACA Bulletin*, December, 1944, p. 319.

GE and UNIVAC: Harnessing the High-Speed Computer

Roddy F. Osborn

"How soon the first complete electronic accounting system can be seen depends not on the business machine companies, and not on the engineers, but on the controllers themselves. One thing is certain: the first electronic accounting system which goes into operation anywhere will start the revolution in every accounting office, and every controller should be forearmed for it." [1]

The revolution starts this summer at General Electric Company's new Appliance Park, near Louisville, Kentucky. The management planning behind the acquisition of the first UNIVAC to be used in business may eventually be recorded by historians as the foundation of the second industrial revolution; just as Jacquard's automatic loom in 1801 or Taylor's studies of the principles of scientific management a hundred years later marked turning points in business history.

The philosophy underlying GE's decision to install this million-dollar digital computer represents, for the most part, a radical departure from current business thinking. It charts a course which many organizations—

Reprinted by permission of the publisher from *Harvard Business Review*, Vol. XXXII, No. 4 (July-August, 1954), pp. 99–107. ©1954 by the President and Fellows of Harvard College; all rights reserved.

[1] This quotation is taken from a speech by Mr. Joseph B. Jeming before the Controllers' Institute in New York, October 1951.

large, medium and small—could follow in harnessing high-speed computers to business applications. Thus the practical problems which had to be explored and solved in the course of GE's pioneering move may be enlightening to the executive still uninformed or troubled with doubts about this controversial new administrative tool.

Here, Roddy F. Osborn, Manager of the Business Procedures Section at GE's Louisville plant, sets forth some of the most critical questions which he and his staff faced.

—The Editors

Getting the Program Started

The high-speed digital computer is here to stay.* Large-scale tape computers have performed miracles for the government, nuclear physicists, mathematicians and even political prognosticators. Yet, while scientists and engineers have been wide-awake in making progress with these remarkable tools, business, like Rip Van Winkle, has been asleep. GE's installation of a UNIVAC may be Rip Van Business's first "blink," which will soon be followed by some real eye openers when a number of other industries complete the installation of electronic computers now on order. At least a half dozen additional giant computers are likely to be in operation in private businesses by the end of this year.

Looking ahead to this development, we saw the need for a master plan of action for GE to follow—facing each obstacle as we came to it and proving each step as we took it. In this way we felt we should avoid both the deadening effect of all the limitations that are so often attributed to electronic computers and the frightening requirement of "rethinking entire operations" according to the prescription of so many of the experts on this subject.

What Are the Stumbling Blocks, and How Can They Be Removed?

When we looked around in industry generally, we found that several stumbling blocks stood in the way of serious management consideration of electronic data-processing equipment: fallacious rumors accepted as truths, lack of vision and foresight, and inability to reduce "spaceship" fiction to understandable realism. Our first step at GE was to try to cut through this confusion—to attack the problem with an open mind.

In particular, four common conceptions which seemed to be discouraging business acceptance were put to the test:

1. "You have to operate a computer 24 hours a day in order to show savings."

* AUTHOR'S NOTE: This article expresses my personal opinions and describes projects which were not all in full operation at the time of writing.

2. "High operating costs of computers make business use prohibitive."

3. "Only large organizations like General Electric Company and the United States Government can afford computers."

4. "Industry surveys indicate that computers are not practical in business applications."

In due time, we found each of these to be false; in fact, they showed up as out-and-out *mis*conceptions.

Our investigations have shown that a high-speed digital computer can be operated on even less than a single-shift basis and still return substantial net savings to the users. A computer does not have to be kept busy 24 hours a day any more than any other piece of equipment has to be used full time. It is not the number of hours of use that is important; it is the cash savings in measurable dollars effected through the use of the equipment.

In our own installation we figured on reaching the break-even point when the computer is used only two hours per day. And, in computing the break-even point, savings were evaluated only in terms of salaries, space rentals and equipment depreciation applicable to those clerical jobs eliminated in four limited routine applications. No value was given to such intangibles as more prompt reporting, the ability of management to make more informed decisions quicker and reduced investment in inventory. Had these factors been included, a break-even point could be reached with fewer applications and less computer time.

We are also certain that electronic computers can be operated by comparatively small industrial organizations. At our break-even point we expect to have only 5,000 employees in our five operating departments at Louisville and to use the computer only ten hours per week. Since computers can be operated continuously seven days per week, our initial applications could be increased a dozenfold. These increased applications would substantially reduce the employment level at which the break-even point would be reached, although not necessarily reducing it twelve times.

In "Electronics Down to Earth" (*Harvard Business Review,* March-April 1954) John A. Higgins and Joseph S. Glickauf point out that one company with 5,000 employees might be able to justify a computer on payroll only. We believe that within a decade certain organizations with as few as 500 employees will be able to rent a UNIVAC at today's prices. At some time in the not too distant future, we expect to use several of the large-scale computers effectively in our five appliance manufacturing units at Louisvile.

Thus, our experience indicates that potential users of this equipment should, as their first premise, cast aside projections based on full-time use and take the position that the smallest usage required to justify the computer economically is what really counts. They can then go on to appraise the practical value of high-speed equipment in an orderly, down-to-earth way.

What Is the Practical Management Approach to Harnessing a Computer to Business?

Judging by our experience, the first step in reaching a realization of what computers can do for executive management is to attack the subject with a fresh mind regarding actual possible uses of computers in the business. This means that it is necessary not only to discard tradition, but also to avoid the distorted impressions produced by certain computer conferences and printed discussions in which scientific interests and business interests are commingled. To hear scientists, mathematicians and engineers discuss the reliability of germanium diodes, the performance characteristics of a vacuum tube, or the use of magnetic cores versus electronic storage serves only to cloud the issue and cause doubt about the practicability of business applications of the equipment now available.

The second step is to get the facts. At GE we felt this called for obtaining a realistic computer education, through such means as:

1. Attending or sending selected individuals to Remington Rand or International Business Machines orientation courses (of one or two weeks' duration) to learn what the equipment will and will not do.

2. Reading pertinent, realistic books, articles, and reports on computer applications and principles; for example, the *Harvard Business Review* article, "Electronics Down to Earth," cited earlier.

3. Conferring with management consultant firms experienced in computer procedures and applications.

4. Getting in touch with computer manufacturers' business research personnel.

5. Visiting business installations of tape computers to see the work being performed.

Employing vision and foresight is another essential step. It is all too easy to be smug and think that punched cards represent the ultimate in office mechanization. Punched cards undoubtedly will continue to be a vital element in office systems, but their role is likely to be limited to input and output media for electronic tape processing. Recent studies by independent consulting firms indicate that many highly mechanized punched-card systems can be converted to electronic systems at substantial net savings.

It is possible that some executives are so tied down with paper work and the increasing complexities of office management that they fail to step aside for brief periods and contemplate the real advantages of utilizing data-processing equipment to eliminate much of the routine work which they and their supervisory group now are required to perform. If they fail to think about the information they need to run their businesses more effectively today, they are even less likely to contemplate what their requirements will be two, five, ten, or even fifty years in the future.

At the same time, thinking ahead does not mean swallowing whole the dramatic headlines and flowery prose in which newspaper and magazine articles picture the ultimate possibilities of this new "miracle toy." Such reporting, however interesting and provocative, is only likely to mislead the otherwise clear-thinking, practical businessman. Or the idea of making a drastic jump from present operations to a completely new system controlled by a mechanical brain will cause him to throw up his hands in despair.

Fortunately, the down-to-earth approach to harnessing a computer for business is not only sounder but easier. Thus, GE's plans for initial use of the computer at Louisville specified the routine tasks of handling payroll, material scheduling and inventory control, order service and billing and general and cost accounting. There is nothing new in the basic material that is fed into the UNIVAC; the difference lies in the fact that it is handled in a fraction of the time with a minimum of human labor.

Eventually, of course, when the potential of the machine is fully realized, far more complicated problems can be fed into it. We believe that only through experience in operating the machine will we be able gradually to pose the more complicated problems we know it is capable of solving. The point is that this is a goal to approach slowly and surely, first taking care of such obvious needs as eliminating the drudgery of office work. But it is a goal, and as such it is an important guide to us in planning successive steps in utilizing the machine.

How Can the Entire Management Group Be Interested in the Possibilities of Using This Equipment?

"Selling" computer applications involves:

1. Offering initial applications to all management functions.
2. Explaining how computers can effect clerical savings.
3. Orienting all management in computer operation and its possible use as a management tool.
4. Stimulating and encouraging bold thinking in terms of determining what additional information executives would like to have to assist them in operating their business more effectively.
5. Weaving the initial and subsequent pieces into an integrated management control system.

In our initial program we intentionally included applications that appealed to all functions. The plans for handling payroll, accounting, order service, material scheduling and so on, obviously were of interest to the *financial, marketing and manufacturing* functions. For *engineering* there also were plans, but not so definite since computers had already been used extensively in this area. In other words, with this program we offered a service and the opportunity for improved operations across the board. We also conducted several seminars to acquaint management further with the equipment, both as to the way in which it operates and as to its potential uses.

In order to explain how electronic computers could effect savings by replacing clerical workers or preventing the hiring of additional clerical help, we presented the following concepts:

1. A very important innovation which tape equipment brings to business operations is that of automatically sequenced operations. Herein lies the opportunity for personnel savings. Tabulating equipment performs limited operations on each machine and accomplishes the desired result when manned by crews to transport the cards from machine to machine. Not so for tape computers. Once all the steps have been enumerated and programed, the computer can follow them automatically and rapidly without human intervention.

2. Equally important, exceptions can now be routinized. No longer is it necessary to have them segregated for manual processing. With a properly coded instruction tape, a computer can handle all operations, including routinized exceptions.

3. Although given greater emphasis by others, the speed of computing is perhaps of tertiary importance only. UNIVAC's speed for processing numbers having as many as 11 digits each in typical operations is:

Addition	1,905 per second
Subtraction	1,905 per second
Multiplication	465 per second
Division	257 per second
Comparison	2,740 per second

   Speed of computations, coupled with the ability to routinize exceptions and perform sequential operations, also makes possible the mechanization of new areas utilizing advanced statistical methods, techniques of linear or mathematical programing and operations research.

Not content with presenting the opportunities as we saw them, we asked all managers and supervisors to review the areas of their respective operations and search for activities in which high-speed data processing could be helpful. We suggested that they report all possible applications, for us to consider until proved practicable or impracticable.

Planning the Uses

Our master plan is designed to solve department problems by (a) minimizing the problem of communication among all functions of a department and among departments of the division, (b) permitting maximum use of common input and output data and (c) minimizing the number and complexity of reports. It coordinates the four initial prosaic applications already mentioned, certain sequential applications that our experience indicates as the logical next stage (budgeting, assembly-line balancing, machine loading, production control and sales analysis and forecasting), and the further, long-run applications which we asked the managers and supervisors to search for and report to us.

How Are the Initial Applications Handled?

The four initial applications, already well underway, represent essentially a conversion of present procedures to the computer system. Certain improvements are being incorporated into the new system, but the input and output are basically unchanged. Here are the details:

1. The *payroll* application provides for computing incentive pay, gross pay, deductions and net pay for approximately 12,000 employees, and preparing the distribution to the appropriate cost accounts. These operations require about two hours of computer time per week. Results are written on magnetic tape to permit the printing of pay checks, payroll registers, personnel reports and cost accounting entries which are handled on the high-speed printer in less than four hours weekly.

2. *Material scheduling* and *inventory control* involve the "explosion" of production schedule into detailed material requirements by days and weeks for any given period. Inventory balances are maintained by posting receipts and withdrawals daily. In addition, open orders on vendors are recorded and adjusted daily.
   Proposals to change production schedules can be analyzed to determine the extent to which they can be satisfied by present inventories and inventory commitments.

3. The *order service and billing* application will process orders received from distributors to prepare shipping schedules, combine less than carload orders on single departments into consolidated car shipments and prepare invoices, sales and cost of sales accounting entries.

4. The *general and cost accounting* application uses the output from the other three—cost distribution, sales and cost of sales entries and so on —as input to be combined with other accounting entries to produce the general and special ledgers, reports, balance sheets and operating statements.

What Is the Role of the Sequential Applications?

We are planning to convert other activities of GE's Major Appliance Division to UNIVAC during 1954. Here the element of new information for management guidance is quite marked, in contrast with the initial applications just described:

1. The preparation of the last *annual budget* and three *quarterly forecasts* required approximately 22,000 man-hours. A program is now under way to prepare monthly, quarterly and annual budgets on UNIVAC. Various suggested combinations of product mix could be analyzed through net income from sales. For the selected product mix, current information would be used to prepare complete budgets and forecasts using last month's—or last week's—information on labor and material cost variances.

2. We have also undertaken a program for improving the *work-load balance* on automatic laundry assembly lines. On the main assembly line approximately 50 hours of desk work are required to distribute the assembly-line work load using present methods. On UNIVAC this takes about two seconds.

   UNIVAC will be asked to prepare several hundred balances from which the one requiring the fewest number of work stations will be selected. Assembly-line balances for normal increments or changes in production levels can be prepared and made available for immediate use when production rates are changed.

3. Investigation of routines for *sales and inventory reports* at all levels of distribution has been started. This will be extended to include initial phases of short-range and long-range projections and forecasts of sales, including multiple correlations with economic and other factors affecting sales of our products.

4. Also, the preparation of *factory machine-loading schedules* is being programed for handling on the computer.

What Can Be Expected From Plans for Long-Range Projects?

Plans for further applications are still in a nebulous state because virtually all of our work to date has been devoted to the programing of the initial and sequential projects. But, since many of these are already reduced to programs which change only slightly from month to month, our efforts now can be devoted to projects like the following:

1. We are examining other aspects of *production control* including the coordination of materials, machine loading and labor loading.

2. We are planning to do a complete *long-range sales forecasting* job which will correlate such existing but inadequately used data as the birth rate and new family formations; disposable income and the level of employment; our models and prices compared with competitors' models and prices and the availability of electricity in new areas and the number of new homes wired for electricity.

3. Our integrated system, when completed, will provide a *dynamic distribution analysis;* it will take information from sales records and projections and provide for management an up-to-the-minute picture of the retail trade and a photo-flash picture of our company's distribution pipelines to all areas of the country. Coupled with budget applications and the production-control application, this should give management the opportunity to adjust selling effort and factory effort to make maximum use of the production facilities at its disposal. Properly handled, it should help us to make the right appliance and deliver it to the right place at the right time. This could have an immeasurable effect in producing more profitable operations.

Evaluating the Benefits

One of the most important concepts in our business-computer philosophy is this "limited perimeter" approach—getting down to brass tacks by concentrating first on the smallest possible areas in which savings can be equated to computer cost, and selecting those areas having substantial amounts of clerical and routine effort and already involving tabulating-equipment rentals.

This limiting of the initial applications permits completion of a survey and a decision on the possible installation of the computer within a reasonably short period of time. Since it stresses the initial conversion of existing systems, it lessens the natural pessimism concerning "blue sky" automation. And, perhaps most important, the results are more comprehensible to profit-conscious executives, who understandably will want the initial conversions to prove themselves in experience before going on to anything like a complete, integrated system. In short, here is the "bread and butter" reason (without the "jam") for getting the computer into the plant.

How Can the Benefits Be Evaluated and Put Into Understandable Form?

The benefits of an initial limited perimeter computer installation can best be predetermined by conducting a comparative survey of existing procedures and computer processing of the same operations. Possible savings can be evaluated in terms of: (a) salaries, (b) "fringe benefits" of clerical workers to be displaced and (c) the related costs, if recoverable, of occupancy and furniture and equipment depreciation. Valid figures can be obtained on the cost of rental or purchases of computer equipment.

Included in the survey report should be sufficient initial application areas to reach a break-even point—in other words, enough to convince management that a computer system can pay for itself in terms of direct dollar savings (people off the payroll), without waiting for the "jam" of more glamorous applications.

The details of conducting the economic survey are too voluminous to be included here, but consist principally of:

1. Determining the routine clerical work and tabulating rentals in selected areas;
2. Determining which of these operations can be performed by the computer;
3. Determining the equipment requirements and cost;
4. Planning the proposed computer runs;
5. Evaluating savings and operating costs.

Selecting the Equipment

Our philosophy regarding electronic equipment may, at first glance, seem impractical. We decided to start at the top of available computer equipment, capacitywise and pricewise, and then, if this could not be economically justified, to work down. We chose to look first for the most versatile data-processing system, not just the cheapest computer which could handle the initial applications. Prompting this choice was the desire not to rule out long-range applications in selecting equipment for initial conversions.

What Equipment Should Be Included or Excluded From Consideration?

The four initial applications were planned and flow-charted. Operating times were calculated for: (a) computer, (b) input devices and (c) output devices. In doing this we allowed both for normal operations and for critical occasions when deadlines for daily, weekly, monthly and quarterly operations all fell on the same day. This gave us a basis for reviewing equipment.

We limited consideration and evaluation to hardware currently on the market and eliminated all that was still on the drawing boards. We saw no sense in waiting for next year's model when savings and experience could be gained by utilizing what was presently available. This is the same idea we use in selling household appliances: the housewife who continually waits for next year's model of our home-laundry equipment will be doing the family laundry on a washboard for the rest of her life. By using the best that is available today great benefits can be obtained; and, when technological improvements warrant, the earlier model can be replaced. It is possible to rent computer equipment (in some cases with an option to buy), leaving a path open for a change to better equipment should it later become available.

We also restricted our review to complete systems, not just a computer alone, and insisted on a high-speed, general-purpose alpha-numeric tape computer (capable of processing figures, alphabetic letters and other symbols), but only when available as a part of a system which included adequate input and output devices all available (or soon to be available) from one company. We needed a complete system guaranteed to operate *as a system*.

At the time of our study and decision in the summer of 1953, we limited our review to the UNIVAC system available through Remington Rand and to one other system from a different but equally reputable manufacturer (International Business Machines' TPM, now called 702). At that time six UNIVAC computers had been in government service, the earliest since 1951, while the other system was not yet available. This served to convince us that UNIVAC should get first consideration.

Since our initial applications required only 10 hours per week (20 hours per week at full employment when the Louisville plant is completed in 1956); and since reports from other users indicated that their UNIVACs had been operable more than 100 hours per week, we felt sufficiently protected to undertake day-to-day operations. Furthermore, since all UNIVACs are identical, we had the possibility of performing our work on a sister machine in other areas such as Washington or New York in the event of a major emergency. (Needless to say, when other manufacturers get more of their computers into operation, similar protection could be available to purchasers of their equipment.)

Why Would Not Groups of Smaller Machines—Electronic Calculators That Use Tabulating Card Input— Serve Just As Well as One Giant Computer?

If we had been limiting our plans at GE to the areas of initial application, we might have considered groups of smaller machines. But, even so, we should have needed five such systems, and the cost of the equipment and the necessary operating personnel were found to be approximately the same as the UNIVAC system and its personnel. Further, mechanization of the initial areas was only an immediate objective. As indicated previously, our ultimate goal is the integrated, long-range, management-tool approach. In one department alone, the management problems already proposed for handling would keep a UNIVAC busy 24 hours a day—and most of them are apparently beyond the scope of lesser equipment.

We understand that management groups in some companies are advocating an approach to the use of computers through card-input calculators. We feel that this is a shortsighted suboptimization, lacking the bold scientific approach of attempting to solve the over-all needs of communication, data processing and operations research—the management-control type of problems which eventually must be tackled.

Winning Top Approval

At Appliance Park we sought top approval to the extent of asking for the necessary funds only when we felt sure we had what those responsible for appropriating the funds would want:

- The understandable concept of converting simple areas to computer operations without disrupting the existing office or factory procedures.

- A break-even point early in the construction of our new plant—and the prospect of annual net savings of approximately $500,000 when construction would be completed and full employment attained—just on the basis of the four standard applications proposed.

- The opportunity eventually to handle many further applications, since the proposed applications would use the computer only half of one shift even after the plant was going at full blast.

Note that, although we knew there would be intangible, but nevertheless real, benefits that would also naturally follow, we did not include applicable dollar values in our report to management. The fact remains that our top executives must have appreciated the values accruing from error-free operations, more prompt reporting of information, and the ability of management to make more timely and informed decisions.

In due course the request for the appropriation of approximately three-quarters of a million dollars to acquire the UNIVAC equipment on a two-year rental plan (with option to purchase) was approved by the local appropriation committee, by the general company appropriation committee, and by the board of directors.

Operating Problems

It is obviously appropriate that people participating in the planning and operation of a computer program for general business applications should be experienced employees with an appreciation of business problems.

How Can an Organization of Specialists Be Set Up for the Detailed Planning, Programing and Operation of a Computer System?

We were fortunate in already having in our Business Procedures Section at Louisville a group of people who had had training and experience in previous systems and procedures, who were familiar with the operation of our business and who had at least a college diploma and in many cases a Master in Business Administration degree. (If our initial applications had included mathematical or advanced engineering problems, it would of course have been appropriate to include representatives from these groups too.)

Out of this group we selected individuals for specialized computer training by means of psychological tests. We were looking for high intelligence and ability to think logically and reason abstractly. And particularly for the leadership of such a group we wanted someone with enthusiasm, vision, foresight, energy and an optimistic point of view; he should be willing to take risks and to devote his entire energies and thoughts to the task at hand.

In addition, because of the pioneering aspect of the program, we found it wise to employ an independent management consultant firm (Arthur Andersen & Co., Chicago), experienced in computer logic and developments. This firm has been particularly helpful in assisting the company group in training personnel, arranging management orientation meetings and planning for conversion of initial applications. We felt that we should neither expect nor permit computer equipment manufacturers to train or supply all the personnel required.

With this setup we were organized to cope with the many problems bound to follow.

What Can Be Done to Overcome the Natural Resistance, Particularly in the Case of Decentralized Management, to a "Giant Brain" Usurping Executives' Activities?

We decided to look on the computer as a data-processing machine only. Our business, like most, includes many varied operations. The Major Appliance Division, which is the one located at Louisville, is operated under a decentralized form of management in which five separate departments manufacture a complete line of large household appliances. Size of the departments ranges from 700 employees in the smallest, to 7,000 in the largest. Each department has a general manager supported by managers of manufacturing, marketing, finance and engineering. If the computer installation was to be effective, we had to make certain that we did not interfere with the decentralized form of management which has been so successful in GE's various operations.

We emphasized the need to solve *department* problems, particularly the problem of communication between functions of a department. We endeavored therefore to conceive of a data-processing center in which routine clerical work could be performed on data which was supplied to the center and returned to the originating department as soon as it had been processed. The important concept here is that it was not centralized accounting or centralized payroll, but rather centralization of the routine "dog" work involved in each of these operations.

With this concept, except for the short time the documents are out of the department for handling at the data-processing center, all data remain in the department, thus enabling the management of the department to operate effectively. In the case of payroll, all inquiries can be answered by the department paymaster by reference to details of pay computation printed for him and to source documents which have been returned to him. In this way, there is no usurping of management prerogatives.

How Can Departments Make Day-to-Day Reference to Their Material When the Information Is Stored on Magnetic Tape?

The problem of using magnetic tape as a medium for storing information can be reduced, if not eliminated, by returning all source data to the department and by providing daily printed records of all input and output transactions in a manner which will facilitate ready reference. When management and auditors have acquired confidence in the computer-system operation and no longer require this information, such printing of all intermediate transactions can be discontinued.

How Can the Necessary Cooperative Effort Be Enlisted?

To get the cooperation needed for the success of the system depends, in our experience, on a combination of factors:

- The data-processing center, which acts as UNIVAC's baby sitter or nursemaid, allows management to forget the problems of computer operation and spend more time on decision-making and policy-forming matters.

- The limited perimeter approach of converting a few routine applications initially, and of processing these in the manner of existing systems rather than making drastic revisions in procedures, also encourages cooperation.

- The people working out the program (including competent consultants) know business problems and computer limitations. It is their function to get the computer to do whatever the departments want done.

- Orientation meetings, and, later, educational sessions, on approved computer procedures conducted by personnel of the computer program and the consultants, inspire confidence and cooperation.

In addition, we found it wise to establish a liaison committee in each conversion area. Department management delegated the authority for approval of proposed procedures to this committee. We included on the committee the most informed individuals in the areas selected, but limited the number of members to three or four people. The committee's function is to approve all aspects of the proposed computer processing in its area, including: (a) manual operations, (b) control of documents and procedures prior to processing and (c) output data and documents resulting from processing. Ideally, the committee should recall all past problems and their solutions and anticipate all possible future problems and their solutions.

Conclusion

If I were to summarize for others the experience of the last two years at General Electric in planning, installing and beginning operations of the first high-speed computer for private business, I would include these guideposts:

1. Employ a competent consultant.
2. Limit areas of initial application.
3. Choose areas where there is a high proportion of routine clerical effort and where tabulating-equipment applications are already present.
4. Use the concept of a data-processing center.
5. Limit equipment review to complete systems available or soon to be available from reliable manufacturers.
6. Get a system—not just a computer.
7. "Use a system in which sufficient checks have been included to avoid a cumbersome superstructure of clerical controls and error correction routines." [2]
8. Start with the most versatile and most expensive equipment and work down.
9. Select the right person to head the program and make ample, capable systems and procedures people available for the required time.
10. Sell management on this practical approach.
11. Interest management and supervision in the possibilities of improving operations through development and installation of long-range and well-integrated plans.

[2] From a speech by M. E. Davis, Vice President and Chief Actuary, Metropolitan Life Insurance Company, "The Use of Electronic Data-Processing Systems in the Life Insurance Business," before the Eastern Joint Computer Conference, Washington, D.C., December 1953.

The Third Generation of Computers—New Tools for Management

John E. Vavasour

Approximately a dozen years have passed since the installation of the first UNIVAC computer at General Electric's Appliance Park facility in Louisville, Kentucky. Since that time, nearly twenty-three thousand electronic data processing machines have been installed throughout the free world, with more than ninety percent located in the United States.

Of the twenty-three thousand machines, some two thousand are of the large scale type, the balance being the small and medium size machines. Nearly all medium to large companies make at least some use of computers and data processing equipment and even many of the smaller businesses are taking advantage of the benefits of computer technology through computer service centers which are rapidly growing in number and size.

Against this background, it would be well for the management accountant to familiarize himself with the new developments in the field of electronic data processing which will have a profound effect upon all of our businesses and upon the future of management accounting itself.

During the first decade of the computer age, improvements occurred at a fairly constant rate and generally consisted of improvement in speed,

Reprinted by permission of the author and the publisher from *Management Accounting*, Vol. XLVII, No. 2, Sec. 1 (October, 1965), pp. 3–6.

memory size, machine logic and programming systems. However, the data processing systems now being introduced, the so-called third generation, contain significant advances over those introduced earlier. In this article, we will review the significance of new developments in each of three areas:

1. Data processing hardware.
2. Programming systems.
3. Advanced uses of computers.

Data Processing Hardware

It is in the equipment itself, that the most obvious improvements have taken place during the last two years. Certainly, the new equipment is capable of doing anything which has been possible with the earlier models. In addition, each new model is faster, somewhat smaller and generally less expensive than the comparable earlier model.

Speed, as we refer to it in connection with computers, is very difficult for us to really comprehend. All of us, I think, can understand the time span covered by one second. But how fast is a billionth of a second?

In terms of computer size, it is much easier for us to visualize changes which have taken place. Vacuum tubes have given way to solid state devices such as transistors and diodes. These, in turn, are giving way to microminiaturized circuits. However, while each of the components has gotten dramatically smaller, the machines have become many times more complex and have required many more components. As a result, the reduction in size of the complete system has not been as dramatic as expected. Furthermore, the reduction has been primarily in the electronic units with relatively little change in the size of the electromechanical devices (printers, magnetic tape units, card readers, etc,), making up the balance of the system.

In the realm of cost, rental and purchase prices have been significantly reduced for the newest models. Considering the ratio of price to performance, the models now being introduced offer anywhere from 1½ to 2 times as much for the user's rental or purchase dollar.

Furthermore, the range of product offerings is broad enough that the user frequently has his choice of replacing his present equipment with newer equipment, having approximately the same performance characteristics at a lower price or paying the same price for a new machine providing 1½ to 2 times the performance.

As a result, potential users of data processing systems who may have looked at available equipment two years ago and decided that the price was just a little too high to be attractive, may now find that the same feasibility study updated with today's prices and equipment performance will result in a decision to install a data processing system.

Another significant advance is the "compatible family" approach. In this approach, which all major manufacturers are using, the product line consists of a series of central processors spanning the range from the very small machine to the very large. The advantage of the "compatible family" concept is that programs written for any model in the family can be run on any larger model with full advantage of the higher speed. This is accomplished by making all members of the family essentially the same in terms of programming features, but with faster circuitry and greater memory capacity on the more powerful members of the group. All use the same peripheral units, although in some of the smaller systems some peripheral devices may not be available.

The compatible family allows a user to start with a data processing system geared to his initial volume requirements with the knowledge that he can convert to a more powerful data processing system as his workload increases, with no need to reprogram the work being performed on the smaller system. With this concept, full advantage of most features of the faster equipment is gained immediately.

Still another significant advance is the concept of multiprogramming, or the ability to process simultaneously different and unrelated programs. As a general rule, few programs make full use of all of the capabilities of the system all of the time.

The ability of a computer to process two or more programs simultaneously permits the system to balance its own workload. It also makes much more feasible "real-time" applications and the use of a central machine to serve many remote locations.

The new data processing systems feature an impressive array of peripheral devices, extending their usefulness into new areas.

Almost from the beginning, computers have been using punch cards and magnetic tape as input/output media and most have been equipped with "high speed" line printers. Some have had the ability to read and write punched paper tape and those designed for the banking field have had document handlers capable of reading and understanding the magnetic ink character recognition (MICR) digits printed on the face of most checks.

Over the years, these devices have been improved, made more reliable, more versatile and faster. In addition to these conventional peripheral devices, such features as optical character readers are reaching the state of practicability. With some limitations, they can read ordinary typewritten letters and numerals and promise to greatly simplify the task of data preparation. Since the cost of data preparation, essentially key punching, frequently represents more than half of the operating cost of a data processing system, the elimination or reduction of the key punch operation will have a profound effect on cost.

On the output side, peripheral devices now include video displays, line plotters, and voice response, all operating under the control of the data processing system. Video displays consist of television-like receivers which can display information being generated by a data processing system on the tube face. Line plotters provide an accurate means for producing graphs plotted directly from data being processed by a data processing system. While the concept is not particularly new, the significant step forward is the ability to operate a line plotter simultaneously with the processing of the data. Voice response is a special peripheral device which accepts output directly from a data processing system and converts it to audible words.

Perhaps the most significant advance of all is the ability of the new data processing systems to tie directly into communications networks. For the first time, this makes the concept of a central computer serving many remote locations both feasible and economical. The equipment now being produced has the capability of bringing information from remote locations over communications lines directly into the computer without any need for intermediate conversion.

Programming Systems

In the field of computer programming systems, it is significant to recognize two trends which all manufacturers are following. The first is the introduction of much more efficient and easy to use computer languages based on the COBOL (common business oriented language) concept.

The principal difficulty in using the COBOL with the earlier machines was caused by the fact that the COBOL language was developed apart from the machines. Each machine required a translator to bridge the gap between COBOL and computer, which resulted in very slow program compilations and generally produced programs of average quality or less.

The new data processing systems recognize COBOL as a direct requirement and accordingly have developed the machine logic around the COBOL principle. This results in fast compilations of programs and efficient processing by the resulting program.

The second trend in computer programming systems is the development of supervisory or operating programming systems for the computer. Nearly all manufacturers producing recently announced machines are planning control programs as an integral part of the product offering.

The operating system, in effect, lets the computer control its own operation, making many of the decisions an operator would make but at computer speed. They permit the computer to operate with the least possible amount of lost time caused by operator error or by not planning the sequence in which the work is to be performed or by not being able to find the program deck needed to run the next job.

The result is an absolute minimum of lost time in terms of computer setup. Where the computer is being used to process several programs simultaneously, or is being used in connection with remote input/output devices, a good operating system can spell the difference between success and failure.

New Applications of Computers

One of the really exciting possibilities made possible by the advent of electronic data processing is the opportunity to develop fully integrated business systems where the total information needed to manage the business is controlled by the computer. Progress in developing such total systems has been extremely slow. In fact, it is in these new uses of computers where the least progress has been made during the last few years.

The job of developing a total system is an unbelievably complicated one, but promises to produce results well worth the effort. While a few major companies have such systems in operation and others are making progress along these lines, we still have a long way to go before we can point to real progress throughout the industry.

Large scale information retrieval systems is another area where great potential benefits lie. Yet progress in developing computer based systems for large scale information retrieval has nearly always fallen short of their goals.

If data processing technology is to continue to advance as much during the next ten years as it has during its first decade, the users must produce the same kind of advances in the use of computers as we have seen during the last ten years in the development of data processing equipment and programming systems. If this does not take place, we will lose many of the benefits promised by the new machines.

This also is the opportunity for the management accountant to make a major contribution to the business, by accepting the challenge offered by the information machine, to learn how it can help in the management of the enterprise and to assume a position of leadership in promoting its use.

Summary

To summarize, the "third generation" data processing systems now being offered represent significant improvements over the earlier versions. The physical equipment is faster, smaller, lower in price, comes in "compatible families," has extensive peripheral equipment, has multiprogramming ability, and can be linked directly to communication networks. The programming systems are based upon the COBOL, or common business oriented language concept, with the equipment being designed specifically to take advantage of the programming language. The equipment is also designed to take advantage of operating systems or programs which control much of the machine's day-to-day operation.

While the users are beginning to make some advanced applications of data processing systems, the real potential they offer has barely been touched. The opportunity is available for the management accountant to assume the position of leadership in the use of information systems based technology within his company. In short, the management accountant must provide not only management information, but the management of information.

4   AUDITING

How Do Electronic Computers Affect Accounting and Auditing Techniques?

Max S. Simpson

The business world of today is characterized by a state of innovation and change unsurpassed in history. This is not surprising when one considers the technological revolution that has taken place in the last 20 years. While man is striving to reach the moon and beyond in space, he is to no lesser extent attempting to apply technical and scientific advancements to optimize the complex art of managing a business in a highly competitive marketplace. One of the major contributing factors in attaining this objective is the electronic computer and associated scientific devices.

What has been the impact of the computer on business management? The answer to this question is difficult and not easily visible at first glance. To say that the computer impact has been extensive is not sufficient. The possibility exists that in the decades ahead history will show that the computer, as a management tool for decision making and control, was the catalyst in revolutionizing business concepts as they are known today. An indication of this premise can be seen in examining the far-reaching effects of the computer on accounting and auditing techniques.

Long-established accounting theory has not been altered by the computer

Reprinted by permission of the author and the publisher from *Financial Executive*, Vol. XXXIV, No. 2 (February, 1966), pp. 38–45.

impact; rather, the effect has been in the area of the changed implementation practices of this theory. Specifically, these machines have provided an environment where not only has labor saving justified their existence, but it has also become possible to service larger geographical areas out of a centralized location and to generate more detailed, accurate information for business management purposes. Further, standardization of accounting procedures and of accounting classification has been stimulated by the centralization of the accounting function, and accelerated processing of data has substantially shortened the accounting cycle.

Computer Evolution

The emergence of these activities has occurred during the past 10 years. From the computer standpoint, this decade was marked by an evolutionary machine development which saw significant advances in higher processing speeds, greater and more flexible storage capacity, and the emergence of communications capability. For little or no increase in equipment costs, speeds and capacities are increasing at a geometric rate as computer improvements continue to be generated. The computers available today can even process various major programs concurrently on a time-shared basis in a communications-oriented data-processing environment.

Along with the development of improved computers, tremendous strides have been taken in knowledge of how to exploit the speeds, versatility and capacities of the modern computers.

Concurrently with computer improvements, significant advances were taking place in the development of related scientific devices: that is, a large array of communications equipment and computer input/output devices without which a modern computer cannot function. In the communications area, telephone and telegraph lines and microwave circuits are used for the transmission of business data, and the use of satellites is in the foreseeable future. In addition, there are about 50 different types of computer input/output devices ranging from such ordinary equipment as punch-card readers and conventional printers to some highly sophisticated and scientific instruments, such as remote console devices, cathode ray tube terminals, and audio-response devices.

Now computer-communication-oriented concepts for the processing of the business and scientific information flow are a practical and highly desirable objective. The most sophisticated examples of this type of processing are generally associated with real-time systems where there is instantaneous response to any physical transaction at the time of occurrence. An example of this in the commercial area is seen in the more advanced current airline reservation systems, in the scientific area in the control of missiles and in space exploration activities.

Advances in Systems Integration

The accountant and the auditor should be familiar with the current developments in the area of systems integration. Certain companies have attempted with varying degrees of success to integrate the data flow from an initial point-of-sale inquiry to the sending of the material ordered by the customer. For example, one of the leading manufacturers of electrical equipment in the United States has in operation an integrated nationwide message switching and order-processing center, which for certain of its product lines permits automatic triggering from sales inquiry to sales order to shipment of material along with the necessary recording of inventory changes and issuance of re-stocking orders. Also, standard accounting applications such as invoicing, accounts receivable and sales statistics are automatically spun off from this integrated system. In this example, everything we need to know about a customer's order is generated by the system whether it be concerned with aspects of marketing, distribution, inventory or accounting—all without human intervention. The extension of this conceptual approach may be further characterized by a company having the capability of updating all records on an as-occur basis, culminating theoretically in an ability to project control statements even to profit and loss on an as-required basis. While this concept is somewhat esoteric in nature and may not be obtainable or economical within the near future, a conceptual direction definitely has been started.

The centralization of the accounting function even in a decentralized company environment has been prompted by cost and control advantages. The computer as a management tool permits large-volume accounting applications to be maintained and processed at a centralized location. Accounting application examples include payroll, accounts receivable, accounts payable, credit accountability, fixed assets and associated summary and analytical evaluation reports. With the inherent records being maintained and processed in this manner, operating divisions are relieved of the administration of these arduous tasks and are permitted to concentrate their energies on other pertinent areas of responsibility. The bringing together of these accounting applications facilitates the standardization and integration of accounting applications.

The computer impact on standardization and integration of accounting applications is already discernible. The standardization provided to a large American steel company by a single wage payroll system affords uniform interpretation of labor contracts with standardized audit procedures regardless of the number of processing locations. The increased control, accuracy and monetary savings of this approach have been confirmed.

An interesting example of accounting application integration is being implemented by a large banking organization in the United States involving the consolidation of payroll, personnel records, expense distribution and work measurement standards. Not only can an employee be properly selected for a job but he can also be paid, evaluated and have his benefits controlled from a composite data base.

Also, through adoption of a uniform chart of accounts, monthly closings processed in a communications-orientd data-processing system can provide for the preparation of financial statements at a much earlier date than was formerly possible. The management benefits involved are significant in providing more timely, accurate information for over-all planning and decision making.

Management Considerations

Such business intelligence systems will go far beyond the limits of classical accounting procedures to process and analyze a broad range of information —both financial and other decision-making data—that are needed by management to run the business. The ultimate achievement would be a system that not only encompasses all information handling requirements but processes each piece of information instantaneously.

Management would be notified on an "exception" basis of any irregular behaviour of business performance requiring immediate action. The environmental aspects would depict a management "control center" where, through the use of graphic displays, pertinent information could be recalled from the computer system and exhibited in chart form for management decision making.

As an accompanying development, operations research techniques would be employed to permit the structuring of composite company profit plans in the form of a "profit model" whereby management could evaluate alternative profit forecasts prior to final selection of the most appropriate profit plan.

A progressive example of current activity in this area is the Financial Executives Institute Research Project, "Impact of Computers on Management and Organization." The project's main objective is to present for general management the constructive uses of computer utilization. Emphasis is being directed toward computer system definition—present and planned, influence of the computer on decision making, management's part in today's and tomorrow's system, and the influence of the computer on organization.

Changing Role of the Accountant

The underlying significance for the accountant in this changing business environment is his emergence in a new role. Traditionally the accountant has dealt with historical facts. The accountant of tomorrow, however, will have the ability to deal with current information at time of occurrence, and with computer-generated projections, so that his services to management can be infinitely greater than was possible with the old tools. The accountant must not only accept and understand the new techniques, he also must take the lead in designing systems which fully exploit the computer and its related sciences. His task then will be adapting to a new profession rather than continuing an old one.

Audit Controls

Insofar as the auditor is concerned, it can be stated that his basic objectives and responsibilities are not altered by the installation of a computer system. The nature of the "control" problem for a computer system is different from other systems, however, and this not only requires new audit techniques but also substitutes new areas of control that must be examined. Since the computer offers a system that replaces manual activities, the auditor will now be more concerned with testing the controls over the system than with controls designed to prevent human error. Although valid for all computer systems, these requirements are intensified in a real-time or on-line data-processing environment.

The American Institute of Certified Public Accountants has recognized the necessity for exploring in depth the computer impact on accounting and auditing techniques. Recently a project has been initiated to develop an applied research and education program in computer technology. Particular attention is being directed toward the capabilities of information processing systems as they relate to accounting, auditing, tax work and management sciences. The research findings will be used in organizing an expanded educational program to service the needs of the Certified Public Accountant on the latest developments of computer technology.

Another perspective of the computer impact on auditing, however, is represented by the use of the computer to conduct various comparisons and tests involved in an audit in a faster and more economical manner than manual methods which would otherwise be employed by the auditor. In this context, reference is made to the use of the computer to facilitate an audit, rather than to problems posed the auditor by the existence of a computerized accounting system. The computer has provided for the auditor centralized control and information accuracy previously not available.

For electronic data processing systems, it is common to designate three areas of control with which the auditor must be concerned.

1. Controls over the movement of data into and out of the computer operations, commonly referred to as "input/output controls."

2. Administrative controls over the organization and operating procedures of the computer department itself.
3. Controls incorporated in the computer programs—that is, built into the sequence of instructions followed by the computer in processing data.

Input/output controls are usually handled by a control section which monitors all data into and out of the computer system. Specific functions would include the monitoring of source data, the processing of rejects and errors due to incorrect input data and insuring accuracy of final output reports.

Administrative controls over the computer operation include the separation of functions that is so important for effective control, such as the separation of the programming section from the operating section of the computer function (Figure 1, "Organization of Functions for Control of EDP Data Flow"). Other controls include the requirement that procedures and operator instructions be fully documented, with flow charts describing each application; also, that log sheets be maintained to account for all computer operating time.

Controls incorporated into computer programs are of many types. Examples of controls that may be used—such as "zero balance" checks, reasonableness checks, sequence checks, self-checking numbers and feedback controls—are generally well described in the many books and articles on the subject, such as Felix Kaufman's *Electronic Data Processing and Auditing*.

Conduct of an Audit

The conduct of an audit should certainly cover a thorough review and testing of the first two areas of control as described above; that is, evaluation of the input-output controls and of the administrative controls over the computer operation itself. The techniques involved in the audit of these two areas are not particularly technical and, indeed, no unusual training is required once the auditor has familiarized himself with the nature of these areas of control. Actual input controls can be compared against a list of those generally acceptable; organization must be reviewed for proper separation of duties; procedures employed must be written and understood.

It is in the third area—controls over actual computer programs—that the auditor generally experiences difficulty. In the past, a technique was employed which involved taking a sample of computer input and manually checking the validity of the output in terms of the pertinent input data. If the sample of output data was correct, the auditor assumes that all of the

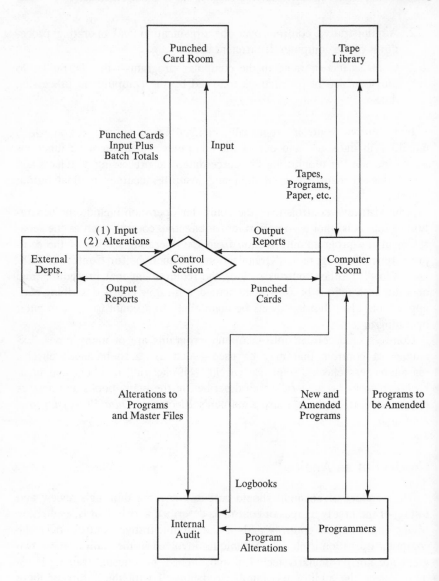

Figure 1. Organization of functions for control of EDP data flow. (Source: *The Impact of Computers on Accounting*, T. W. McRae.)

processing procedures were also correct and that they had sufficient control features.

With the growing complexity of computer programs, the greater use of exception reporting, and the trend toward integrated processing without separate printout between operations, it is necessary that the auditor now assume a direct responsibility for auditing the adequacy of the computer programs themselves. To an increasing degree, relying only upon the evaluation of an input-output sample will not represent an efficient or adequate check of the operating controls involved.

Audit Review and Tests

The best time for initial audit review of computer programs is while the programs are being designed. In this manner the auditor may make suggestions for improved controls to be built into these programs—suggestions which could be extremely expensive to implement were they to be developed after the program was in operation. Some large companies, in addition to developing training programs and manuals for computer auditing, have established procedures whereby agreed-upon program documentation of all new computer accounting applications is forwarded to the internal audit department for evaluation of control requirements. Principal elements in this documentation generally consist of a flow chart showing the flow of data through the various processing steps, and a narrative description of the system, including the various control procedures over the processing within the computer.

In addition to evaluating controls incorporated in computer programs, the auditor needs techniques for testing transactions to insure that the programs, as written, are producing accurate and complete results in actual operation. The two techniques that have so far been found to be most practicable are sample testing (perhaps using the more refined statistical sampling techniques) and simulation. Indeed, statistical sampling can be aided by designing a computer program to select the proper sample.

For the auditor who has sufficient computer knowledge, probably the most desirable technique is simulation, using what are commonly referred to as "test decks." These "test decks" of punched cards or magnetic tape simulate actual transactions involved in the system's processing. They can be introduced into the system like actual transactions and are a relatively inexpensive method of testing transactions since no programming requirements are involved. The system, in effect, checks itself to insure that the necessary outputs are reliable, accurate and appropriate.

The computer also presents the auditor with a unique opportunity to use its services in performing many of the time-consuming tasks normally involved in an audit. Computer programs can be designed which will test the records maintained on magnetic tape and which will select data from a tape file and print it out for audit. Other computer programs can be designed which will perform such functions as comparison of activity between periods, measure actual versus budget figures, or material on hand versus normal stock levels.

One of the international oil companies has developed a computerized payroll audit program which prints out for the auditor all changes since the previous audit in master payroll tapes and also develops a statistical sample of those items to be given detailed audit verification. This same program also makes certain comparisons to test for such cases as salary or overtime outside of normal limits, incompatibilty between base pay and income tax deductions or between base pay and employee savings deductions.

Challenges and Opportunities

In review, ours is a changing world, changing at a technological rate that challenges comprehension. One of the prime motivators of this revolution has been the computer. The computer impact has been significant on business practices, and specifically on the accountant and auditor and the techniques utilized in the administration of their functions.

The accountant must accept the challenges posed by his changing environment. He must adapt to a new profession rather than continue an old one. He must provide management with unbiased, timely recommendations on day-to-day business activities and future predictions to optimize long-range plans and goals. If the accountant does not accept this premise or is not up to this responsibility, he runs the risk of being relegated to a restricted role as various organizations are formed to carry out these "management service" functions. Certainly these functions must be performed if the company is to wage a successful battle in the increasingly competitive worldwide marketplace.

Similarly, the auditor must recognize the full impact of the computer revolution. He must view a computer as a centralized tool of control previously not available to accomplish his objectives. A "through the computer" approach must be adopted along with the necessary knowledge involved to insure that factors of reliability, timeliness and control inherent in computer systems are realized.

Finally, the years ahead will be marked by opportunity. The accountant and the auditor have an unparalleled opportunity to exploit the utilization of the computer as the prime tool in servicing management's needs. This opportunity must be seized eagerly but with intelligence, lest we forget that the computer must supplement and complement, though not pre-empt, man's role in achieving his business objectives. As Gilbert Burck states in *The Computer Age:*

> The machines compel men to formulate their problems so much more intelligently and more thoroughly than they ever have that men can

hardly be unaware of the shortcomings of their programs. . . . Nothing would make a company more vulnerable to smart competitors than to abdicate responsibility to the neat, clean, consistent judgments of a machine.

By keeping this belief basic to our professional philosophy, we can successfully respond to the changing accounting and auditing techniques demanded by the computer and other scientific devices.

Plain Talk About Auditing in an ADPS Environment

Irving J. Sandler

In July 1965, the contract audit services of the Army, Navy and Air Force were consolidated into a single agency within the Department of Defense called the Defense Contract Audit Agency (DCAA). During this reorganization, the impact of automatic data processing systems (ADPS) on the contract auditor was critically appraised. As might be expected, this self-appraisal involved differing degrees of emphasis regarding the nature of the problem (or opportunity, depending on your point of view). These views, to a large extent, mirrored the concern of others in the profession. There was apprehension over the potential loss of audit trails in computerized accounting systems. Certainly, a need existed to search for causal relationships which might explain why the audit community has shown less than enthusiastic acceptance of ADPS-oriented techniques. The mere fact that it was possible to audit without any significant involvement with the computer lent some credence to the view that the time for change might not be quite here. Still, there was merit to the view that the accounting profession should assume its proper and rightful role in the design, development and direction of management information systems, particularly as they may affect financial decisions. Furthermore, an optimum solution was not yet in sight.

Reprinted by permission of the author and the publisher from *The Journal of Accountancy*, Vol. 125, No. 4 (April, 1968), pp. 43–47.

The resultant DCAA charter contained a positive policy commitment to exploit the use of improved audit techniques. Inherent in this commitment was the hypothesis that while expansion of the common body of knowledge would undoubtedly fortify the auditor of the future with the necessary background to face his environment, more can and should be done within the present capabilities of auditors and accountants.

This article discusses some of the ADPS opportunity areas explored by the DCAA in the past two or three years, some of the misconceptions developed since the advent of computers, and some of the ways in which the agency's objectives are accomplished in giving recognition to audit in an ADPS environment.

The Challenge

One of the agency's initial research projects in the ADPS area concluded that (1) in over 90 per cent of the major contract audit engagements, field auditors were faced with an active ADPS environment, (2) there was a positive current trend toward integrated defense contractor management information systems, (3) a current need existed for definitive minimum standards of what is expected of the auditor in the field and, more important, there was a current need for dialogue on the role of the audit supervisor in an ADPS environment, (4) there was a need for improved current and comprehensive ADPS guidance and related reference material and (5) a need existed for an aggressive action plan to catch up with the computer.

Combating Common Misconceptions

While this research program did generate immediate enthusiasm regarding the explosive potential of computer audit applications,[1] the need to clarify misconceptions about auditing in an ADPS environment continues to be of concern and worthy of emphasis. The major items impeding audit progress in an ADPS environment are for the most part related to basic requisites. Is auditing in an ADPS environment more difficult? Does it require extensive specialized education? Does it require programming skills? Should the auditor become involved in console operations? Are comprehensive test decks required? Is a change in basic auditing concepts necessary? In the judgment of the DCAA, the answers to all of these questions can be found to be negative.

---

[1] See Irving J. Sandler, "(D)ial for (C)omputer (A)udit (A)ssistance," *The Federal Accountant*, Federal Government Accountants Association (Fall 1966–67) for a discussion of the use of time-shared computer services to solve problems in statistical sampling, improvement curves, correlation analysis and regression analysis.

1. Our auditors, who use advanced techniques, find that ADP systems offer better internal control capabilities and greater reliability than they had previously realized. They find that ADPS-oriented techniques facilitate rather than hinder the audit.

2. Many courses of relatively short duration are offered by equipment manufacturers, business schools, universities and professional organizations which can indoctrinate the auditor in ADPS. Self-study programed texts[2] are available. These courses in "ADP basics" should provide the auditor with a springboard to learn by doing. DCAA has found that this exposure, coupled with in-house training, effectively overcomes auditor reluctance to apply ADPS-oriented techniques. Formal ADPS training is conducted at the agency's Contract Audit Institute at Memphis, Tennessee. The two-week in-house course accents on-the-job experience through case studies. Workshops in advanced audit techniques are conducted at the agency's field audit offices on a continuing basis to supplement this training.

3. While programming skills are useful to the agency in research activities, an extensive background or proficiency in programming is not required of its field auditors. Furthermore, experience has shown that review of complex computer programs is unproductive and generally impractical.

4. Independent operation by auditors of computer consoles, other than authorized remote inquiry stations, has not been practical or necessary.

5. The test deck technique for contract audit purposes is still in an experimental stage. Experience to date indicates that best results are obtained in less elaborate applications. The auditor should try to include all reasonably likely types of valid and erroneous transactions, but attempts to include every possible combination of data in a test deck may generate excessive audit time with little corresponding return. Use of data from contractor test decks and/or actual transactions can facilitate the development of audit test decks.

6. The agency has found that auditing in an ADPS environment accents discipline required in the identification of basic audit objectives. It demands an effective survey—thorough analysis of internal control procedures and practices and effective correlation of all sources of audit reliance. There is no change in basic auditing concepts.

Financial management controls are an intrinsic part of a modern ADPS. The same programs which record costs may analyze their pattern and trend

---

[2] A number of our auditors find Leeland R. O'Neal's text *Electronic Data Processing Systems—A Self-Instructional Programmed Manual* (Prentice-Hall, Inc.) to be most informative. It can be completed in less than 20 hours of self-study.

and compare them with budgets, past performance, production levels and other standards. An alert auditor, even with limited ADPS exposure, can readily appreciate the importance of these computerized reports to such functional audit areas as (1) evaluating financial management controls, (2) evaluating employee utilization, (3) identifying idle or under-utilized facilities and (4) evaluating the effectiveness of estimating systems and practices.

The agency has found that a nontechnical approach to ADPS is helpful in developing audit programs for these and other functional areas. This type of review is directed at identifying (1) source document flow, (2) computer reports utilized for management decisions which have an audit import, (3) automated processing routines, (4) areas which have automated internal control, (5) areas subject to automated exception analysis and (6) areas where audit steps can be shifted from manual review to the computer.

For example, one auditor's first hard look at an airframe manufacturer's ADP system elicited the following comments:

The survey disclosed that existing edit routines permit greater audit reliance than had been realized; automated exception analyses provide immediate audit visibility to error conditions; redundancy in certain audit program steps was evident, indicating necessary shifts in audit emphasis; while changes in the focal point of audit are indicated, no conceptual change in audit objectives is required. . . .

"Around" or "Through"—A Case in Semantics?

An inhibiting factor to the adaptation of ADPS techniques to the audit situation has been semantics—in particular, two terms: *auditing around the computer* and *auditing through the computer*. While the meaning of these terms has been rather clearly delineated many times, the writer suspects that their very definitions may have been used to rationalize decisions to ignore the computer. As long as these terms appear to offer a choice between two alternatives, an avenue for inaction through semantics exists.

Most defense contractor ADPS are structured to permit management to identify, isolate and trace back, to its origin, every significant transaction. The ability to obtain this information for analysis and to permit informed decision-making is a practical necessity in today's business world—hopefully, with a minimum of cost. This prerequisite will, in the writer's opinion, continue to be valid for future systems, real time considerations notwithstanding. The who, what, why, how questions must be answered, even if the computer has to be programed to do it itself. Consequently, auditors, if they choose to do so, may be able to "trace" transactions indefinitely. Unfortunately, under the guise of auditing around the computer, they may be ignoring ADPS opportunities available to them.

Minimum Standards

While DCAA does not prohibit the use of around the computer techniques, minimum audit standards in an ADPS environment have been promulgated which encourage more efficient methods. These standards, together with the Appendix C,[3] "Guidance for Auditing Automatic Data Processing Systems," to the Defense Contract Audit Manual, provide the field auditor with basic building blocks for greater sophistication in the use of computers to facilitate audit work. To this end, original DCAA postulates remain valid:

Each resident auditor or branch manager responsible for the audit of contractors employing ADPS is expected to:

1. Have a nucleus of staff members who are sufficiently trained in ADPS concepts to direct surveys, evaluations and audits of the ADP system employed by the contractor, including source data and system output. All staff members should receive sufficient ADPS training to participate.

2. Institute a survey and evaluate the adequacy of the contractor's ADPS system and update the survey on a continuing basis thereafter. Conclusions derived from such surveys will serve as the basis for development of new or modification of existing audit programs.

3. Obtain an inventory of computed and punched card accounting machine reports (ADPS output), also to be updated on a continuing basis, and determine the usefulness of such reports to audit.

4. Obtain or prepare flow charts showing the audit trail from source documents through the contractor's cost accounting system to amounts shown on cost representations and/or billings to the government. Flow charts are to be maintained on a current basis for audit management and training purposes.

5. Obtain copies of the contractor's internal audit programs and reports relating to ADPS and evaluate their usefulness in contract audit effort.

6. Arrange with appropriate contractor personnel to obtain specialized periodic ADPS print-outs to reduce audit effort in tracing costs, reconciling costs and selecting costs to be audited. It is intended that, insofar as possible, these reports be a by-product of the contractor's normal processing routine and that reprocessing of accounting data solely for audit purposes be held to a minimum.

---

[3] Appendix C to the Defense Contract Audit Manual may be obtained at a cost of $2 per copy from the Defense Contract Audit Agency, Attention CA-DX, Cameron Station, Alexandria, Virginia 22314. Requests for this Appendix should be accompanied with a check made payable to the Treasurer of U. S.

The Importance of the Survey

One of the early truths emerging from DCAA research involves the significance of survey activities in an ADPS environment. It is axiomatic that an effective audit program cannot be prepared without a thorough understanding of the processes employed by a contractor or client and the impact of ADPS on the area to which the program is to be applied. However, it would be less than candid to infer that an overwhelming ground swell exists for placing the highest audit priority on accomplishing the ADPS survey. There are still those who defend the *status quo*. On the other hand, the ever-increasing weight of evidence suggests that audit productivity, quality and effectiveness may be adversely affected until this type of survey becomes an integral part of audit planning and programing. The auditor need not be a computer expert to accomplish this survey effectively.

To illustrate, an ADPS survey of a defense contractor revealed extensive automated accounts payable edit routines. Receiving report quantities were automatically compared with invoiced quantities; purchase order prices were matched with invoice costs; necessary extension checks were performed by the computer, including the deduction of trade and cash discounts; and the propriety of accounting distribution codes was evaluated by computer comparison with appropriate bills of materials. Audit programs were revised, in part, to shift emphasis in order to ascertain that (1) the programed internal controls, which cause computer rejection or transaction exception, are operating effectively and (2) the contractor's methods of researching, correcting and reintroducing rejected transactions into the system are acceptable.

The ability of a computer to perform in a consistent manner—to handle all like transactions in exactly the same way—is an established attribute of all ADP systems. This predictably consistent characteristic, once identified, substantially reduces the need for extensive testing in certain areas. For example, computerized internal controls to purify input, disclosed during an ADPS survey, could have a decided influence on the depth of audit to be accorded source transactions.

Another survey disclosed that the computer was programed to and did effectively screen labor transactions to detect significant variations from standard, to identify invalid work order authorizations, to verify currency of payroll information and many other items of audit significance.

While considerable flexibility is permitted in the management of individual field audit offices to accommodate differences among defense contractor accounting systems, minimum DCAA standards pertaining to ADPS survey activities are required of all locations subjected to an ADPS environment. Reporting of ADPS survey progress is required of each field audit office.

This progress is monitored and measured against established goals at regional levels and, ultimately, the progress of the respective DCAA regions is compared and evaluated.

The Importance of Using the Computer

The savings in auditor time made possible through use of computerized sample selection have been demonstrated in many field applications. Increased emphasis in this area is now required because of the advent of time-sharing. Computerized selection is often the only practical means of obtaining highly stratified samples. By reducing variability, stratification permits auditors to obtain greater precision in sample results while examining fewer items. Sampling from more than one or two strata has been inhibited in the past by the complexity of the calculations required to determine the optimum allocation of sample sizes among strata and to appraise the results of examining the selected items. In view of the capability of programs in the DCAA time-shared computer system to perform these calculations, this complexity should no longer be a significant factor.

Successful computerized sample selection applications for audit purposes have been achieved in the following typical areas: purchased materials, other direct charges, overhead expenses, intracompany transfers, subcontract billings, inventory transactions, travel vouchers, forward pricing estimates, spare parts costing, accounting for government property, and labor floor checks.

Development of computer programs to evaluate a contractor's or client's procedures and practices is well within the current state of the accounting art. This approach is sometimes referred to as an *automated audit of procedural attributes*. While it is under active research consideration by the agency, preliminary investigation suggests that, in view of wide diversity of defense contractor management information systems, high development costs may not be as easily recouped as from successful internal audit applications in widely dispersed but standardized military supply systems and public accounting applications in brokerage accounts or other uniformly maintained records.

Alert auditors are always on the lookout for unusual or odd transactions which could signal control breakdown. The potential of specialized computer exception analyses for audit purposes appeals directly to the advocates of concurrent auditing. Their objectives are more related to the cost avoidance potential than to remedial alternatives. The exception analysis process capitalizes on the computer's ability to make compatibility and limit checks.

This computer explosion of audit visibility provides even greater assurance that automatic data processing systems facilitate the work of the auditor.

How To Succeed in Auditing by Really Trying

Experience is still the most valuable teacher. Only by trying can audit be successfully adapted to the ADPS environment. The primary ingredient is the development of a sense of urgency. Because the benefits of a successful audit in a computer environment are so significant, the necessary investment of resources to exploit this potential is justified. An aggressive action plan suggests the following considerations.

1. *Fight apathy.* The individual auditor should include "ADP basics" in his self-development program to be updated on a continuing basis.

2. *Develop applications.* An in-house capability should be developed to conduct ADPS training and periodic workshops. This effort should be designed to meet the specific needs of the audit agency or firm.

3. *Establish minimum standards.* Audit management should make a positive commitment on minimum standards of what is expected of the auditor in an ADPS environment. In this regard, the ADPS survey is paramount. The survey can alter the line of least resistance in auditing around the computer.

4. *Exploit existing opportunities.* Audit management should adapt organizational structures to permit moderate research activities in advanced audit techniques to exploit changing technology.

5. *Initiate action.* This research/operational talent should be used as a catalyst for field implementation right now. Properly motivated, a team concept of analysis, advice and action can propel audit progress in an ADPS environment.

6. *Follow through.* Audit management should develop a workable mechanism to control, follow up, evaluate and influence ADPS audit progress.

Ultimately this effort should be reflected in an improvement in the quality of the audit product, greater efficiency in the use of audit resources or, ideally, both.

5 INTERNAL CONTROL

Use of Controls in EDP Accounting

Joseph V. Miccio

There are several questions to be answered about data processing controls. What are the objectives of controls? Who is responsible for them, how do we control the source data, how do we assure everyone that computer programs are reliable, how do we control the actual processing, how do we check the output and how do we satisfy other interested groups, such as public accountants, federal tax authorities, etc., that information given to them is correct? Let us take these points one at a time.

Objective

First of all, the major objective of control is to insure that only valid data is accepted and processed and that no invalid data is introduced during processing. Controls should prevent loss of information or incorrect processing of data. Loss of information might result from loss of a field in a record, loss of a whole record, loss of a reel of tape in a multi-reel file, or even loss of an entire file. Controls should also ensure the accuracy of file results.

Reprinted by permission of the author and the publisher from *Financial Executive*, Vol. XXXV, No. 8 (August, 1967), pp. 50–54.

114

Keeping the Audit Trail Alive

An important function of controls is the provision for audit trail. With data processing, audit trails can become lost in the collection and summarization of data. There are several ways to keep the audit trail alive in data processing, and they all involve essentially the same concept: keeping a detail file of the transactions as they occur. The detail file might be kept by printing daily proof listings of each day's transactions. It might be kept by printing a transactions journal showing opening balance, detailed transactions and closing balance for each active account over a short period of time. Or it might be kept by assembling all transactions on a journal tape. This tape could then be the input for an audit program which would extract the transactions for selected accounts and print them in such a way that the accountant or auditor could trace the status of an account, transaction by transaction.

Are controls economically feasible? To answer this question, we must balance the incremental cost of controls against the risk of loss that could result from the lack of controls. The cost resulting from lack of controls, which might consist of rerun time, a dissatisfied customer, an out-of-stock condition in inventory and many other intangibles, is difficult to measure. The incremental cost of controls is not difficult to measure, though some of it is involved in other functions and is, therefore, not essentially an out-of-pocket cost. I think most data processing people would be willing to pay the cost of controls just to avoid reruns.

Divided Responsibility

The responsibility for controls should be divided. If the responsibility is laid entirely upon the data processing department, not only is there greater risk of error and possibility of fraud, but some errors can become self-perpetuating due to lack of feedback. In general, the responsibility should be divided into four parts. The operating department should be responsible for the accuracy of the input and should be provided by the data processing department with those items necessary to check the accuracy of the input data, such as error lists and batch proof totals. The data processing department should be responsible for processing from keypunching through printing of the reports even when the keypunching or data preparation is done in other departments. The user or the final recipient of the report should be responsible for the output. The systems and programming sections should be responsible for the reliability of the systems and program.

Let us review more specifically each of these four responsibilities. First of all, how should input data be controlled? The procedures for the recording of the source input documents can have a great deal to do with the accuracy and the ability of the data processing department to control these documents. Although this is a step that is somewhat removed from the data processing department, document design and recording procedures nevertheless have a very great effect on the accuracy and costs of data processing, particularly keypunching.

The operating department creating the source data should be responsible for providing batch controls. Simple adding machine tape of the hours contained in a batch of time cards or the dollars in a batch of invoices can save much grief later on. The computer, of course, should then calculate a total of the detailed transactions for matching against these batch controls.

Various edit controls are designed to catch keypunch errors or possible transcription errors in the preparation of source documents. The editing is done by the computer on first entry of detailed transactions into the system. One approach is in editing to match the details against the master file to insure the accuracy of account numbers, payroll numbers or names, with exceptions being printed out in an error list. Other things would be:

- Testing numeric fields against absolute or reasonable limits which they are not allowed to exceed;
- Checking against format to see that a numeric field is all numeric or does not contain blanks;
- Checking that a field which is expected to contain information does contain the information;
- Checking logical relationships in the data; for example, a man whose job code represents a maintenance function would only be able to charge to indirect labor;
- Using a *check digit,* whereby the digits in an account number, including the check number, must add up in some predetermined manner to a predetermined figure. With the use of such check digits, it is usually not necessary to match details against the master file merely for the purpose of checking the accuracy of account numbers.

Rework Is Expensive

The next area of responsibility is program reliability. This pertains to the systems and programming function whether it is a separate department or part of the data processing department. Proper systems design is of paramount importance to control. It is the responsibility of systems design to specify the use of batch totals, the use of a journal tape to keep audit trails, the use of edit programs, and most of the other things that I have already talked about.

Following good systems design, of course, must be good programming. In connection with both of these functions, I would like to state as an aside that senior talent is cost effective in these areas. Competent people may be expensive, but mistakes and problems and rework are more expensive.

Another step to insure program reliability is good documentation. More and more data processing departments are realizing the importance of documentation. We see better documentation these days than used to be the case.

After the program is written and documented, it should be tested first against test data and then against live data. Sometimes the live data test can be a parallel run, although the changes in system design are quite frequently so radical that a parallel test is impossible. However, just running a batch of live data not parallel with anything can be useful in pointing up exceptional conditions that were not considered in the test data or perhaps not even provided for in the systems design.

Before the program is implemented, preferably early in the design stage, the systems design should be reviewed by the accountant. The systems department and the entire computer operations can be in serious trouble if it is discovered after several production runs that the auditor does not approve, for example, of the method of round off. The auditor might suggest exception tests and reasonableness tests which will help to pick up serious errors in design or errors in data preparation.

After the program is implemented and running and everyone is satisfied with results, the problem of future changes to the program arise. Changes to the program should be controlled; they should not be made without documentation and review by the systems manager and the data processing manager. These reviews are necessary to insure that the changes do what they are supposed to do and do not have unforeseen effects.

In addition, the program itself should contain controls in order to assure that proper tapes are used and that records are not lost. These would include controls for:

- Tape labels.
- Record counts which are checked from program to program as a file passes through the system.
- Hash totals for the same purpose.
- Redundant identifiers, such as an alpha code corresponding to the last name of an account.
- Memory protection and file protection to prevent valuable information from being wiped out in error.
- Suspense accounts for the accumulation of the amounts of error records which are discarded from the system.

Suspense accounts help in balancing the data and point out the errors to be corrected.

Restricted Area

The next control area is the computer room or processing shop, which comes under the aegis of the data processing operations manager. There are several control possibilities in this area. The first is to restrict access to the computer room. Programmers, analysts and outsiders should submit jobs on a job request form and should not be allowed to enter the computer room unless they receive the permission of the data processing operations manager. A good programmer will not resent this; it gives him more freedom to continue with his work. In any event, a programmer is too expensive to be acting as an operator. It is usually necessary for a programmer to attend the initial runs of a new system, although some computer operating systems are set up with memory and tape dumps so that the programmer does not need to attend even the initial runs.

Another important point is that of operator intervention. If a program does not run through to the end of the job or if it required that the operator take action of any kind, this information should be logged either manually in an operator log or on the console typewriter. Programs should be written in such a way that operator intervention is minimized and, when it does occur, that logging is required.

The importance of control over tape or disc libraries cannot be over-emphasized. Anyone who has had a master file or an important transaction file wiped out realizes the importance of having a tape library set up with logging of tapes in and out. There are other advantages of tape libraries: we can keep tape histories and get information on life of tapes and be able to forecast tape usage so that supplies can be purchased enough in advance to prevent exhaustion of the tape supply.

Backup and rerun procedures come under the control of the data processing department. Backup procedures require knowing what compatible equipment is available, making an arrangement with the user of that equipment and setting up procedures so that the operation can be run on the alternate equipment. Rerun procedures are related to the tape library policy to prevent rerun unless there are backup files for the rerun. It is necessary to insure that father and grandfather generations of master files be kept, that the detail files be kept on hand for a fixed amount of time (usually at least one and preferably two accounting cycles). It is also necessary to make provision for storing copies of master files and program tapes in a remote location from the computer room. This is called vital records control and provides protection against fire and other eventualities. Proper vital record control can result in reduction of insurance premium if insurance is carried against computer room damage.

The user is responsible for checking the output. In some cases, this is merely a test to determine if the figures are reasonable. In other cases, the user can check against other related totals to see that the totals bear a proper relationship. The user should control exceptions, such as where a report flags numbers that are outside some predetermined range. It is up to the user to check the exceptions to see if they are reasonable. The user can also perform statistical analysis of the output data to insure that it is correct.

Who Is Interested in Controls?

In addition to the people who have direct responsibility for controls, there are other groups that are interested in them. The corporate controller is usually, by corporate charter and by law, directly responsible for the accuracy of the company's financial reports. Any data processing operation involving the accounting function of the business is of interest to the controller. And both the internal and external auditors naturally have an interest in data processing controls.

There are many outside agencies interested in controls: the federal and local tax authorities are interested in the accuracy of the financial reporting of the corporation, as may be military procurement agencies if government contracts are involved. Unions and many other regulatory bodies may also be involved.

The accountant will frequently want to determine the controls in the EDP system, appraise their accuracy, and check their operation. A preaudit by the internal auditors or the accounting department can be a great benefit to all levels of management, but particularly to those designing and programming the system. It is easier to make changes before and during the design of the system than to make them afterwards. With the concentration of the data processing function in EDP equipment, auditors will usually find it necessary to make audit tests of the processing by the equipment. On many occasions they will wish to use the EDP equipment to perform some of their audit tests. Since it is in the best interest of all concerned that any system errors be detected, it is vitally necessary that the data processing department cooperate with the accountants in establishing such procedures. The data processing department can save considerable effort by enlisting the assistance of the accounting and auditing departments in the early stages of systems design. The accountants and auditors can ensure that the results of the data processing effort will reflect good accounting practices if they give as much assistance as possible throughout the design effort.

New Generation EDP Control Considerations

Robert F. Moloney

Fast-response data processing systems, generally referred to as "real time" or "on-line systems," have made rapid progress over the past several years. Much of this progress can be attributed to the introduction of third generation computer equipment and supporting software capable of handling the complexities inherent in these systems.

The traditional control concepts, painstakingly built up over the past decade for batch-type operations, are no longer adequate. The use of communication facilities operating in an on-line mode, duplex equipment configurations, multiprocessing and multiprogramming necessitates the development of additional control techniques if these systems are to process all data accurately and efficiently.

The purpose of this article is to discuss some of these new control requirements which systems analysts, programers and auditors should be considering in the design of any real time system. These controls are considered in this article in four categories: on line controls, data protection controls, diagnostic controls and emergency procedures.

Reprinted by permission of the author and the publisher from *Management Services*, Vol. V, No. 2 (March–April, 1968), pp. 15–22.

On-line Controls

The use of communication lines to transmit data in systems of this type requires the use of an on-line terminal device by which messages are transmitted to or received from a computer. The most important consideration when operating in this mode is to ensure that the data being transmitted are received and properly processed. It is always possible for messages to be lost or garbled or perhaps for a line or terminal device to go out of order during transmission. To prevent this from happening the system should provide program routines to check on messages sent through the system. These routines should provide for at least the following:

Message Identification Handling Procedures To Ensure That Each Message Is Properly Handled. Every message received at the data center should be identified by a message header showing such information as message number, terminal, date and action code. This information is necessary for the initializer routine to route the message to the proper program for processing. If a message with an incorrect header is received, it should be routed to a control group for corrective action or rejected with a request to the originating terminal for retransmission of the entire message.

Message Transmission Controls To Determine That All Messages Transmitted Over the Lines Are Received. This is done by assigning each message a number, usually within a block, and subsequently verifying the sequence of the message numbers received. Unaccounted-for numbers are considered exceptions to be investigated. Another control is the confirmation by the computer or terminal of all messages received.

One such system used a combination of these two methods. Each location was assigned sequential numbers 000 through 999. As an item was transmitted to the computer, it was assigned a message number, which was stored internally by the computer. Periodically a routine checking of these numbers would produce a report of out-of-sequence numbers and those remaining unused. These were forwarded to each originating location, which checked them against a log maintained for that purpose. Lost messages were retransmitted. Additionally, every message received by the computer was confirmed. This told the operator downline that it had been received by the processor and enabled him to verify the accuracy of the data.

Rerouting Procedures To Handle Messages Sent to Downline Stations Which Are Not Operating. When this happens it is necessary to provide routines to reroute the message to another terminal or store the message internally in the computer until such time as the down terminal restarts operation. The procedures for dealing with this type of operation are sometimes called "willful intercept." (The action to be taken when the computer breaks down is not discussed here since this topic will be covered under the category of emergency conditions.)

Check Characters To Detect Transmission Errors. Two data verification procedures generally used to check the accuracy of transmitted data are the character and message parity checks. The character parity check, with which most accountants are familiar, verifies the accuracy of each character transmitted. The message parity check is a check digit compiled at the originating terminal, based upon the number of bits in the message sent, which is tacked on to the end of that message. The receiving terminal, similarly, compiles a check digit based on the number of bits received, and both check digits are compared. If they agree, a "transmission correctly received" signal is sent to the terminal or processor. If the communication lines have introduced errors, the system should provide for an alert signal to the terminal notifying it of the error or, preferably, for the automatic retransmission of the entire message.[1] In the latter case, if the error condition still exists the terminal should be alerted.

Data Protection Controls

The on-line capability inherent in a real time system creates a problem of data protection. Information stored in the files may be made available to terminal operators at their request. This raises the question as to what procedures are necessary to prevent data from being accidentally destroyed or used by unauthorized personnel. The question is especially critical when the information involved is highly confidential or the system operates in a time sharing mode. The problem becomes even more complex in a multi-programed system: What assurance is there that program segments read into core storage will not be accidentally loaded over data currently being processed?

For purposes of this discussion data protection includes those measures incorporated in the system to prevent concurrent updating of stored files, unauthorized use of stored files and accidental destruction of data in core storage during processing by the computer. Applicable control considerations are discussed in the following three sections.

Concurrent Updating. The normal types of errors which can occur during the transmission of data over the communication lines do not pose

---

[1] For a more thorough discussion of this topic refer to IBM Corporation, "Message Control System Concepts," Reference C20-1609, p. 5.

serious problems as the majority of these can be discovered through the use of a strong edit routine and the incorporation of the on line controls previously discussed. But what about the problem of concurrent updating, as when two transactions in a multiprogramed system attempt to update the same file simultaneously. For instance, transactions A and B retrieve the same file and update it. If the updated version of the file resulting from transaction A is stored first, it will be lost when transaction B is stored. What is needed is a procedure which permits only one transaction to update a file at a time. In the IBM system software package this is referred to as "exclusive control."

"Exclusive control" can be achieved by requiring each transaction to "request" permission of the supervisory program to update a file. If the file is available, the supervisory program grants the request and the transaction updates it. During this time no other transaction is permitted access to this file.

Data Security. The prevention of unauthorized access to stored data can generally be accomplished by the use of lockwords, authority lists and dedicated communication lines. Lockwords, sometimes referred to as "keywords" or "passwords," consist of several characters in a data file which the input transaction or inquiry must match in order to gain access to the file. The use of this device to control file references may be further refined by supplying several lockwords. For instance, one set of characters may permit the file to be retrieved for reading purposes only (read-protect), and still another set may permit both reading and writing.

When using lockwords, consideration should be given to the type of terminal used. If the lockword appears on each document printed by the terminal, it may defeat its own purpose since it becomes relatively easy to compromise it. There are devices available from which the lockword can be entered into the system in a non-print mode. This type of terminal should be used where feasible.

Authority Lists

Authority lists are another form of protection. In this instance, the lockword is used to identify the person transmitting from the remote location. After the initial identification has been established, reference is made to an authority list which indicates which type of data the sender is authorized to receive. As with lockwords, the authority list may classify references to the files as read only or both read and write.

The previous discussion regarding the use of these two techniques does not exclude the use of other approaches to accomplish the same ends. For instance, "if an inquiry is received from a remote station. . . . . asking for confidential data, the computer might break the connection and then redial it, after checking to see that the station is authorized to receive the data."[2] The extent to which these controls are used will depend on the type of system and the nature of the stored data.

When lockwords and authority lists are not used, terminals may be identified by means of dedicated communication lines. This generally implies the use of only one terminal on the line. Where terminals are attached to a party line or a similar network, answerback would be used in lieu of a dedicated communication line. With answerback a signal is sent to the terminal, and the latter responds within a prescribed amount of time with its code indentification. Because this system can be compromised, it is not recommended where the security of stored data is of major importance.

The first two methods discussed should successfully exclude unauthorized personnel from the stored data files. However, even the best coding system can be broken if an individual can work on it. What procedure, then, can be incorporated in a system of this nature to prevent an unauthorized individual from transmitting data to the processor in an attempt to decode the lockword and gain access to the system? A monitoring routine could be established which would count the number of unsuccessful attempts to enter the system and after a certain number had been reached, say, three times in succession, a message might be printed out at the data station with instructions to call the downline station for an explanation. The point to be made here is this: If the data are important enough to require the use of lockwords and authority lists in the system, it is important to ensure that these controls are effectively accomplishing their assignments.

Boundary Registers

Memory Protection. In a multi-programmed system, a number of different data elements will be in core storage at the same time. These will consist of the control program, a portion of which will permanently reside in core; a number of operational programs; and various queues of messages awaiting processing or in the process of being handled by the computer. Because of the possibility of a programming or a machine error, an operational program could address portions of core storage outside the limits of its own coding, work areas or other applicable areas. The result could be the alteration or modification of another program; the destruction of data on tape, disk or drum; or perhaps the creation of a series of endless loops. To keep this from happening the system should provide for some form of memory protection.

[2] Corning Publications, Inc., *EDP Analyzer*, March, 1966, Vol. 4, No. 3, p. 12.

One technique currently employed is the use of boundary registers. This requires additional equipment in the form of an upper and lower boundary register. In the simplest form of this system the boundary registers are loaded with the upper and lower core storage addresses of the program when it is loaded into the processor. If during the course of the program the address portion of the instruction exceeds the boundaries indicated in the registers, an interrupt occurs, and control is passed to the supervisor program for appropriate action.[3]

The IBM and the Spectra 70 use storage and protection keys. Core storage in these systems is broken up into blocks. Each block has a four-bit storage key assigned to it. The program status word for each program has a four-bit protection key. Before any program references a block of core storage for the purpose of writing data, the storage key and the protection key must be matched; otherwise the operation is aborted, and control is passed to the supervisory program.

It is easy to see that there are a number of different approaches, depending on the equipment used, to provide memory protection. Since this topic has been thoroughly discussed in various EDP publications,[4] it will not be discussed further in this article.

Diagnostic Controls

One of the characteristics of a real time system is that it must operate without stopping for fixed periods of time. The duration of time will depend upon the equipment configuration. A duplexed system can be designed to operate 24 hours a day, whereas a simplex system operates for only part of the day. Suppose, however, that there is a malfunction of some component part or that a programing error occurs while the system is operating. Should the processing halt, as was usually the case with second generation equipment, or should it continue processing after branching to some routine to handle the problem? The general rule is to keep the system operating if there is some way of circumventing the trouble. To accomplish this objective, it is necessary to build into the system some way of detecting and isolating error conditions so that appropriate action can be taken. This can be done through the use of diagnostic programs.

"Diagnostic programs are a tool used to test computers, isolate component malfunctions, and improve overall computer system operations."[5] We

[3] For a more thorough discussion of this topic refer to William H. Desmonde's "Real-Time Data Processing Systems, Introductory Concepts," Prentice-Hall, Inc., Englewood Cliffs, New Jersey, 1964, Chapter IV.

[4] See especially Corning Publications, Inc., op. cit., pp. 10–12.

[5] James Martin, *Programming Real Time Systems*, Prentice-Hall, Inc., Englewood Cliffs, New Jersey, 1965, p. 125.

are interested only in those on-line routines which detect the fact that errors are happening and isolate, where possible, the cause of the error.[6] Once the error has been isolated it is up to the supervisory program to determine what action is necessary. According to Martin,[7] one of six actions can be taken:

1. Re-execute the faulty instruction and continue processing.
2. Restart the program in question.
3. Transfer to an exception routine characteristic of the program in question.
4. Initiate switchover.
5. Initiate closedown.
6. Halt.

Each of these alternatives will be discussed in the section on emergency procedures which succeeds this section.

The number and types of diagnostic programs in a particular system will depend on the design of the system and its equipment configuration.

For purposes of illustration, the following is an example of how these programs might work:

Consider a real time system communicating with a number of remote terminals. Suddenly a terminal breaks down. When this happens, a diagnostic program checks the communication network and establishes that there is a problem. Another diagnostic program checks each line until the down terminal is isolated. Once the error has been isolated, control is returned to the supervisory program, which might close down this line until repairs are made and route all interim messages to an adjoining terminal for manual handling.

It is always possible, of course, that errors may occur which will not be detected by such routines. The only protection against invalid data created by such errors is to have adequate file reconstruction procedures.

Emergency Procedures

Once an error or malfunction has been isolated, it is up to the supervisory program to take appropriate action. As was stated previously, it has a number of choices. The first three of these—re-execute the faulty instruction, restart the program or transfer control to an exception routine—do not present any unique problems. They have been satisfactorily tested in the traditional batch processing systems, and similar procedures can be incorpo-

---

[6] Although there will be a number of off-line routines peculiar to real time systems, we are not interested in them for purposes of this discussion since they do not affect the system while it is operating and are generally used only by the systems engineer.

[7] Martin, op. cit., p. 224.

rated into real time systems. The last three alternatives—initiate switchover, close down part of the system or halt—are unique problems and require careful consideration if the system is to provide for all contingencies.

Failures that can cause a system to switch computers or close down a part of the system are generally due to hardware malfunctions. When a system is able to switch its operation from one computer to another, as is possible in a duplexed system, without changing its method of processing data, we say a "switchover" has occurred. On the other hand, if an equipment malfunction occurs in the system which requires the system to close down some part of the operation and modify its method of processing data to circumvent the error, we say it is functioning in a "fallback" mode. Whenever either of these conditions arises it is necessary to provide procedures to ensure that they are efficiently handled.

Switchover, as stated previously, assumes the use of duplex computers so that if the operating computer breaks down its supporting unit will take over processing. When the change from one unit to another takes place, whether it is automatic or manual, the machine operator should be informed via the console or printer what action he is required to take, if any, and the reason why the change was made. For an automatic switchover to take place, the on line computer should initiate action. However, if the malfunction is serious, this may not always be possible. To ensure that a changeover is effected when such a malfunction occurs, the standby computer should periodically check its counterpart. If it detects a malfunction, it should initiate the switchover. Whenever this transition takes place, a message notifying terminal operators of this fact should be sent downline.

During the transition it is vitally important that transactions not be lost. Messages that have not actually entered the system present no problems since these will be noted as missing when the sequence check (discussed under on line controls) is made. The problem lies with those that have entered the system and are awaiting processing on input, work, or output queues. This problem may be resolved by recording the message sequence number after a record has been updated rather than as each message enters the system, or perhaps both actions might be recorded and subsequently compared to each other. Another method is to post the message sequence number to the file as it is updated. In the event of a switchover the comparison of the transaction and file message number will prevent a file from being updated twice. It may or may not prevent messages from being lost depending on the system design.

Graceful Degradation

Fallback or "graceful degradation," as it is sometimes called, occurs in a non-duplexed system when a part of the equipment configuration breaks down but the loss of the particular piece(s) is not serious enough to shut down the entire system. When this happens, the machine operator should be informed by the control program as to the current status of the system and what action he should take. In some instances terminal operators should also be informed. Procedures should be available to advise supervisory personnel what clerical action is necessary to support the system until it recovers and, finally, what action is necessary to restore the system to the condition that existed before the fallback occurred.

The results may be catastrophic when a real time system halts. If the halt is due to a complete breakdown of a major component the only thing to do is repair it as rapidly as possible. Procedures should be available for supervisors so that they may take necessary emergency action and guide clerical personnel in work which must be done while the system is down and initially after it recovers.

It is imperative that restart procedures be incorporated in the system. The restart is based on a complete checkpoint record written on a peripheral device such as a disk file. The checkpoint record, provision for which should be incorporated in the system, is a complete record of all messages, counters, logs and status indicators in the system at that time. When a restart is necessary, the checkpoint record is used to restore the system to its condition at the time the checkpoint record was written. Each terminal is advised of the restart and the number of the last message properly received from the terminal at the time of the checkpoint. Subsequent messages are retransmitted, and the system is again operational.

If the halt occurs because of a system overload the problem is not as serious. System overloads can occur when a number of messages are read into core and subsequently it is discovered that there are not enough available core blocks to complete all the work the computer has started. This problem can occur in a multiprogramed system using random input. There must be some emergency procedures in the system to handle this dilemma.

It is possible to prevent this from happening, except in rare instances, by anticipating when the level of core blocks available for processing data in the computer is reaching a danger point. When this level has been reached, the computer should shut down and refuse to accept any more input. This means the computer must be able to control the volume to input during peak periods. This control is exercised in a system utilizing "polling" techniques by not "polling" the transmitting locations until the overload is ended. Another method that may be used is for the processor to send a signal either requesting the operator to re-enter the message into the system or locking the terminal pending further notice from the computer.

If the overload does occur, however, the system should be able to handle the problem by first determining the application programs temporarily in core which are not currently being used and making their applicable blocks available for the further processing of data. If this doesn't solve the problem, the system may have to destroy messages in the system, preferably on a last-in basis, and request the applicable terminals to repeat the messages.

Conclusion

Real time systems are here to stay. If systems analysts, programers and auditors are to design and review these complex applications, it is necessary that they understand what a real time system is and, more important, the controls necessary to ensure that the desired results are produced. An understanding of the traditional controls is not sufficient when operating in a real time environment. Although these controls, such as matching and batching or validity and limit checks, are just as necessary to the effective operation of a real time system as to a batch system, the nature of the real time system has necessitated additional controls to ensure that the system operates as desired.

This article discusses many of those control considerations. It is not intended as an all-inclusive statement of control requirements in real time applications, since these will be dictated by such factors as system design specifications, the equipment used, security requirements and many other factors. It merely summarizes some of the more common control considerations basic to a well designed real time system.

6   SYSTEMS AND
SYSTEMS PLANNING

STARFIRE—An Advanced Financial Information System

Michael R. Tyran

The external and internal requirements for more varied and detailed information cannot be generated under the conventional information sys-tems. Each new requirement or change has to be programmed separately which is a time-consuming, laborious, expensive effort at best. As can be understood, once a system becomes operational, it essentially becomes fixed. Because of the high implementation costs, this forces you to use the me-chanical program over a period of time even though it does not maintain pace with the needs from today's ever-changing reporting climate.

As an inevitable result of these deficiencies, many organizations began to develop "prop" systems to extract data from "official" reports to meet their needs. Naturally, this entailed expenditures of manpower effort and other associated costs to obtain financial and operating data for planning, report-ing and control purposes.

Equipment Aspect. Until recently, the state of the computer art was not sufficiently advanced to handle large masses of data in storage which could be updated in a timely manner and retrieved instantly on an "as needed"

Reprinted by permission of the publisher from *Management Accounting*, Vol. XLVII, No. 9, Sec. 1 (May, 1966), pp. 3–16.

basis. Recent technical strides, however, have changed this situation and more sophisticated equipment with compatible program language capability is available.

Current Mechanical Program Status. Many of our programs at Lockheed Missiles and Space Company (LMSC) were generated over a ten-year period of time and in various program languages—FORTRAN, Autocode, 9 PAC, etc. Changes were difficult to make, particularly if the original person who programmed the system was no longer available to make changes or additions. Furthermore, many of the programs were inflexible for making changes and, therefore, "patch type" additions to the program had to be made, which lead to considerable error susceptibility.

Need for a Change

In view of the above, the Financial Systems and Procedures Department at LMSC conceived and designed the STARFIRE concept which will make possible the immediate accumulation of all financially oriented data, mechanically manipulate this information and make it instantly available for retrieval to the user. This single file concept will make possible a fully integrated mechanical system which will achieve the ultimate in data processing. Its flexibility advantages will overcome the current problems associated with making changes to satisfy current as well as "unthought of" future needs.

The system, identified by its acronym—STARFIRE:

**SYSTEM
TO
ACCUMULATE &
RETRIEVE
FINANCIAL
INFORMATION WITH
RANDOM
EXTRACTION**

organizes financial reporting so as to give us greater flexibility, report timeliness, mass storage capability, built-in controls, etc. The name is actually insignificant; it serves only as an identifier to the system.

Figure 1 summarizes the processing evolution which will occur from the implementation of the STARFIRE system.

The general and detailed steps involved in the development of this new system are discussed in the following presentation.

The Overall Concept

Figure 2 depicts the overall system. As can be seen, remote stations located in the various concerned organizational units such as payroll, cost accounting, budget and forecast, etc., make daily input to the files from their locations. This information is entered through card media, magnetic tape and input/output devices.

Authorized input and output organizational units are established. Only those thus designated have the means to enter data in certain files and retrieve that information to which they are authorized. This eliminates the problems of security (need to know, entitled to, responsible for, etc.,) concerned with data development and usage.

The transactions are validated against the master audit file which checks for data completeness, proper charge numbers, valid organizations, em-

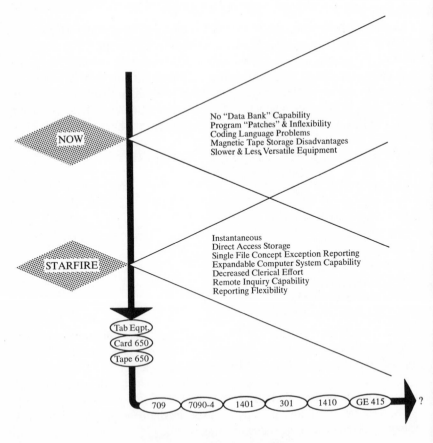

Figure 1. Process evolution.

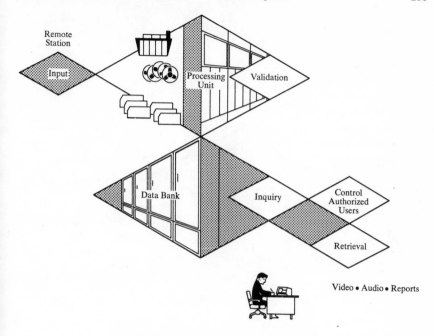

Figure 2. Data flow under STARFIRE.

ployee numbers, etc. Incorrect data are rejected and an error message is sent back automatically to the inputting units. The correct data enter the various data banks where program routines update, add or delete information in the files.

Each day the processing unit forwards to each of the submitting organizational units a listing of the transactions made that day. These listings then serve as checklists for their verification and future reference.

The information is obtained through devices such as video display, input/output keyboard print, audio (in the future) and routine reports. The reporting can be either on a real time basis (instantaneous) and/or batch processing. The main consideration in this whole system is that it be user oriented—give the responsible organizations the capability for immediate access and retrieval of routine or unique information that they need to perform their function effectively.

The Current System vs. STARFIRE

Under our present system, we input various data as shown in Figure 3. This is done through transmittals to keypunch from the concerned areas.

The information is processed and the resultant report data is outputted, "massaged" and in many instances again re-inputted to obtain the final

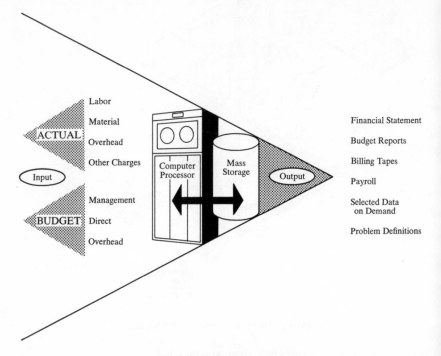

**Figure 3. Current data process vs.
STARFIRE.**

result. This is necessary because we have no mass storage capability for complete processing of the data to its ultimate end from the initial source document. Under STARFIRE, this capability is available and will give two additional features that we do not possess today—capability to "call out" of the files only that specific information we need and exception reporting. By exception reporting, it is meant that there will be programmed parameters in the system which will automatically report deviations from the norm. For example, if the actual direct labor hours against a contract exceed the budgeted allotment by a certain percent, then this information will be automatically reported to the concerned organizational unit for investigation and subsequent action.

Data Flow. In Figure 4 you will note that, under our current system, timecard information is processed weekly and reports are generated. The problem is that the result is only achieved through continual resubmission of data in order to obtain the next hierarchy or summary level of reporting. Weekly summaries are received and resubmitted for monthly totals. Monthly

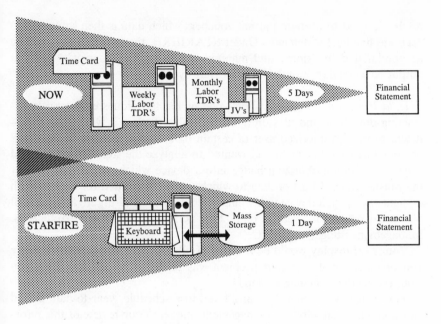

Figure 4. Data accumulation and report generation.

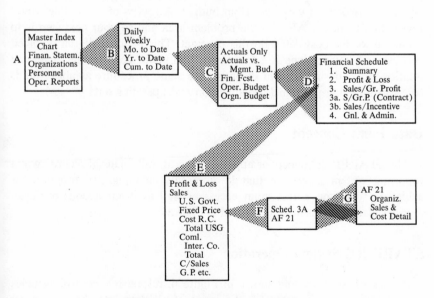

Figure 5. Example of a STARFIRE technique.

totals are used to prepare journal vouchers which data is then submitted to generate financial statements. Under STARFIRE, the timecard data will be accumulated daily, stored and manipulated to achieve financial statement output on a one day, month end processing cycle.

Data Retrieval.   Figure 5 shows one of the techniques employed in extracting data from the files on a video display device. It works like this—if you were an authorized user of certain data, had a problem in the detail of your financial statement and wanted to analyze the situation, you would insert your data authorizing badge into a device which would then display the Master Index Chart of data to which you were entitled for access. With a "light ray" pencil device you would select in Step A of Figure 5 "Financial Statement," then the "year to date" time period in Step B and "Actuals vs. Management Budget" in Step C.

Your next display would be a listing of all your financial schedules. Since you predetermined that your problem was in the profit-and-loss area, you would select that schedule in Step D.

Now you have in Step E a profit-and-loss schedule, year-to-date period and a comparison with the management budget. Your review of this information indicates your unexplained and largest variance to be in your cost reimbursement contracts. In Step F, therefore, you select "Cost Reimbursement Contract" for more detail which would be a listing of CRC contracts with their associated variances from budget. A review of this listing would reveal that Contract AF21 is the problem area and so your next step is to obtain all of the cost detail on this contract. This is not really an involved process and having done it a few times, you could go from the beginning inquiry to the desired end in seconds. The same procedure as above holds true for obtaining personnel, organization and operating data.

Data Bank Concept

The STARFIRE concept as applied to the overall financial recording and reporting system is new in that it represents an integrated program for achieving real time, direct input access as well as instantaneous retrieval. A generalized process flow is reflected in Figure 6.

STARFIRE System Operation

As described above and shown in Figure 6, responsible control agencies or stations are accountable for the input of all data into the system, its manipulation, validity, monitoring and distribution control of the output.

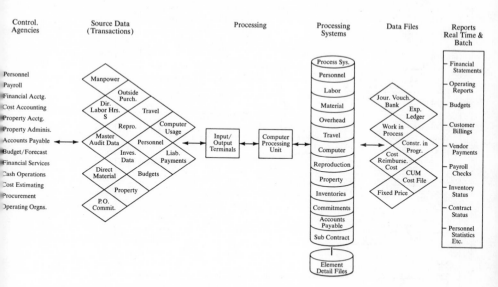

Figure 6. STARFIRE data bank concept.

The flow of the data, as shown, is through remote station located input/
output devices. Input will be on a daily basis (as is possible) with file
updating occurring on off shift hours. Listing of all transactions will be
outputted to the concerned organizations daily. Program routines will manipulate the data into the various usage files so that "update" can be accomplished in a number of areas simultaneously.

As you will note in Figure 7, the detailed elements of the source documents (Reproduction Dept.) are shown along with the files and reports
with which they are associated. For example, certain reproduction request
data is entered in Journal Voucher 291 (Reclassification of Reproduction
and Photographic Charges), subledgers (Cost Reimbursement Contracts,
Work in Process, Expense, Billing), cumulative cost file and various batch
reports. No real time reporting is required in the reproduction area. A
single transaction can, as stated above, "trigger" the appropriate entries in
all of the affected files.

Detailed element files are maintained and updated daily (direct labor,
material, etc.). The data banks are also updated to reflect certain summary

Figure 7. STARFIRE—direct reproduction costs: data element to output relationship chart.

Source Document/ Process/etc.	In TC	Data Element In (x)	Data Element Out (O)	JV 291	CRC	WIP	EXP	Billing Date	Cum. Costs	Real Time	A	B	C	D	E	F	G	H	I
Reproduction request, Engineering job, Release ticket, Blueprint request		Plant (Facility)	Converted repro. charge no.	o		o		o	o		o	o	o	o	o		o		o
		Requesting orgn.	Major class	o		o		o	o		x	x	x	x	x	x	x	x	x
		Request date	Project	o		o		o	o		x	x	x	x	x	x	x	x	x
		Major class	Work order	o		o		o	o		x	x	x	x	x	x	x	x	x
		Minor class	Work authority						o		x	x	x			x	x		
		Project	Minor class (8)						x		x	x	x	x			x	x	
		Work order	Reproduction amount, week				x		x								x	x	
		Work authority	Reproduction amount, month				x		x		x	x	x				x	x	
		Segment/task	Responsible project orgn.															x	x	
		Source document number	Responsible work order orgn.			o									x			x	x	
		Units (quantity) reproduced	Journal voucher number															x		
		Reproduction cost code	General ledger account no.	o	o	o	o	o			o		o							
		Vendor cost	Subsidiary account no.	o			o	o			o	x	o							
		Indirect analysis code	Orgn. O.H. pool identifier	o	o	o	o													o
			Group code		o															
			Labor (reproduction) amount						o		o	x	o		x		o	x	o	
			Analysis/element code	x			x	x			x	x	x		x			x		
			Dir. repro. amt., last 12 months									x								
			Reproduction amt., year to date									x								
			Repro. amt., contract to date									x								
			Indir. (repro.) amts. by O.H. pool (3 months)						x		x	x	x		x		x	x		
			Suspense code						x		x	x	x		x			x	x	
Reproduction cost code/ rate transmittal		Cost code, total rate (price)	Reproduction amount, week	o	o	o	o	o	o		o	o	o	o	o	o	o	o	o
		Cost code, labor rate (price)	Reproduction amount, month						o											
		Reproduction type	Labor (reproduction) amount	x				x	x		x		x		x			x	x	
		Reproduction cost code	Dir. repro. amt., last 12 months						x		x		x					x	x	
			Reproduction amt., year to date																	
			Repro. amt., contract to date																	
			Indir. (repro.) amts. by O.H. pool (3 months)																	
			Suspense code																	
Reproduction budget Transmittal		Major class	Year to date budget amount						o	o	o	o	o						
		Minor class	Contract to date budget amount						x	x	x	x	x						
		Project	Schedule status (indicator)							o	o	o	o						
		Work order	Variance project to date							x	x	x	x						
		Work authority																	
		Segment/task																	
		Requesting organization																	
		Responsible project orgn.																	
		Responsible work order orgn.																	
		Budget amount, month																	
		Scheduled completion date																	
		Estimated completion date																	
Labor distribution system		12 month direct labor hours	Repro. rate per direct labor hour			x		x	x		x	x	x			x				
		Major class	Dir. repro. amt., past 12 months			x		x	x		x	x	x							
		Project			x			x			x	x							
Master audit file		Converted repro. charge no.							x		x	x	x	x					x
		Major class		x				x	x		x	x	x			x				x
		Project		x				x	x		x	x	x			x				x
		Work order				x			x		x		x	x						
		Work authority		x				x	x		x		x						x	x
		Responsible work order orgn.							x											
		Gen. ledger account number							x											
		Orgn. O.H. pool identifier							x											
		Subsidiary account number							x											
		Division							x											

Note: Although Journal Vouchers and Ledgers indicate a monthly update above, it is anticipated these will be updated more frequently than this, possibly daily.

information which will be used to prepare financial statements, operating reports, budgets, customer billings, etc. The complete process from source document to the final reports will be mechanical under STARFIRE and the data bank concept.

Implementation Considerations

As you can imagine, there are many activities to be considered in designing and initiating a system such as STARFIRE. The steps are outlined in Figure 8 and discussed below. It should be noted that the tasks are not necessarily performed in chronological order. In other words, varied tasks can be performed simultaneously by different teams.

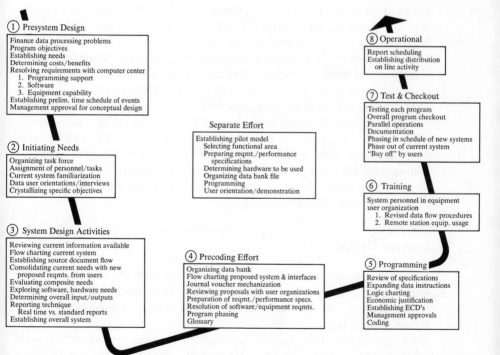

Figure 8. STARFIRE—implementation considerations.

Pre-system Design

After reviewing our data processing problems and establishing our objectives and needs, a series of meetings was held with the computer personnel to resolve programming, software and equipment requirements. The computer center management readily recognized the benefits which would accrue in their operations from the improvement and streamlining of our many current programs and systems. Decrease in computer processing time, fewer reports and reruns were the definite achievements anticipated from this system. A generalized approach to this new endeavor was formalized and presented to LMSC management for approval to proceed with a detailed system design. After management concurrence, effort commenced on this project.

Initiating Needs

Our next step was to organize a task force for this activity, composed of the systems department and programming analysts from the computation center. This made an ideal team in that all aspects of the system could be covered—from the source data flow to the preparation of the specifications, programming and system implementation.

The total effort was segregated into ten functional areas of two individuals each. In other words, separate teams were assigned to the direct labor area, overhead and manpower, property, payroll, personnel, etc.

The teams familiarized themselves first with the current systems and mechanical programs involved in each area. Presentations of the program objectives and how the system would work were made to all levels of management and concerned operating organizations. Subsequent meetings were held with various data user organizations to verify their current needs and establish any new requirements. As a result of this effort, program objectives were more specifically determined.

System Design

In the review of current information available, flow charts were prepared to show the data flow, data processing and the reporting involved. Every source document was tracked from its point of origin to its resultant contribution in the reporting cycle.

Current reports, both manual and mechanical, were charted by functional areas showing report identification, recipients, issue schedules and all of the data elements contained therein. New requirements were also added to these charts so that a composite picture of all needs was reflected. This allowed us an opportunity to view the total data flow and determine duplications and irrelevancies, and streamline requirements for the overall system.

While the above effort was going on, a separate computer center team was engaged in evaluating software/hardware needs. There was close co-ordination among all of the personnel assigned to the STARFIRE project.

Precoding

One of the main requisites of this system was to develop an overall data bank. The data banks were generated by each functional area and then consolidated. In the consolidation, there were approximately 1500 line items which were categorized by primary usage.

It should be noted further that the consolidation reflected the added feature of classifying the elements as to their involvement in the procedure of editing, auditing, sorting, updating, data collection and reporting. This bank will assist the programmer in organizing the data on disc file for the instant access and retrieval operation.

Under the STARFIRE system, it is envisioned that all journal vouchers possible will be mechanized. In some instances, it is not practical to mech-anize because of the judgment factor involved in their preparation. However, even with those manually generated, the data will be inputted into the system through the input/output devices located in the area where the information originates.

One standard computer program will be prepared to handle all of the "hand-feed" type transactions. The mechanized journal vouchers, which constitute about 95 per cent of the total, will be automatically prepared by the equipment from other information already in the computer system. The consolidated journal voucher data reflect document number, the organization preparing, processing description and ledger account detail involved. For the future, it is anticipated that journal voucher data will be outputted in the form of a listing of the debit and credit entries and the support detail will consist of mechanical reports rather than the bulky support attachments of today.

The STARFIRE system requirements generated were reviewed with the user organizations. Any changes required were negotiated. The specifications reflect all the needs, if practicable and justified, of the user organizations.

The program phasing schedule indicates the programs in priority order for coding and mechanizing. This was a very necessary process in that certain programs are dependent upon others for source and/or manipulated data.

A glossary of all terms used in this program has been compiled. It totals approximately 1,800 definitions of terms used in the STARFIRE system. This will definitely lessen the communication problems for all concerned

personnel in the understanding and usage of these terms. The glossary consolidation includes an abbreviation for each term (programming and referral
ease), number of characters and the definition itself.

Programming

This phase of development will entail the activities noted in Figure 6.
Some of the current programs will only require minimum adjustment to
tie-in to the STARFIRE concept. In others, there will be major changes to
make them compatible with the new system.

Training

This effort is extremely important to the success of the system. In the
initial implementing stage and in order to effect a successful transition,
remote stations will be established only in the current information control
areas such as payroll, accounts payable, property, etc. The system will be
expanded to include operating organizations after they have been trained in
the usage of the program and input/output devices and have established a
need for a tie-in to the overall network.

Test and Checkout

Each program will be checked out individually and then in total. Parallel
operations will be a necessity before there is a "buy-off" to go productional.
Phasing in of the new programs will be based on the priority of individual
program data needs and their relationship to the overall system requirements. Results of the test and checkout process will govern the production
schedule; however, prototype runs will be made and used as "authentic data"
in the interim period.

Pilot Model

In order to determine what the problems might be from the standpoint of
a STARFIRE system implementation, a pilot model operation was conceived and placed into operation. An input/output device was obtained and
located in the financial systems' area. It was tied in to a remote computer
file in order to simulate a typical STARFIRE process of accumulating and
retrieving information on a real time basis as well as batch processing. A
series of charts was prepared for demonstration purposes which showed
the data transmission parameters, a general system flow chart of the opera-

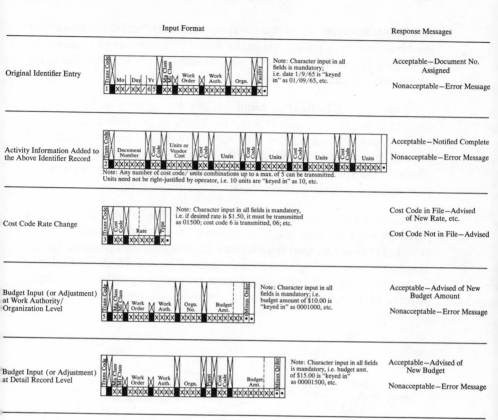

Figure 9. Input transactions to update system records.

tion and the format for inquiries as well as what the response messages would look like. Figure 9 shows one of the charts used in this demonstration.

This pilot model was prepared to reflect all conditions that might occur in a "live" situation. Detailed specifications were prepared and programmed. Many problems were encountered before successful "runs" were made. This model will assist us immeasurably in implementing the overall program. All concerned user organizations have been oriented to the equipment usage and also given an opportunity to observe firsthand the operation of the STARFIRE concept.

Cost Considerations

To undertake a system of the STARFIRE size and magnitude, a thorough investigation was required in order to establish the justification of the anticipated costs involved. The initial question posed was "will the system achieve the objectives on a paying/benefiting basis?" The answer of course is yes. In making this evaluation, our Figure 10 was used as a guide. The factors considered are discussed below.

Equipment. STARFIRE could conceivably operate with the current equipment but the real-time aspect would have to be eliminated. It was determined that the much faster processing of data and the improvements in the current programs would more than offset any additional requirements added to the mechanization process. Further, the reductions in current reruns and added equipment capabilites would result in dollar savings.

Programming. In essence, the initiation of STARFIRE gave us an opportunity to redirect programmer support for the development of an integrated system to meet our requirements in an organized, systematic manner. The same programming support will be used for the STARFIRE effort as on the current financial programs. Future programming will certainly decline because of program additions and improvements under the new system.

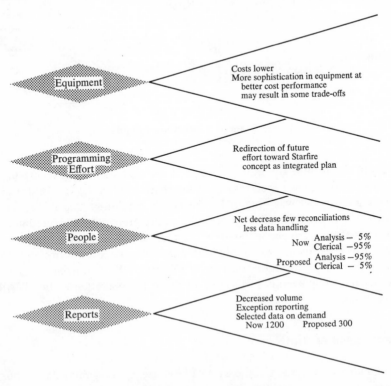

Figure 10. Cost considerations.

Further, the language to be used is similar to English and, therefore, this minimizes programmers' effort on machine characteristics and allows greater concentration on the important system aspect of the program. Here, too, we can expect programming effort savings.

People. Presently, much clerical effort is necessary. Under STARFIRE, with its mechanical implications, clerical effort will be reduced and more time will be devoted to analytical endeavors of "what does the information developed really mean."

Reports. A decreased volume is definitely anticipated because of the real-time capability and exception reporting. The concentration will be on obtaining selected data as needed which will allow for more immediate decision-making.

All of the above considerations lead us to believe that the cost savings under the new system concept will more than offset the cost of STARFIRE implementation. Further, the need for certain information to control and guide operations is immeasurable in terms of dollars. Benefits from the new program are discussed below.

Benefits

User Oriented. The user can now have direct access to the file on an instantaneous basis and extract data that heretofore he has been unable to obtain.

Flexibility. Changes to the system will be easier to program, more information is available and new applications can be added by increasing disk storage units and terminals. You can also custom fit the system to the job because of the capability to select the proper devices for doing the task.

Mass Storage. All data can be stored on disk for immediate access. There is unlimited storage capacity off-line, because data cells can be removed and stored. Magnetic tape, as used today, has the disadvantage of volume tape storage, dust accumulation, etc. All concerned organizations can use centralized files for data reporting and retrieval.

Decreased Clerical Effort. Resulting from exception and real-time reporting.

Built-in Controls. The capability to recognize program errors vs. machine malfunction and to reject data not cleared through the master audit file. In addition, the input from remote stations will be displayed either on printed report or visual device for a last-minute check before it is released to the files.

Improved Operations. Data is available immediately for decision-making and the results of the decision made can be more effectively monitored and reported. More information will be available.

Revitalization of our reporting system will be achieved in order to accommodate changing management, customer, governmental, etc., requirements.

Summary

The STARFIRE program represents a telescoping communication, direct access and mass storage integrated plan for financial reporting. It is an advancement in the "state of the art" of financial data processing. It is a necessary tool from both the standpoint of data needs and the introduction into the system of the new generation of equipment with its associated capabilities.

The above benefits represent only part of the story of why the trend to more sophisticated data accumulation systems, mass storage and retrieval continually advances. Competition for business is accelerating. Reduced data processing costs, more timely and meaningful information for operation effectiveness and reporting necessitate such a concept as described above—STARFIRE!

A Positive Look at Management Information Systems

Robert Beyer

The phrase "management information systems" is among the most used—and abused—in industry today. In recent years it has been applied to virtually every kind of computer application, ranging from pure payroll processing to closed-cycle control of production machines. As a result, it is frequently misunderstood and often unjustly criticized.

The controversy has resulted in part from differences in nomenclature and in part from the variety of opinions on how management information systems can or should be applied to management problems and when they will be universally adopted. But the main source of confusion lies in the lack of à consensus on what management information systems are supposed to be and how they should be designed to meet the growing needs of management today,

Lest we become lost in the miasma of speculation and expensive false starts, we must return to fundamentals and try to develop a fresh perspective on management information systems, unobscured by the magnification of "nuts and bolts."

The movement toward more fully integrated systems is already underway and will not be retarded by unresolved questions, however legitimate. This

Reprinted by permission of the author and the publisher from *Financial Executive*, Vol. XXXVI, No. 6 (June, 1968), pp. 50–57.

movement is evidenced by the growing number of major U.S. concerns that have already installed centralized management information systems or are planning to do so. Moreover, as management is subjected to increasing pressure for faster, more complete, and more fully coordinated information, it is only reasonable to assume that the trend must gain momentum, especially with the advent of the third generation computer.

These rather general statements, of course, do nothing to dispel the confusion and misconceptions that have arisen in some quarters. The objectives of this article, therefore, are first to define more clearly a management information system; second, to examine some of the current trends in system development; third, to show how systems are serving top management in a variety of settings; and, finally, to provide some guidelines for information system design.

The explosive growth of the data processing industry during the last 20 years has created many language problems. What is called a "compiler" by one company may be an "assembler" to another. What is "automation" for one firm is "process control" for the next. What is "on-line" in one environment is "off-line" in another. What is "real-time" in many areas represents nothing at all in others.

Despite differences in nomenclature, it is possible to define a management information system in terms of what it should do rather than in terms of what it is. Once this point is established, we can see what effect modifiers such as "total," "integrated," etc., have on its meaning.

The *raison d'être* for any information system should be a need to know. While payroll records in a huge organization constitute information, there is no need for top management to know that a particular man accumulated six hours of overtime in a given week. On the other hand, if a particular manufacturing section should happen to go 15 per cent over its budget for the week, the appropriate top-level manager should be informed. The more timely and accurate the information presented to the manager, the better equipped he will be to take whatever action is necessary.

Around the turn of the century the need for information could be satisfied in a most elementary fashion. In a typical system, data acquisition and processing was achieved by jamming an invoice or bill onto a spindle, payables to the left and receivables to the right. Recording this information in a central data storage bank meant, quite simply, copying it into a ledger book. The ledger book was usually kept within arm's reach of the manager; if he wanted to get an idea of the day's sales, he simply opened the ledger or, even more directly, checked the cash drawer.

This rudimentary system, however, had one major drawback: it got tired and careless under high volume conditions. And during the next 40 years volume was to become the byword of American industry.

Information Explosion

From about 1900 to 1940, U.S. commerce expanded at a prodigious rate. The railroads pushed west, north and south to open new markets. Mass production techniques doubled, tripled and quadrupled manufacturing output. Industries grew into giants. Interchangeable parts ensured that items purchased in one part of the country could be serviced in another. American ingenuity produced 1,330,000 new patents in the first third of the 20th century alone.

But along with change came the information explosion. The data itself wasn't that much different. There was just so much more of it. Managers were confronted with the problem of sorting through great amounts of information to find meaningful data. Often the time and cost of searching it out didn't pay off.

Of course, there was some information that had to be found. Many techniques and machines were developed during the first half of the 20th century for this purpose. But, for the most part, the kind and form, of information flowing to top management wasn't commensurate with the decisions they had to make.

With the advent of the electronic digital computer, management had a tool capable of drastically increasing information flow. Characteristically, the early data processing systems were concerned primarily with replacing previous manual systems rather than with presenting specific data to management. This was to be expected. The tool was new, and industry first had to understand its nature before actually taking advantage of it.

But it didn't take long for management to realize that their new tool was the depository of a huge amount of company information. To process payroll, for example, meant recording all personnel, salary and labor data in punched card or magnetic tape form. The accounts receivable file, by the same token, contained a wide variety of customer, sales and credit information. And computerized inventory records held much more than just the current stock status of a given item.

Management soon discovered that programming made it possible to retrieve all or part of a given record either periodically or on demand. Moreover, by applying certain mathematical parameters to the file, they could pick out only those items or accounts falling under or over a predetermined safety margin.

Thus, the next step was development of systems for exception reporting on a routine basis. These systems were, in effect, the forerunner of present-day computerized management information systems. Instead of overloading management with reams of routine data—a printout of the entire accounts receivable list, for instance—the computer was programmed to pick out only those items that called for management attention. In this way, top executives were able to get information they wouldn't or couldn't get otherwise because of the time, effort and money involved in searching it out. And they were able to get it in time to take decisive action.

Two-Dimensional Data

Unfortunately, these early management information systems were on a segmented or vertical basis; i.e., they were restricted to one particular area or aspect of the company's operations. The inventory system, for instance, concerned only the flow of goods and took no cognizance of current sales, financial conditions or long-range planning. The payroll exception reporting system did a good job of calling management's attention to labor oddities, but ignored the effects of manufacturing output on present sales conditions. Thus, management was provided with only two dimensions of what is really a three-dimensional picture.

Traditionally, a top-level manager makes his decisions as a result of many inputs. These inputs include both internal and external data. Internal information, of course, is concerned with virtually everything that happens within the company. External information comes from such sources as government economic reports, independent market studies of product movement, weather reports affecting seasonal products, salesmen's reports on competition, even newspaper and magazine assessments of world, national and local conditions.

In its broadest sense, a "total" system is one in which all information—external and internal—is channeled into a single centralized source. This source doesn't have to be a computer, but where volume is high nothing else will do. Furthermore, no other form of system can process data with comparable speed and thoroughness.

Coordination vs. Segmentation

The computerized total management information system is, admittedly, a complicated concept. It means capturing raw data as close to its source as possible, feeding this data directly or almost directly into the computer, and then allowing the computer to apply the information to several files at the same time. After that, it means presenting the information to managers in a coordinated rather than segmented fashion. Thus, where management formerly got information directly, the computer now serves as an intermediary.

A total system is only a concept. Integration, on the other hand, is the means of implementing this concept. It involves taking a wide variety of information—internal and external, formal and informal—and through programing and the computer's mass storage abilities blending it into a meaningful whole. Thus the executive gets an over-all corporate picture.

Perhaps the most common example of an integrated system is that of automatic inventory reorder. In a typical vertical system, the processing of a customer's order would include only preparation of an invoice and updating his accounts receivable file. In an integrated system, however, the item and quantity information on the order would also be used to update inventory records. As the computer examined each order it would note the quantity of the item requested, go to the proper stock record to see of the order can be satisfied, and automatically subtract the figure from the present total.

The computer would also be programed to make certain logical decisions. If the present order caused the stock amount to fall below a predetermined standard, for example, the computer would print out a purchase order or a factory job order. In more sophisticated applications, it might even determine the various assemblies, sub-assemblies, and raw materials involved, examine their respective inventory levels, and generate purchase or factory orders wherever necessary. And, going even a step further, it could take into consideration the manufacturing and shipping lead times of each part and generate orders so that each element in the final product arrives at the specific time needed.

If all this sounds a bit too farfetched, bear one thing in mind: integrated data processing systems of even greater scope are in existence right now. What's more, they are doing an extremely successful job of concentrating company information in a single source, using this input for a variety of necessary accounting and administrative jobs, and providing meaningful output to managers in a concise, timely and accurate manner.

Now let's turn to the third of the three important trends in management information today, the dynamic system. Here we tread on the thin ice of controversy.

Despite a certain amount of skepticism, we are once again met by the fact that the dynamic systems are already here and that there is considerable evidence that their use will grow. For this reason alone they are worth close appraisal.

The "dynamic system" is characterized by three essential aspects. First, key data is input on an immediate or real-time basis, usually at the point of origin. This could mean, for instance, using a punched paper tape created by a cash register as direct input to a computer, or setting up some sort of card or optical reading device at the point of sale which feeds information directly to a computer. In any case, the objective is to capture vital information as early as possible so that it can be processed and presented to the proper management for immediate use.

Second, the dynamic system often involves a simulation exercise. That is, some aspect of the business—or the entire business—is mathematically modeled within the computer so that management can present hypothetical "what if" questions to it and receive a reasonable answer. With key variables being fed to this model on an almost immediate basis, management can determine in minutes, rather than in days, the profitability of several different courses of action and arrive at the most effective combination.

Finally, the dynamic system is designed to minimize the time, cost and effort of system changes. Today, for example, a change in computer hardware or a major system change too often necessitates re-programing and re-education of the users. With the dynamic system, these changes can be made without upsetting existing procedures or reassembling existing data banks.

It is worthwhile at this juncture, however, to put these total, integrated, dynamic systems in perspective. Because there is almost no limit as to what can be processed and presented to management on an on-line basis, it is tempting to misuse these systems. Management doesn't need *all* information on an immediate basis. For example, fixed costs won't change minute by minute. Using hardware to present this information on a real-time basis is a waste of time and money. Rather, these systems must be used to identify and control only key data—data on those aspects of the business which demand immediate top-level action.

Control Limits

A second danger lies in management's over-reacting to data furnished by the system. I doubt we'll ever reach the point where systems will explain the reasons for *every* minor fluctuation in sales. Therefore, instead of over-reacting to random, minor fluctuations, management should establish control limits to identify those fluctuations which deserve attention.

A major insurance company in New York processes about 15,000 new insurance applications at any given time. Each application must go through a variety of departments, including medical, underwriting, policy service, and so forth. Finding one application out of the many used to present quite a problem.

Today the company is using a total, integrated, dynamic management information system to keep track of each application. As an application hits various processing points, on-line input/output devices are used to feed control information directly into a computer. The computer applies this information to application records stored on its direct access disks. When a manager wants to know where the application is located and what has been done to it, he simply picks up a phone on the terminal, uses the touch-tone buttons to key in the application's number and the "voice" of the computer provides the answer.

Another example of "voice-answer-back"—wherein the computer actually formulates a verbal response to a management query—is at the New York Stock Exchange. In this case member brokers need only dial a computer to get the up-to-the-minute activity of any stock on the exchange. And while this response may be only a matter of seconds or minutes faster than the ticker tape, it accomplishes a vital management job by providing information when and how it is needed.

Still another example of the dynamic management information system is found in the office of the president of one of the nation's largest manufacturing firms. The executive has a visual display unit in his office on which he can call up a wide variety of company information. He can, for instance, get the weekly sales figure, the month-to-date figure, the year-to-date figure, and a comparison of all of these with figures for previous years. He can also ask for production data, check to find out the current status of accounts receivable and accounts payable, and get a precise listing of all pending orders. While this information is presented to him as a series of totals, he can break them down simply by pointing to the figure with a light pen. He gets information when and where he wants it, he gets it in confidence, and he gets it without cluttering up his desk with a lot of extraneous paperwork.

The "decision room," where top executives can get visual display of key data on demand, examine alternatives and see the result, is a reality today in a number of corporate situations. Available and practical at present only to the largest and most progressive companies, such facilities portend the future in one form or another for all corporate enterprise.

Many legitimate questions are still to be resolved about management information systems. These questions, however, should not obscure the fact that integrated information systems are already here and are being used effectively by many firms. Neither should they lessen the sense of urgency felt by those close to systems design for the development of more effective systems.

There is a wide range of opinion concerning when companies should develop and implement these systems. There are some who suggest a "let's wait and see" attitude. After all, they reason, it took 20 years for EDP to reach its present point, and another 20 years won't make that much difference.

At the other end of the pole, there are those who won't or can't wait another day. In a sense, they over-react to urgency by installing the hardware first and worrying about system design later.

In my opinion, the "middle of the road" is the best approach. On the one hand, things are happening and, unless positive steps are taken now, the lengthening lead time for effective system development will make it difficult for a company to catch up with its competitors. On the other hand, a headlong plunge may do more harm than good.

Precise, Professional Planning . . .

What is needed is precise, professional long-range planning, planning that will show the company where to go, how to get there, and how to employ its resources toward that end.

The starting point of such thinking should be at the very top of the company. A management information system isn't simply a beefed-up accounting report. It is, quite simply, a flow of data designed to answer specific management needs. And the only way these needs can be ascertained and planned for is by having systems objectives originate at the highest level.

It must be stressed that management isn't always in a position to ascertain these needs. This is the old problem of not being able to see the forest for the trees. For this reason the first step in management system design might very well be the securing of professional personnel either by hiring capable system analysts or securing outside consultant services.

From this point management should proceed to a series of pertinent questions: How are we doing in comparison to our competitors? How is the company holding up in the current economic environment? Are we meeting the goals set last year, five years ago, and ten years ago?

While these questions might seem elementary, the answers may very clearly reveal gaps in existing management information and even point the way toward organization of data so that it better serves the decision-making needs of management.

If, for example, a company begins to lose its competitive position, more questions are in order: Are we suffering talent gaps along the way? Is top management getting a clear sales picture—and getting it fast enough? Is there a breakdown in quality control and, if so, where is it? Are we being responsive enough to customer needs? Is a firmer hand needed, and where?

These questions, in themselves, indicate a breakdown of communication between top executives and operation management. And answering them on a once-in-a-while basis isn't the solution. If there is real concern about the inroads of competition, this information should be available on a routine or on-demand basis.

What about the effects of the current economic environment? Here, too, an answer might reveal a major problem. If the company is suffering from the effects of dynamic economic changes, the reason may be a basic inability to anticipate these changes. In this instance the problem isn't one of fast action and fast decision but of effectively using current information to anticipate future conditions.

What I am talking about here is the use of simulation to prepare alternative courses of action in order to meet various forms of change. The information system takes current data and applies it to a mathematical model of the company. Thus, where management once had to depend on intuition, it can now make decisions based on scientific consideration.

... at the Highest Level

Setting goals, too, is aided and enhanced by rapid, selective and scientific use of routine company information. While formulation of long-range plans usually is a function of middle management, the ultimate responsibility for achieving the goals lies with top management. Therefore, still another objective of a management information system is the presentation of data in a form and manner that provides support to this responsibility.

Planning a total management information system is a managerial and organizational rather than technical activity. It should start at the highest level of the company. Thinking should not be in terms of "what kind of information can I get from our accounts receivable reports" but in terms of "what type of data do I need in order to run the company more effectively and more profitably." Once these questions are answered, management can tackle the problems of how to organize raw data for input to an information system, and how to process this raw data for effective output. Only at this point should the questions of hardware be considered.

It has been said that nothing can delay an idea once its time has come. Given the new capabilities of the third generation computer, who has the courage to say that the time for management information systems to take a giant step toward totality has not come? It suggests at the very least that, since the rate of change affecting the techniques of management and organization will not remain constant, the question of where a given company will be 20 or even 10 years from now may be determined by what plan and course of action in systems design are taken now. Catching up may be a thing of the past.

Information Systems and Managerial Accounting

Peter A. Firmin
James J. Linn

The Pervasive Character of Management Information Systems

Is Our Current Preoccupation with Systems Justified?

Interdisciplinary literature in business administration, behavioral sciences, and computer sciences, as well as the literature of accounting and management science, abounds with discussions of and references to "management information systems," "total information systems," "the 'systems' approach," and other similar terms. Does this preoccupation presage revolutionary shifts in organizational structures and in our perception of organizational behavior? Are we on the threshold of unparalleled gains in managerial effectiveness? Or are we squandering our talents on fad and fetish? To answer these questions we must explore such fundamental problems as: "What is a 'management information system'?" "What do we mean by the 'systems' approach?" "What does all of this mean for [managerial] accounting?"

Reprinted by permission of the authors and the publisher from *The Accounting Review*, Vol. XLIII, No. 1 (January, 1968), pp. 75–82.

What Is a Management Information System?

The essence of *system* is interrelationship among elements. *Information* is purpose-oriented organized data and is a requisite for survival of *all* organizations. The interrelated networks (with their content) which transmute data into information throughout an organization constitute its information system.

All purposive organizations (even the "self-governed" ones) must be "managed"—directed towards a goal or purpose. The information system which enables the process of management is the management information system. The term "total information system" when applied to the management information system connotes *all* of the information needed by management and implies a "systems approach" to the study of management's information requirements and their satisfaction. The "systems approach" (in the context of the organization) connotes a perception of the organization as a set of interrelationships rather than as a set of independent elements or sub-systems.

A management information system is a system for accepting data as raw material and, through one or more transmutation processes, generating information as a product. It is composed of the following functional elements which relate the organization to its environments:[1]

1. Perception—initial entry of data, whether collected or generated, into the organization.

2. Recordation—physical capture of signs and symbols.

3. Storage—presupposes some expected future use, recordation, and a location.

4. Retrieval—search for recorded data.

5. Processing—transformation according to the *specific* needs of the organization.

6. Transmission—the flows which occur in an information system.

7. Presentation—reporting, communication.

8. Decision making—a controversial inclusion, except to the extent that the information system engages in decision making that pertains to itself.

What Is the Relationship Between the Management Information System and the Electronic Data Processing System?

Since management information systems inhere in organizations of all kinds, conceptually-oriented studies of them need not relate to implementa-

[1] James J. Linn, *The Concept of the Information System of the Organization*, a paper presented at The Institute of Management Sciences 1966 American Meeting, College of Measurements in Management, Dallas, Texas, February 16, 1966, pp. 3–11 (multilithed), contains a comprehensive discussion of these elements.

tion methodology. The existence of an electronic data processing system, for example, is not necessarily an essential part of a management information system. In any organization, the *management information system* may be a loosely joined set of sub-systems designed to serve the purpose of providing information for management. Such systems may be formal or informal, planned or *ad hoc*, integrated or separate. Their totality still could be called *a* management information system. Most systems analysts, however, would choose to call such disjoint sub-systems several separate systems instead of one integrated management information system as the term is now used.

But it is exactly the computer-oriented revolution in information technology that has created the currently prevailing surge of interest in management information systems and which has kindled the hope that the "total" information systems dream might be realized. Electronic data processing systems have made practicable serious efforts to utilize the "systems approach" in the design and implementation of management information systems. Electronic data processing systems also have made feasible the radical changes in the nature of data input and information output required by management science models. As a consequence of this improvement in technology, management information systems both on drawing boards and in various stages of implementation usually include management science planning models as an integral part of the information generating process.[2]

Are Total Systems Feasible?

Most systems analysts and corporate managers who talk about and aspire to "total" information systems realize that the ideal may be extremely difficult if not impossible to achieve. There has unquestionably been a great deal of overzealousness as well as extreme disillusion. As Anthony has remarked, "It is because of the varied and unpredictable nature of the data required for strategic planning that an attempt to design an all-purpose, internal information system is probably hopeless. For the same reason, the dream of some computer specialists of a gigantic data bank, from which planners can obtain all the information they wish by pressing some buttons, is probably no more than a dream."[3] Others have been less kind and have labeled the concept of the total information system as a myth or a chimera.

[2] Neil C. Churchill and Andrew C. Stedry, "Some Developments in Management Science and Information Systems with Respect to Measurement in Accounting," in Robert K. Jaedicke, Yuji Ijiri and Oswald Nielsen (eds.) *Research in Accounting Measurement* (American Accounting Association 1965), p. 45.

[3] Robert N. Anthony, *Planning and Control Systems: A Framework for Analysis* (Graduate School of Business Administration, Harvard University 1965), p. 45.

At the very least we can agree with Churchill and Stedry, who pin the label of "awesome" on the concept of "total information."[4]

Implications of the Information Systems Concept for Managerial Accounting

Managerial Accounting Systems Are Subsets of Total Management Information Systems

The product of any managerial accounting system, like that of all other information systems, is information. The nature of accounting is that of an information system, as the American Accounting Association's 1965–66 Committee on Basic Accounting Theory has pointed out.[5]

As an information system, accounting deals selectively with problems of the same order as more general information systems. Managerial (and financial) accounting systems are comprised of the same eight functional elements which were listed earlier to describe the general class "management information system": Perception, recordation, storage, retrieval, processing, transmission, presentation and decision making. (Some would object to the last, "but the relationship between the processes of the information system and . . . decision making are close enough to raise the question of including decision making as part of the information system."[6])

Ideological support for this position has been expressed by others. Managerial accounting has been tentatively defined by another committee of the American Accounting Association as a composite of data-gathering techniques embodied in a system whose focus is managerial planning, decision making and control.[7] Anton has suggested that an effective accounting system, in addition to providing continuous data gathering and processing, must be integrated with the planning and control system.[8]

Finally, like general purpose information systems, the output of accounting systems purport to educate the recipients of that output.

Clearly, the hypothesis that the managerial accounting system is a subset —if not a *proper* subset—of the total information system is tenable. Both have the same purposes and can be described in the same general terms. How, then, has recent preoccupation with total information systems impinged upon conventional managerial accounting systems?

---

[4] Neil C. Churchill and Andrew C. Stedry, *op. cit.,* p. 41.

[5] Norton M. Bedford, "The Nature of Future Accounting Theory," *The Accounting Review* (January, 1967), p. 82.

[6] James J. Linn, *op. cit.,* p. 11.

[7] Draft statement of the American Accounting Association Committee on Managerial Models, 1966–67.

[8] Hector R. Anton, "The Effect of Computers on the Reliability of Accounting Measurements," in Robert K. Jaedicke, *et al., op. cit.,* pp. 127–128.

Fundamental Changes in Perspective Have Occurred

Until the advent of electronic data processing, integrated information systems in the large-scale enterprise were exceptional. Often, the managerial and financial accounting systems were (and still are!) the only formal information systems in the business organization. Such systems do not fulfill *all* the planning and decision-facilitating information needs of management. But they do represent viable models of the business organization. And management does use the output of these systems for decision making. In cases where management does not feel that the output of these systems is sufficient for its purposes, additional and often *ad hoc* systems are created.

One of the early effects of the "information systems syndrome" on managerial accounting was produced as a secondary result of computer-induced changes in the organizational structure of the enterprise. Many lower-level clerical and middle-management jobs have disappeared, and activities formerly performed at these levels have been "taken over" by the compuuter. In other organizations, middle-management positions have assumed even greater importance than before as planning and control functions have been moved to lower organizational levels. Concomitantly, top management has been able to devote more attention to understanding system interrelationships. In either case, fundamental changes in organizational structures (and hence in information systems) have occurred.

One of the obvious results of the introduction of computer technology has been a revision of reporting requirements, as well as, in some cases, a centralization of record-keeping activities and of information processing. These revisions of reporting requirements—in many cases involving more variety—have forced many to restructure their management information systems to take advantage of the ability of the computer to accept, store, rearrange and process data with a great deal of flexibility.

And many organizations have begun to suspect that it may not make sense to support separate, disjoint, and uncoordinated functional area information systems for marketing, production and personnel—and for management and financial accounting as well. This observation reflects one of the more subtle but perhaps even more important effects wrought by computer-induced information systems revisions. Even where the organization is some distance from a total information system, partial implementation of this concept through the use of electronic data processing equipment has changed the way we look at the organization. There is now a propensity to view the organization as a total entity and to attempt to analyze it as an interrelated system, not as a collection of subsystems.

These four factors—changes in organizational structure; perception of the organization as an interrelated set of subsystems; heightened sensitivity to possible undesirable redundancy of effort in separate information systems; and rapidly escalating capability of data processing equipment to deal simultaneously with varieties of input and output characteristics—have fostered an expanded concept of the transaction.

New Models of the Organization Exist

For many years the accounting model of the organization sufficed (however well or badly) as the major formal information system on which management decisions were based. The last two decades have witnessed the introduction of many newer and more sophisticated models of the organization and its subsystems. These models advance managerial effectiveness by furnishing new perspectives on organizational behavior and new approaches to decision-making. They require the use of varied data not limited to monetary measurement or historical orientation, and in some cases they mirror the fact that information flows needed by management are not always accompanied by resource flows. Such varieties of information do not always fit the traditional accounting mold.

These models include cost-effectiveness models reflecting the behavioral or modern theories of organization that business enterprises may have goals other than profit. They also include scheduling, planning, decision, control and evaluation models which require data embodying non-monetary and non-historical measures.

New Organizational Models Have New Data Requirements

Different models may also require data of different degrees of accuracy and precision. Planning models may be extremely sensitive to certain parameters representing estimates of demand or production constraints, while some evaluation models need only consider broad ranges of performance. Planning models may require non-monetary statements of resources available and rates of resource consumption as well as requirements in dollar equivalents.

Some models which combine planning and decision functions require that decision rules be incorporated in the model so that certain types of decisions —usually routine—might be "made" automatically. Particularly in decision models, and to some extent in evaluation models, is it necessary to consider subjective factors which may defy quantification and which may not be expressible in monetary units.

Decision models should reflect the decision rules of the decision maker. But studies of decision making in the organizational setting have revealed that a vast amount of decision making is heuristic in nature and that the overwhelming number of uncertainties surrounding the decision frustrate optimization. In making decisions, the decision makers consider such difficult-to-quantify factors as the compatibility of intended decisions with existing operating constraints, optimum time for decisions, optimum amounts of information, conflicts of interest, the organizational scheme for rewarding successful decision making and penalizing failures, the relationship between payoff and risk and degree of understanding of the decision which exists in the minds of subordinates.[9]

A New Concept of a Transaction Is Needed—and Is Feasible

The characteristic of electronic data processing systems which makes it possible to collect in one file various types and time-phases of data and to store this data separately for later interrelationship and analysis has supported mounting demand for integrated measures and data collection schemes. The potential ability to collect data on an integrated basis has eroded also the need for a common denominator of measurement, since we are now able to construct and utilize information vectors specifying an almost unlimited number of properties of the objects that we are attempting to measure.[10]

"Accounting [traditionally] has been concerned with communicating the effects of economic events . . . "[11] Not all economic events are recognized by the conventional accounting model, however. Accounting theory defines a set of properties that an economic event must possess before it can be accepted as an input to the accounting system—before it can be recognized as a transaction. These properties include, for example, objectivity, quantifiability, verifiability and freedom from bias.[12] Thus, many economic events relevant to decision making are not recognized by the accounting system. Price-level changes, increased employee skills, and intra-entity changes in asset values are but a few examples of such "non-transactions."

If multi-dimensional vectors are used to depict added (non-monetary) dimensions of the conventional accounting transaction, some progress toward data integration in the perception function of the information system will be made. But what is needed, in addition, is a concept of the transaction that will allow the point at which the system recognizes an entry to vary with the type of information flow. Some research has already been directed toward this objective.[13]

[9] Samuel G. Trull, "Some Factors Involved in Determining Total Decision Success," *Management Science* (February, 1966), B-271-B-280.

[10] Peter A. Firmin, "The Potential of Accounting as a Management Information System," *Management International Review* (February, 1966), pp. 45–55.

[11] "(The) Institute of Management Science Committee Comments for Common Body of Knowledge Study," *Journal of Accountancy* (December, 1964), p. 80.

[12] Committee to Prepare a Statement of Basic Accounting Theory, *A Statement of Basic Accounting Theory* (American Accounting Association 1966), p. 8.

[13] John Field has offered a view of the conventional accounting transaction based on the information patterns of technical information flows, operational planning information flows, contractual rights flows, credit flows and property flows.

"The principle of this approach is that underlying the complexities of day to day phenom-

One of the most significant imports of the preceding discussion on data input requirements for various types of models and expanded transaction concepts is that the total information systems approach requires the design of data bases permitting and perhaps demanding the collection of data in the smallest whole unit which characterizes the most basic or elemental property of the object being measured.[14]

Implications of the Expanded Transaction Concept

The expanded transaction concept requires that the resources of the firm be reflected not only in monetary but also in other multi-dimensional forms as they move through the organization. Meaningful integration of such data in a total management information system involves the contribution of many different disciplines. Many types of models require operational facility in many aspects of mathematics. Planning, control and evaluation models require a knowledge of probability theory and statistics. They also require an understanding of behavioral science as it relates to problems of motivation and goal perception; individual, organizational, or group conflicts; and responsiveness to controls. Above all, problems of measurement and communication as well as other aspects of information technology must be understood.

The expanded transaction concept has implications for preserving the reliability of information, and it has audit implications as well. When information is not accompanied by resource flows, the discipline enforced by the double-entry system of accounting is lacking. Lack of duality in the system requires that other forms of discipline be imposed. Problems of information reliability and system control, with their audit implications, also imply a need for new methods to evaluate system reliability and effectiveness.

What Are the Implications of the Information Systems Concept for (Managerial) Accounting Education?

Educators Have Two Roles

To answer this question, we must first ask, "What role do we play?" One dimension of our role as educators is to convey the current state of the art

---

ena are a relatively few elements or building blocks. The world of information revolves about transactions. All information, starting with research and ending with financial statements, is directed toward either activating a transaction or recording its occurrence. Particularly interesting is the fact that each transaction has a definite information pattern and that the patterns are remarkably similar to one another."

John Field, "Determining Information Patterns," *PMM & Co./Management Controls* (April 1967), pp. 77–82.

[14] James J. Linn, "A General Asset Model." Working Paper No. 188–66 (Massachusetts Institute of Technology, 1966).

to the student. We need to perceive the state of the art in contemporary managerial accounting, and we need to teach about this system. As a corollary, we need to sense changes in the state of the art and we need to evaluate and respond quickly to these changes.

In this dimension of our role, we have an obligation to "keep-up" with management. But this dimension of our role does not require us to pioneer or to lead management—we merely selectively transmit information about its state.

What does the state of the art reveal—and what are the portents for the future?

As we survey the state of the art, we note that in those organizations which have attempted to implement—even partially—broader concepts of management information systems, the impact on the traditional role of the management accountant has varied. The seriousness of this problem is reflected in the plethora of articles in our literature about "Who'll Be in Charge?" These articles discuss the importance of the role of the information system controller, and they issue repeated warnings that the controller or management accountant will lose ground unless he has the will and the capability to broaden his horizon. There are hints that management accountants are too involved in their own discipline and too restricted in their vision to appreciate the problems of the entire organization. Hence, they are not capable of operating in the richer world of the information specialists. Beyer and others urge that accountants change their attitudes— that they recognize accelerating change as a characteristic of our time and that they develop a total corporate viewpoint, accept new techniques and participate actively in the process of change.[15]

As teachers, we have a second and more important role—that of pioneer, developer, catalyst, innovator, leader. Not only do we have the obligation to register the current state of the art, but we must anticipate and foresee the future. For in a very real sense, we create today the accounting profession of tomorrow. The students of today will be the policy-making management accountants and partners in CPA firms of tomorrow, just as we and the management accountants and partner-level CPAs of today are the products of our educational system of yesterday. If we foresee that the accountant of 1980 will have to deal with expanded transaction concepts, and if we teach these concepts, he (and not someone else) *will* deal with them.

What Do We Need To Know?

Accounting *is* concerned with the furnishing of information. It is an information system. The important question is, "To whom is the information

[15] Robert Beyer, "Management Information Systems: Who'll Be In Charge?," *Management Accounting* (June 1967), pp. 3–8.

being furnished, and for what purpose?" The answers, of course, are "To management," and, "To facilitate management decision making, planning, control and evaluation." If new tools exist which can facilitate these functions, and if the utilization of these tools requires the construction of different kinds of data or the revision of information frameworks, and if these newer methods are effective—then we must recognize them and become proficient in their use.

We must focus—as always—on the requirements of the user. The implication here is that we must understand the user's job and his need for information. *Therefore, we need to understand management and all of the functional areas of business.* On top of this understanding we *then* superimpose our expertise in the design and control of information systems. This is not a new suggestion—this has always been our hallmark. In constructing traditional accounting models, we fashioned accounting reports along lines of classification which we believed would be useful. These classifications were predicated upon certain analytical methods. If these reports are no longer as useful as they once were because better methods of analysis and new uses exist, then we cannot ignore the new methods.

If understanding these newer methods requires that we become operational in mathematics, statistics and other aspects of information technology, and if it requires that we comprehend fundamental concepts of behavioral science, then we must.

What Is Managerial Accounting?

The essence of [managerial] accounting—the thing which distinguishes accounting from other functional areas—is that our product is information. The "specialty" which we have is the ability to assess information needs and to design appropriate systems for satisfying them. We must construct reliable systems, borrowing as necessary from the bodies of knowledge in other disciplines. If the computer is to be a basic part of information processing, we must understand the computer. If the transformation process involves the application of a management science model, our accounting system must literally "wed" the model involved.

Some have raised questions as to whether this kind of activity—implementing a broadened concept of accounting or the information systems concept—is accounting or something else. Such inquiry is sterile. As Bedford has pointed out, accounting has always evolved, and the accountant of today might very well not be called an accountant by the accountant of yesterday.[16]

By whatever name, the accountant of the future is going to have to be a systems analyst. In the literature on systems, there is already evidence of a desire for better communication between systems and audit specialists.

---

[16] Bedford, *op. cit.*, p. 82.

John Carey, in "The CPA Plans for the Future," foresees a whole new profession of information specialists.[17]

It is abundantly clear that the fragmented information system of the past will not be optimal—if even useful—for the industrial enterprise for the future. It is also obvious that the information specialists who will design and implement tomorrow's accounting (information?) systems must have capabilities far beyond those now possessed by most accountants.

However, people do adapt to pressures of change. Ten years ago, it would have been hard to find a doctoral program producing the kind of accountants that we suggest will be typical of the future. Today, such programs exist and the output of such programs are already teaching in various universities in this country. Ten years ago, it would have been difficult to find a mathematical symbol in the literature of accounting. Today, our literature contains such articles. No longer can we say that management accountants must become part of the evolution of information systems—we *are* part of this evolution—a fact which is abundantly reflected in our literature and by such discussions as this.

[17] John L. Carey, *The CPA Plans for the Future* (New York: American Institute of Certified Accountants, 1965), pp. 244–245.

The Accountant's Role in Management Information Systems

H. Bruce Joplin

Present computer technology has put management information systems within the reach of any company willing to spend sizable sums on systems development. Believing that a substantial payoff will accrue, many companies are now developing workable management information system models. It is safe to predict that within a short time management information systems will be the new status indicator for managers in industry and in government. What is a management information system? What will be the accountant's role in management information systems? These questions are explored in this paper.

Many students of management theory hold that the quality of management is directly related to the quality of information available to the manager. Information available today, while greatly improved over past years, is not entirely adequate. This is so primarily because information is not sufficiently selective. The manager must use a shotgun when he needs a rifle. Second, most existing data systems are merely many separate systems which are not truly integrated. Third, most systems do not produce information on a timely basis.

Reprinted by permission of the author and the publisher from *The Journal of Accountancy*, Vol. 121, No. 3 (March, 1966), pp. 43–46.

Those involved in information theory reason that what is needed is a completely integrated system of data gathering, data storage, data retrieval and information communication. Such a system would accept data as raw material and, almost simultaneously, would generate information as a product. Such systems are called management information systems, or total information systems.

Data vs. Information

At this point, a distinction must be made between data and information and between data processing and management information systems. This is done at the risk of overgeneralization. Data are here used as a collection of isolated facts. Information is used to mean units of knowledge developed from the skillful management of data.

Management information systems build on data processing techniques but go much further. Data processing is basically a process of *analysis* or the breaking down of events or conditions into minute units. Management information systems use the analysis method but are essentially a process of *synthesis* or the building up of data into meaningful units of knowledge. Another point of difference is that data processing can be said to be one-dimensional in character. That is, typically only one facet of an event is recorded. As will be discussed later, management information systems require a multi-dimensional approach to data gathering.

At present, in most companies, there are many separate systems such as the accounting system, the inventory system, and the production system. Each system may record and store the same or different facts about a single event or condition. Although there is an interchange of information between files, these systems are seldom truly integrated.

In a management information system all information will enter the system only once, in a universally acceptable standard coding and simultaneously with its creation. The various aspects of a recordable event might be measured in terms of volume and weight, or in terms of time, as well as in terms of money. The one record of this event will be used by different managers for quite different purposes. The total impact of the record will be reported to top management.

The Accounting Function

How does the accounting function relate to management information systems? Accounting has historically been defined as the art of recording, classifying, summarizing, evaluating and communicating financial data. These various functions are not independent but rather build, one upon the other, culminating in the communication of financial information. The recording, classifying and summarizing of data are techniques which the accountant uses to accomplish his primary objective as a communicator of financial information. Thus the accountant's product, that thing of value which he contributes to the enterprise, is information.

Contrast the accounting department with the production or marketing departments. These departments produce and even process data in some instances. They do not, however, regard information as an end in itself but as a means of attaining other goals, i.e., the production and sale of goods. Thus the accounting department's position is unique in that it is the only major department which has been established for the sole purpose of generating information. That is, such was the case before management information systems.

The accountant may tend to consider himself in competition with the total systems concept. In this light, the accountant's role in management information systems takes on an aspect of self-preservation. That should not be the case. The accountant is well equipped not only to survive in a management information systems environment, but to become an indispensable member of the total systems team.

Organizational Factors

Top management will decide whether the accountant is primarily responsible for the management information system or whether he is one of a number of participants in this function. It is to be hoped that the accountant will have a voice in this decision. It may be reasoned by management that the accountant, because he has extensive training and background in data collection and in the communication of financial information, is the most logical person to develop the management information system.

Present trends indicate that the accountant who is in charge of management information systems may be the exception in years to come. More and more, other considerations are dictating that a separate department, independent of financial management, be established to develop the system. In government, for instance, it is not unusual to find that statutory provisions prohibit the chief financial officer from assuming primary responsibility for the management information system. The extent to which other managers view the accountant as a progressive, dynamic innovator who is sensitive to their problem tends to increase the probability that the accountant will be selected to head the total system effort.

Broader Viewpoint Needed To Prepare for
Management Information Systems

A certain broadening of viewpoint on the part of the accountant will be necessary if he is to contribute to the management information system. The traditional one-dimensional approach to data gathering is no longer applicable. Rather, the multi-dimensional aspect of business activity must be recorded. This approach stems from recognizing that information needs are not limited to departmental boundaries but draw from all functional fields such as marketing, production, personnel and finance.

Consider the information requirements of governmental units relative to a given parcel of land. There is a need to know who owns the land and what use is being made of the parcel. If a structure is on the land, what type and size is it, what age and what condition? If it is occupied as a residence, how many persons live there and what are their ages, incomes and conditions of health?

The zoning department is interested in the type of structure and its use. The fire and building and safety departments are interested in the age and condition of the building. The education and police departments are interested in the ages of children residing in it. The health and social welfare departments are interested in living conditions, health and income data. Finally, the tax assessor is interested in the value of the property.

Not only is such information useful on a selective basis but it must be combined with information regarding other parcels on the block to form an overall community pattern.

The accountant can best prepare himself for management information systems by becoming more aware of the informational needs of his colleagues in other departments. Often we, as accountants, view the engineering department as people with slide rules and drawing paper, when, in reality, much of the engineer's time is taken up in summarizing vast files of data. Do we appreciate the complex system of recording the movement of materials and job status data that occupies much of the time of the production department?

How long has it been since we have met with other managers in their "shops"? Have we considered with them their particular network or flow of services, materials or products? The marketing vice president may need to know the effectiveness of an advertising medium. The personnel manager may need to know the impact of prehire screening or productivity, safety and turnover. We, the accountants, ought to learn about these needs.

Often information needs are not well defined. The manager may have only a vague idea of the absence of knowledge about a certain area of responsibility. Or he may know exactly what he wants but have no idea that under the total systems concept previously unavailable information is now within reach. The accountant should go out of his way to acquaint himself with the informational needs of the entire enterprise.

Converting Data into Information

When first coming into contact with data processing, one is impressed by the apparent high value placed on the *quantity* of data and the low value placed on the *quality* of information. In one data processing system it was found that a given transaction was being reported, in its entire detail, to eight different managers. Considering that over one million transactions of this type occurred each year the eight managers must have devoted a great deal of time to this one report. One could say that these managers were drowning in data while starving for information.

This surfeit of data will undoubtedly carry forward from data processing installation into the first management information systems. Much study will be necessary to determine the real needs of the company for information. Corporate managers have had financial information available to them for a number of years, and they know what classifications and reports are useful in decision-making. The need for other types of information is not so clearly defined.

For example, what does your company know about its work force? What does it need to know? Data are probably available regarding the cost of fringe benefits, sick time off, average salary costs, etc. Consider, however, other important questions. What is the potential within the work force for management development? What is the average age of present middle management? What will be the need for managers five or ten years hence? The answers to these questions will aid in developing recruitment and promotion policies.

Who among the work force is preparing himself for more responsible positions? How is he doing it? Who is stagnating in one job or department and why? Who has special skills, speaks a foreign language, wants to move, is limited by health problems?

In an organization of 100 employees and 10 managers such information is easily obtained. In an organization of 100,000 employees and 10,000 managers the collection and handling of such information gives rise to a number of problems.

Historical Information

The accountant involved in management information systems must monitor closely the introduction of financial data into the system and the preparation and dissemination of financial information as output from the system.

The accountant is familiar with the type and relatively rigid format of information which the organization must make available to the outside world. He must determine that the system provides the information which is required by law, by stockholders and by the public.

We are all familiar with the use of direct costing for internal purposes while only absorption costing is allowable for external reporting. Some real problems arise in the efficient management of these two systems within a company. A number of persons, some in the accounting field, hold that the traditional classification of expenditures is not useful. Many alternate reporting schemes are suggested, one being a report of expenditures by cost centers. Still others believe that reporting should be on an "encumbrance" or commitment basis rather than on a completed transaction basis. Consider also the current emphasis on appraisal or price-level accounting. These methods, while valuable techniques for internal management, are not, at the present time, acceptable for external reporting.

The accountant must stress the fact that the format of historical financial information is "given"; it is not a "variable" subject to negotiation. The accountant can perform a valuable function by incorporating currently acceptable classification techniques into the system.

Controls

The accountant must determine that the management information system provides for the development and preservation of information in what is commonly known as an audit trail. This is necessary not only for the use of those outside the organization but also for management's use in monitoring the system.

New electronic equipment, with emphasis on direct access devices and real time systems, does not easily lend itself to controls. Data stored in the internal memory of direct access equipment are continuously altered as a result of the intentional posting of updated data over the prior data, automatically erasing the prior data. For example, in processing an order from a customer the inventory accounts would be relieved of the amount of the shipment, the invoice would be computed and printed, the customer's account would be charged and the pertinent cost and sales data accumulated. Assume that this order was made by the use of a transaction recording device by which there would be no printed copy produced. The only visual record would be the invoice printed by the computer. No record, visible or otherwise, would remain of the condition of the inventory or accounts receivable files before this transaction was posted. When the next transaction is posted the present records will be altered.

The emphasis in management information systems on being up-to-date may result in failure to preserve necessary historical records. One company engaged in systems design work has stated that "in-line accounting is usually adopted where it is important to maintain data on a current basis and therefore it may not be practical or economical to delay the processing to establish usual historical records." The accountant must guard against this attitude's becoming paramount in systems design.

Controls and audit trails are developed at a cost which can be measured in loss of time and efficiency as well as money. In one installation the cost of controls was determined to be 30 per cent of the total systems costs. At the same time the entire process was slowed up approximately 25 per cent as a result of incorporating these controls. One can correctly argue that, in the long run, controls reduce error correction procedures, and thus save more than they cost. However, it is often difficult to sustain this argument in the early stages of systems design.

These factors make the development of controls and audit trails doubly difficult. Many information theorists involved in the management information system are not familiar with well-established control requirements from both inside and outside the company. The accountant can be of great help in this area.

Security

A primary objective of management information systems is to make data in the system available to all departments in the company. This concept, if not restricted, can lead to unauthorized persons obtaining access to confidential data.

In present systems, a number of departments maintain separate files of data. Each department typically uses only its own files. In a management information system these various files would be combined into one file with multiple usage. Consider information about employees. The operating department, health office, personnel section and the accounting department all store some data regarding a given employee. Some of this data will be stored in an informal medium, other data will be in a formal file. In a management information system, all data would be in one central record available to each using department. The design of adequate controls over this type of record requires considerable ingenuity. The accountant who is familiar with company security requirements can contribute this knowledge to the development of proper controls over confidential data.

Opposition to Total Systems

There may be a tendency on the part of some accountants to oppose the development of a total system for the enterprise. Such opposition may stem from a realization of the great expenditures of resources necessary to build such a system, the payback of which may not be measurable in dollars and cents. The cost of developing total systems will be much greater than the cost of present data processing systems. A preliminary estimate in one company is that the cost will be five times greater. One reason for this is that most data processing systems were built upon existing channels of information. Total information systems often must be built where little or no data was previously collected.

Some accountants may reason that the present procedure of having separate systems for each department is adequate. Indeed, a form of such systems, called subsystems, will continue to exist long after a total systems program is begun. However, management's thirst for more complete, accurate and timely information will eventually make separate systems obsolete.

Generally speaking, the accountant is ill advised to assume a position which is categorically opposed to management information systems. Economics and competition, combined with technology, will eventually force all large companies to develop one. The accountant's role in management information systems will depend on the position he takes toward such systems in the early stages of their development. I believe that most forward-looking accountants, faced with this challenge, will wholeheartedly join in the development of management information systems.

7 FEASIBILITY STUDIES

ADP Conversion Planning

Walter J. Kennevan

Fundamentals

The following alliterative tabulation provides a concise summarization of the primary components of an ADP system. These are:

> Personnel.
> Procedures.
> Programs.
> Peripheral equipment.
> Processor.

This alignment, beginning with the human element and concluding with the data processor, is proposed as being the order of importance of the various basic components to the development of the system. This is a deliberate inversion of the order of importance as usually depicted in articles extolling the "Glamorous Gizmos" and should be understood readily by those concerned directly with the field of data processing.

From the point of inception to the intelligent use of the product, the human element is of paramount importance. It is man who does the original thinking which results in determining requirements, designing procedures,

Reprinted by permission of the author and the publisher from *DPMA Quarterly*, Vol. 1, No. 3 (April, 1965), pp. 2–23.

devising instructions, preparing input data, operating and maintaining the equipment, directing the output, supervising and controlling the entire operation, utilizing the product, determining and overcoming deficiencies and improving the system. In brief, it is *people* who prescribe the *procedures* which are paraphrased in the *programs* applied to the *peripheral equipment* and the *processor,* to produce the product for use by *people!*

An orderly plan is the catalyst used to meld these components into a successful data processing system. The broad sequential steps of such a plan should include these elements:

> Feasibility study.
> Detailed Systems Analysis.
> Preliminary Systems Design.
> Equipment Evaluation and Selection.
> Conversion Planning.
> Detailed Systems Design & Documentation.
> Programming.
> Performance Evaluation.

Because electronic data processing is still in its formative years, it has the same problem of lack of clear expression and definition encountered by all "teen-agers." It has, therefore, produced a cabalistic jargon understandable only by the initiated. This would not be any more of a problem for the layman to cope with than that of interpreting the esoteric terminology of other professions, if it were not for the fact that the lingua franca of the computer has so many dialects.

As a result of the work of the various standards committees and the advent of common programming languages, such as COBOL and ALGOL, this problem should be resolved in time. But until an electronic Esperanto is developed and universally applied, it is necessary that terms be defined precisely. Accordingly, to reiterate in capsule form the fundamentals of devising a data processing system, as well as to isolate and focus attention on the Conversion Planning phase of control of systems design and evaluation, definitions of the major subdivisions of the over-all plan are required.

Feasibility Study

Of all the terms used in this field, the word "feasibility" has the broadest range of definition. As used in this article the term represents a determination of the need and desirability of using automatic data processing equipment for specific applications, rather than a full-scale justification including equipment selection. Therefore, recognizing the feasibility study as being the preliminary phase of systems planning, it can be readily segregated as an independent segment in the over-all study of the design and installation of an automatic data processing system.

Although in the later stages of development and application the significance of the spadework performed during the feasibility study will appear to diminish, the importance of the findings of the study group cannot be overemphasized. Their conclusions must be keyed to the possibility of effective, efficient and economical application of automatic data processing systems to appropriate processes of the organization. It should be on the basis of the study group's recommendations that management makes the decision to proceed with plans for conversion or for abandoning or deferring the project.

In order for management to make a valid decision, it must be furnished with sound information. The possibility of obtaining such intelligence will be enhanced if, at the time the study group is established, careful selection is made of members from appropriate staff and line functions, and a top management representative is designated as chairman to serve on a full-time basis. This action should be combined with a precisely defined charter which specifies the following:

> Objectives of the study.
> Scope of the study.
> Authority of the study group.
> Responsibility of the study group.
> Organizational representation.
> Designation of chairman.
> Necessity for cooperative effort.
> Final written report.

The objectives should not be nebulous. A statement that the study group is to "determine the applicability of using computers" is not as effective as a clear-cut expression of a specific goal in terms of ascertaining whether monetary savings, manpower savings, better information or more responsive information can be obtained. The significance of this item justifies accentuation. The objectives will be reviewed and reappraised at many stages as the study progresses. During subsequent performance evaluations they will be one of the principal bases for analysis.

The sanctioning of the project by the highest echelon can be a valuable factor in obtaining a penetrating and dependable evaluation by those concerned directly with the study, as well as those who may be affected by its results. This is also an important consideration in establishing the authority of the group to conduct its probings and receive support and assistance in obtaining information at all levels.

Representation by appropriate organizational subdivisions is also vital to the success of the mission, as is the necessity for well-qualified personnel capable of supplying a broad outlook, rather than those who may be inclined to take a parochial view of the task. The appointment of a chairman who commands the respect of the group because of his knowledge of the over-all organizational structure and who is not oriented toward a specific function, such as production, sales, comptroller or purchasing, will represent another asset in making a meaningful feasibility study. This will enhance the co-operative effort and assist in avoiding a dogmatic approach to the data processing problem.

It is advisable to establish a firm deadline date for submission of the final written report and provide general guidance as to what the report should encompass. Although this will vary, dependent upon the basic objectives, the minimum requirements should include a statement of conclusions and recommendations with supporting justification. These are the fundamentals needed to properly conduct a feasibility study in order to have a solid foundation on which to build the remaining phases of the systematic plan.

Detailed Systems Analysis

If, as a result of the conclusions reached during the feasibility study, it is decided to proceed with plans for conversion, the detailed systems analysis can begin. The feasibility study can be construed to be the preliminary systems analysis and, thus, this second step in the over-all plan is a continuance of the determination as to the appropriateness of converting to automatic data processing.

The importance of this element of the over-all plan can be noted by observing that the term "systems analyst" is widely used throughout this field to cover the function of those who not only analyze systems, but who also design systems. Seldom is the term "systems designer" used, although the greatest proportion of the effort of the typical systems analyst is spent in devising procedures, and this is the area where good systems must be initially conceived or all that follows (e.g., programming, recording, reporting and analysis) is of little value.

But in order to be able to devise a system which will furnish meaningful information, it is necessary, first, to analyze in detail the existing procedures, in terms of input, processing and output. By discussions with appropriate suppliers and users of data and by personal observation, determination must be made as to whether management's needs are being satisfied or if deficiencies exist.

The ideal approach to systems planning would be to outline the information which represents management's needs, then analyze the present system, after which the selection of equipment and detailed design and development of procedures could take place. But, as a matter of practicality, the approach generally followed is to analyze the present system and then make a determination as to modifications necessary to satisfy the demands of the organization. The principal reasons for this sequencing of events are the time factor and imposed requirements.

The time factor is important because, if the current system is discounted and an entirely new collecting, recording and reporting plan is developed, a disproportionate amount of the time will be required to construct the system from the basic building blocks to the finished product. This, together with the "imposed requirements," which are the control demands made at echelons higher than the organization for which the system is being designed, serve to mitigate against a completely new approach.

Having obtained the fundamental information concerning the system which is in being and an objective understanding of the revisions desired by management, it is now possible to proceed from the preparatory stage to a crystallization of the objectives envisioned in the feasibility study.

Preliminary Systems Design

In the detailed systems analysis, a study was made of the current procedures for collecting, recording, reporting and using information, and an initial determination was made as to management information requirements. The next step is to formulate the over-all design of the proposed system to the extent that appropriate specifications can be developed for equipment selection. This is the first approximation of the ultimate system and, in addition to providing the basis for equipment specifications, at the conclusion of this stage the study has reached a critical point at which management, before proceeding further, should evaluate carefully the advantages anticipated.

In this transitory development of the analytical effort to a general systems plan, emphasis is concentrated on a generic description of data processing requirements. The ultimate result is a basic systems design which is conceived after reviewing the broad scope of management's needs. An important precaution to be noted is that the design should be sufficiently flexible to assure that the system can be applied to various available equipments.

The development of accurate and complete systems specifications is vital to the acquisition of the most appropriate equipment configuration to accomplish the data processing needs effectively and economically.

In order for the manufacturers to furnish definitive proposals, they should be given a summarization of the present data processing system, its constraints, and the objectives of the proposed system. This information should supplement the specifications which describe input (methods, mediums, peak loads), internal processing (volume, record length, file maintenance methods, interrogation, types of computation, random access), and output (medium, peak loads, deadline dates). The manufacturer should be requested to supply other pertinent data, such as time estimates, reserve capacity, maintenance information, modularity, etc. With this information as a base, the manufacturers can make realistic proposals as to the equipment which they consider to be appropriate for the system.

Equipment Evaluation and Selection

One of the immediate considerations in evaluation of the manufacturers' proposals is to be certain that they have been prepared in accordance with the terms of the specifications. Some manufacturers may suggest deviations from the specifications or systems design and these may be acceptable to management. However, in order to assure that an unbiased analysis is made of all bids a common denominator is needed. Thus relative capabilities, such as time and cost factors, can be compared in a logical manner.

Although there are valid reasons, other than cost advantage purposes, for converting to automatic data processing systems this factor is nearly always of prime concern. Therefore, when evaluating manufacturers' bids, it is essential that all of the many cost elements involved in devising, installing and operating an automatic data processing system are considered. As a result, it is frequently necessary to go beyond the information contained in the bids and evaluate other comparative factors such as cost of site preparation, installation, detailed systems design, programming, training, conversion and operation. The manufacturers may furnish information concerning these elements, but it is prudent for well informed management personnel to independently evaluate this and all other information received from the vendor.

When the determination has been made by the study group as to the equipment considered to be most appropriate for the job, the information supporting the selection should be summarized and presented to the approving authority.

The summarization will consist of the findings of the feasibility study, the systems analysis and preliminary design, the equipment evaluation and selection, and the conclusions and recommendations. Together they comprise the justification, on the basis of which system is proposed for management acceptance. If it is to be accepted, the justification must clearly outline the benefits which will accrue as a result of the conversion.

This requires careful documentation since the summarization and its underlying supplementary information will serve a variety of purposes for a considerable period of time. These are in addition to the principal use of the justification material in providing a factual and analytical report for management's use in determining whether or not to convert to automatic data processing operations and authenticate the equipment selection.

Other purposes which the justification serves include its use as the basic reference during development and installation of the system to resolve misunderstandings and differences of opinion as to what the system is intended to accomplish and the extent or limitation of its impact. In the Federal Government, as well as in many private industry installations, the justification is used as a key element in conducting a "readiness review" during the period of 30 to 60 days prior to equipment delivery. The purpose of this review is to ascertain whether or not the prospective user is prepared to apply the equipment in a productive manner. Also, after the system has been operative for a sufficient period of time to warrant performance evaluation, the justification is the initial check-point in ascertaining the degree of accomplishment of the original objectives.

Conversion Planning

In the sequencing of the items involved in the formation of the over-all plan, it will be noted that consideration of Conversion Planning is proposed immediately after equipment selection. At first blush this may appear to be premature, but as all of the elements involved in converting to automatic data processing are reviewed the necessity for advance planning will become more apparent.

In its broadest sense, planning for conversion to automatic data processing begins with the gleam in the eye of the first person who visualizes the practical use of a computer in his organization. It continues through all phases of the justification stage, i.e., from the initiation of the feasibility study to the selection of equipment. But it does not acquire substantive form until after the selection of equipment has been approved. At that time, if it has not already been determined, one of the most crucial decisions must be made—who will coordinate the entire project?

This decision warrants the assiduous attention of top management. Of all the assignments to be made, none is more important than that of the project coordinator. Since he will be the focal point of contact with the upper echelons of both the staff and line organizations, his role in the success or failure of controlling the conversion should not be underestimated.

Depending upon the size and scope of the installation, this may or may not be a full-time assignment. But whether full-time or part-time, it requires the appointment of a capable administrator who can achieve cooperative relationships among all of the organizational components and levels involved in the systems change. His responsibilities should include prescribing the method of scheduling, controlling and reporting on the progress of the installation. An intimate knowledge of the organization, its key personnel and management information needs is invaluable. When the coordination assignment is conducted at the vice-presidential level, or its equivalent, it offers the advantages of such intimate knowledge, as well as authority and prestige. It also provides the top management representation which is of inestimable value in resolving difficulties between or within staff elements and line departments.

It is virtually impossible to read a book or an article on ADP without finding a mention of the necessity for top management support. In every line of endeavor this same cry is heard. Everyone considers that his problems, his needs, his findings are of sufficient importance to warrant top level attention. The data processing fraternity is well in the forefront in this clamor for recognition. And they, like many others, have a logical claim on the time and attention of the principal officials of the organization.

ADP is quite a new profession, requiring use of costly equipment, expensive systems, high salaried personnel and considerable time before a break-even point is attained. These reasons would be sufficient within themselves to cause the higher echelons to be concerned. But there are many more reasons for giving prime attention to the installation of an ADP system, because decisions having a penetrating and far-reaching effect on all factors of operation must be decided upon.

These decisions may involve major organizational adjustments—establishing a separate Data Processing Department or its location in an existing component is a patent example of this. Personnel changes, planned far in advance of the equipment installation date must be anticipated—not just key personnel but all levels in many units. The difficult question of whether to buy or rent ADP equipment demands careful deliberation. Budgetary planning, including the possibility of necessity for an extra monetary allocation which may be required during the period of parallel operations of the old and new systems, may be one item of significant import. Such funds may be needed to pay for overtime or temporary personnel as well as rental fees for two kinds of equipment. These are problems which may well demand that decisions be made at the highest level.

The possibility of integrating data processing wherein the same basic information is used for more than one purpose, e.g., purchasing, accounting and production planning and control, while having the potential benefit of significant economies, also encroaches on a number of distinct organizational entities. Approval by a regional or central office is oftentimes needed before a system is installed, and the top local official is responsible for furnishing adequate justification. Modification of policies and administrative regulations are typical concomitants of major systems revisions. And last in this partial listing of reasons for top management support, is the necessity for the unqualified endorsement of the project by the individual or group in which final authority resides, in order that the most favorable climate will be provided to encourage cooperation at every level.

The appointment of a capable coordinator from the top management level, or one who has ready and direct access to that echelon, can overcome resistance, instill interest, achieve cooperation and facilitate efficient and harmonious planning. Ideally, he should be relieved of all duties other than those of planning the systems installation. But as a practical matter, this may not be possible. Also, it may be more satisfactory to have a coordinator of high management calibre on a part-time basis rather than a full-time appointee whose capability is unquestioned but who may be unable to facilitate the resolving of inter-departmental disagreements, thereby impeding the progress of the long-range project.

The first task of the project coordinator will be the drafting of a tentative conversion plan. To do so, he must be well acquainted with the conclusions and recommendations in the justification for the new system and be fully cognizant of the scope of the proposed ADP system and intent of the basic objectives.

After developing the nucleus of a detailed conversion plan, the coordinator can meet with key personnel and assess the degree to which the responsibilities should be divided. An effective method of doing this is to establish a control team headed by the coordinator and comprised of department heads. This team should have authority to establish policy and act as a decision-making body. Those charged with controlling the conversion plan have the responsibility for guiding and directing the conversion, but they should not be involved directly in the detailed implementation of the plan. Under the guidance of the coordinator, they would be responsible for establishing the firm conversion plan and schedule. This approach is conducive to the creating of a rapport and coadunation leading to the envisaging of the project as a cooperative effort in which the entire enterprise is contributing to the mutual benefit of all.

Guidance would then be available to determine whether conversion teams need be established, how many would be required and the composition of the groups. The degree of the parceling will depend upon the magnitude and complexity of the systems development. Recognizing that the size and extent of the systems installation will have a significant bearing on the mechanics of converting, the most successful approach to the transition to automatic data processing has been the subdividing of the conversion responsibilities to segments controllable by task forces or teams.

In order for the over-all conversion plan to be executed in a disciplined manner, the control team must be certain that the subsidiary groups conduct their assignments with an appropriate degree of uniformity to permit correlation of progress reporting and evaluation of the status of the project at regulated intervals. To assure this, documentation is required of the method to be applied.

The particular local situation will determine which method of documentation is appropriate, the brief and informal or the detailed and formal. But whichever approach is taken, the same basic purpose must be served, i.e., to insure that the user will be prepared to apply the automatic data processing equipment in an efficient and productive manner when it is installed.

If the informal approach is followed, as a minimum, a memorandum should be prepared setting up the task forces, outlining their basic responsibilities, allotting the personnel complement, prescribing the reporting requirements and establishing a general time schedule for completion of the major events. Or it may be found to be more appropriate to direct the transition to an ADP system by preparation of a conversion manual which, in addition to the items outlined above, would include an introductory statement on the background of the study and the objectives of the system, for the purpose of the manual, definitions, prescribed charting and diagramming formats, master schedule and progress reporting methods, documentation techniques, and detailed information concerning each principal and subordinate element involved in the conversion process.

For some installations, the establishment of two distinct types of task forces may be the most effective manner in which to develop an orderly plan for conversion. One type would be organized on a functional basis e.g., Production Control, Order Processing, Inventory Control; and the other would be on a project basis, e.g., Data Clean-Up, File Conversion, Site Preparation.

The composition of the groups concerned with the individual projects should, whenever possible, consist of a specialist from the functional or project area, a senior systems analyst or senior programmer, and other members such as management engineers, internal auditors and industrial engineers. The best mix is one which would include a representative of the ultimate user of the product and a representative of the design group, as well as staff or line personnel who are experienced in analytical or investigative fields.

The work of the task force is such that it does not demand full-time attention of the members. It is possible and advisable for some key personnel to be represented on several of the task forces. But care must be exercised to prevent the expenditure of a disproportionate amount of the time of key personnel, with the resulting derogation of their regularly prescribed duties.

The basic responsibilities of the task force are to review the developments in its assigned area, resolve problems or refer the problems to those who can take corrective action, and act as the liaison in reporting progress to the over-all planning committee. They may also be responsible for subdividing their assignment into distinct reportable segments for the purpose of more effective control. The more sophisticated of the large-scale systems designers are beginning to use scientific techniques, such as Performance Evaluation and Review Technique (PERT) and Critical Path Method (CPM), as pantologic aids in scheduling the intermeshing of the many factors involved in conversion planning. These are methods of measuring current progress against planned objectives in terms of where the program is with respect to where it should be.

A word of caution is advisable when considering the scheduling of progress reporting to the control team. It is difficult to plan the most efficient schedule of written and oral presentations. Too frequent meetings and too many written or verbal reports are as much of a handicap as are too few of those items. But there must be regularly scheduled meetings and periodic progress reporting, or advancement will be impeded because of unrelieved obstructions. A method of identifying critical items can be readily devised and the time and effort of the control personnel can be focused on those areas, until the problems are resolved and they are no longer categorized as critical items. All other areas can be covered by routine reporting on a monthly or any other appropriate regularly scheduled basis. Some planning systems use the exception method of reporting wherein information is furnished only for those items requiring attention.

The extensive use of graphic aids is also of much value in conserving the time of reviewing authorities, by highlighting the areas on which special action should be concentrated. The key to successful use of graphic presentations is in the initial devising of a realistic estimated time schedule and providing for a valid method of comparing accomplishments with the plan. Frequent revisions to the original schedule or inability to determine the current status on a factual basis will negate the value of the reporting system. Careful attention to development of this type of projection is necessary so that it can be used reliably in conserving management's time.

As noted earlier, the problem of communications in the field of data processing is complicated by the lack of precise definition of widely-used terms, the use of some words for multiple purposes, and the defining of others in a completely different sense than is applied in their common usage. A few examples of words which have been given these unique treatments are—cycle, erase, clearing, extract, feasibility, application, program and operation. To proceed from confusion to chaos, common terms such as "flow chart" and "block diagramming" are defined in an astonishing number of ways in various publications, particularly those prepared by equipment manufacturers.

Because of its wide use by everyone who has a major or minor interest in the system design and implementation, the conversion manual is one of the best places to list the definition of terms. The conversion manual is used internally by systems analysts, programmers, the project coordinator, equipment operations personnel, internal auditors, and, most importantly, by the line and staff department heads and their key personnel who will be the principal users of the computer product. It will also be used by personnel outside of the immediate organization, such as review authorities, consultants, outside auditors, and many others with a direct or indirect interest in the project.

Whether shown in the conversion manual, analysts' manual, programming manual or other means of documentation, a standardized method of preparing flow charts and block diagrams should be prescribed. If a "block diagram" is used as the graphic illustration of operations that a computer is to perform, and if a "flow chart" depicts the flow of information among the organizational and subdivisions, the terms must be restricted to those definitions and applied uniformly.

Consistency is a keynote in controlling successful systems development. The portrayal of the system profile in a manner which will permit ready understanding by all analysts, programmers, reviewers, operating management and other interested personnel, will be beneficial long after the development stage is completed. Management's information requirements are not static, and since they change from time to time, the system for producing the intelligence needed to properly conduct operations must also be conducive to modification.

The value of standardization, documentation and consistency is most apparent when analysis is made of an operating system in order to determine what revisions are necessary to meet current management demands in an expeditious and economical manner. Also, this is one of the principal reasons why handbooks and instructions must be kept up-to-date throughout the project. It is only by doing so that the systems analyst, who at a later date may be charged with revising a procedure, can do so with a minimum of effort and with assurance that the changes do not contravene the balance of the systems design.

This is further indication of the value of planning for all phases of conversion immediately after approval of the justification for installation of ADP equipment. Before the systems designers and programmers put pencil to paper, they should be furnished with guidelines as to the narrative and graphic evidence required to support their work. The guidelines may be developed by consultants, senior analysts or systems reviewers from the home office, representatives of the equipment manufacturer, or any other source of experienced or qualified personnel. An effective method of developing guidelines is to have local representatives affiliate with experienced specialists in formulating the requirements. This offers the dual advantage of local participation and a definite understanding of the intent and force of the guidelines.

The guidelines should describe and illustrate, not only major items, such as block diagrams and flow charts, but also the symbols to be used in those schematics, including those used to represent equipment, documents and notations. Other detailed guidance should be provided, such as prescribing the content and format of run books and manuals. Such documentation control will facilitate communications, aid in resolving conflicts, prevent delay and can also serve as a means of certifying the proposed system by having department heads and other key users of the computer product, review and approve the handbooks, manuals, run books and other pertinent validations.

When the method of accomplishment of the conversion to ADP operations is well planned, e.g., guidelines formalized in a conversion handbook and committees and subcommittees organized and staffed with responsible and capable members, then attention can be concentrated on each of the major considerations involved in installing and using ADP and related equipment. These major considerations are:

> Organization Realignment.
> Personnel Selection.
> Training and Orientation.
> Systems Design.
> Programming.
> Testing and Debugging.
> Narrative Procedures.
> Data Clean-Up.
> File Conversion.
> Site Requirements.
> Installation Scheduling.
> Emergency Planning.
> Readiness Review.
> Public Relations.
> Accrediting by Top Management.
> Transition Schedule.

Organizational Realignment

Much has been written on the question of organizational location of the data processing operation. There is no universal answer to this problem since the basic factors of legal requirements and management philosophy will determine the proper structure to be established. But the prime concern of the conversion planners is not the manner or form of the organization, it is the implementation of the proposed action.

The conversion coordinator may have the authority to approve the organization plan, or he may have the responsibilty for devising an organization structure with approval action retained at a higher level. Whatever the approach, the objective is to assure that the plan has been approved, in final form, sufficiently far in advance of the equipment installation date to permit definitive action to be taken.

One of the major actions required is the timely issuance of an approved organization chart and functional statement outlining the structure, authorities and responsibilities of the data processing component. After this has been issued, it is desirable to acquaint the other line and staff elements of the organization with the expected impact of the realignment. The goal is to have the ADP duties and prerogatives recognized and accepted, throughout the organization, sufficiently far in advance of the operations stage, to create an understanding of the benefits which can be realized through a cooperative relationship between the producers and the users of information.

Personnel Selection

The interest of the conversion planning group in this function should be to establish or review the policy on the transfer of employees to the data processing organization, the hiring of new employees, utilization of temporary personnel and the possibility of dismissals resulting from conversion to ADP. Also, attention should be given to the standards used or other methods followed in selecting systems, programming or operating personnel.

Management may also use the conversion control team to interview, screen and recommend the candidates for the position of head of the ADP organization. Whether recruiting from within or from some other source, the selection of the manager of a business data processing installation requires careful deliberation. The aim is to obtain a manager who will command the respect of the other department heads and whose managerial and administrative abilities are such that he can conduct the internal operations of his department in an efficient manner.

Other interests, in this area, with which the conversion group is concerned are the prompt establishment of job descriptions and development of a suitable salary structure in order to be able to attract and retain qualified people. Examination of the practices followed concerning these items and the factors mentioned in the preceding paragraphs, together with a review of progress by use of graphic reporting techniques, should assure management that this phase of conversion will be properly controlled.

Training

The training of personnel is a program which should be initiated immediately after selection of those who will perform the various ADP systems planning, design and operational functions. Although equipment manufacturers, consultants and educational institutions are all used for this purpose, the emphasis has been on the courses offered by manufacturers. They are usually well equipped and staffed to conduct this function and their training programs are precisely oriented to the particular equipment configuration which will be installed.

After selecting the courses required, a training schedule must be devised in such a manner that sufficient personnel will be available to perform their specific functions at the proper time in the over-all systems development cycle. For example, it would be logical to start the training program by concentrating attention on the systems analysts, and the programmers then, later, tape librarian, console operators, auxiliary equipment operators and other support personnel. This alignment represents the usual order in which those specialists would be developing or applying their contribution to the total system.

Orientation

The orientation phase should be designed to provide for introduction to ADP and indoctrination in the system concepts of all those who are not directly concerned with the ADP installation, but who will be affected by the system. Equipment manufacturers' executive schools and introductory seminars are excellent aids in acquainting all levels of management with the fundamentals of ADP and a description of how such equipment will be applied in their company. This also provides an opportunity to stress the objectives and the benefits which are expected to be attained.

This is an area with which the conversion team should be especially concerned. It may be advisable for the planning coordinator, the head of the Data Processing Department, or another key official to assume the personal responsibility for arranging for the orientation of the top management group. The knowledge acquired as a result of viewing films, film strips or other visual aids, supplemented by appropriate oral presentations, will be very helpful to those executives who may be confronted with the necessity for making a decision affecting the data processing function.

In addition to the intrinsic control obtained by inclusion of Training and Orientation as an item in the charting of the conversion plans, a roster of officials and other interested personnel from all departments should be compiled, and arrangements made for all to be given some form of orientation in automatic data processing systems. Special effort should be made to conduct the program in a manner which will be tailored to the convenience of the attendees. The object is to expose the greatest possible number of members of the organization to the fundamentals and applications of ADP in order to overcome any possible prejudice against the system caused by lack of knowledge as to its composition and purpose.

Systems Design

In order to control the planning for design of systems, it is frequently necessary that this broad function be divided into well-defined parts. Divisions of the systems study usually consist of these sections:

> Design of output data.
> Design of input data.
> General flow charts.
> Detailed flow charts.
> Narrative procedures.

Inasmuch as systems design is one of the major factors in conversion to automatic data processing, caution must be observed in preparing progress reports which indicate the status of the actual accomplishments to date as compared with the planning estimates. The combining of the sub-items shown above under the heading of "Systems Design" on a progress report may be meaningless if the composite picture presents a distorted view of the development. Therefore, more detailed reporting of the information involved in the devising of systems is sometimes more useful than consolidated reporting.

In addition to the usual task of keeping the entire project on schedule, the conversion team can be of assistance in the Systems Design area whenever situations occur where there is a controversy between the functional groups and the systems analysts. The conversion coordinator must be certain that appropriate action is taken promptly to resolve the differences and relieve the bottleneck. He can also be of assistance in resolving questions concerning the determination of priorities on development of the various applications.

There is another item which can cause delay in completing the systems design. That is the lack of agreement as to the final format of input data, reports, records or other material items of concern in devising the system. This common problem is caused by the reluctance of systems analysts, or those responsible for the use of the data or information, to settle upon a format until the last possible moment. When this situation is encountered it can be corrected by having the coordinator provide for the establishment of a fixed date for final submission of changes and freezing the design at that time.

Programming

There is no more difficult feature in the installation of an ADP system than that of preparing a realistic estimate of the time required to prepare a program. The experience of many commercial and Federal Government installations indicates that the time required to complete the programming is frequently 50 per cent to 100 per cent greater than the estimated time.

This widespread experience and external difficulties, such as delays and modifications in systems design, decree that prudent estimating and rigid control must be enforced. An appraisal of the programming effort indicates that 85 per cent of the time is consumed in defining and analyzing the prob lem, outlining a solution and detailing the solution. The remaining 15 per cent is spent in encoding and debugging. Therefore, the attention of the conversion planners should be focused on those items which have the greatest potential for time savings.

As in systems design, the establishing of a rigid deadline beyond which no major changes will be accepted, can be one of the most valuable guides in both realistic estimating and control of the project. The deadline can be fixed when the formats of the input data, output data, files, forms and reports have been agreed upon.

Testing and Debugging

The interest of the conversion team in this area extends far beyond the analysis of the progress as compared with the plan. Programmers may need assistance in obtaining computer time or in resolving an equitable schedule for the program teams. This may necessitate decisive action as to which applications are to be given priority in the development of the entire system. The conversion coordinator must either have the authority to make these decisions, or see that they are made, in order to keep the project on schedule.

Because of the many facets involved in preparing for program testing, a disciplined method of test preparation should be defined. Such things as program halts, restart options, completion of desk checking, review of flow charts and coding, and compiling of fabricated or canned data must be accounted for. The basic responsibility for assuring that test planning is complete may be that of a senior programmer, but the conversion team must ascertain that the fundamental requirements have been established in order to minimize delays in the testing and debugging process.

Fabricated data is that which contains a sampling of all possible known situations which may affect a program run. Canned data represents infor-mation which is based on actual experience. Obtaining this material for test purposes can serve the collateral purpose of acquainting those who will furnish the data and those who use the finished product, with the program, its purpose and how it operates.

Narrative Procedures

In analyses of the results of computer operations which reveal failure to achieve the original objectives, there is one item which is reported consistently as a contributory factor in the lack of success. That is, neglect in adequately documenting procedures and programs.

Narrative support and documentation of programming is the least troublesome item. Methods of preparing run manuals and run books, as well as their content, are given much attention in manufacturers' brochures and other guides used in systems design. But there is a dearth of information offering guidance on documentation outside of the program area.

Since the necessity for documentation of procedures is highlighted in the results of reviews of performance evaluations of ADP systems, it is apparent that those responsible for conversion must give special consideration to this factor. Accounting for progress in preparing written procedures should be included in the oral and written reports on the status of the installation and this item should also be included in the control charts as a major consideration in the development of the entire system.

The method for documenting procedures should be decided upon as soon as possible after approval has been obtained for use of ADP equipment. This applies not only to the programming function, but to all systems design, control, scheduling, auxiliary and clerical functions.

Data Clean-Up

There are many stories told of disclosure, upon conversion to automatic data processing, that repetitive errors have been occurring in the previous manual or mechanized system for extensive periods, without being detected. Such stories, like those which denounce the ADP system as one which produces misinformation at electronic speeds, are often exaggerated. The less sophisticated processing methods should be expected to contain a greater proportion of errors than the more modern methods.

Users of ADP equipment report that practical experience has proven the necessity for close scrutiny and purification of data, prior to systems conversion. Although the data of a manual or machine system may be subject to rigid predetermined manual control and there is an audit trail after processing, it must be analyzed because the content is not static and changes may occur at any time.

The editing of the file data and other records, for completeness and accuracy, is a demanding assignment which requires precise attention and control. The responsibility of this task is one which should be specifically assigned, sufficiently far in advance of the conversion date to insure that the data will be purified and balanced before the conversion date. Also, after the data clean-up has been accomplished, data must be controlled, updated and kept up-to-date, so that accurate initial data will flow into the ADP system.

File Conversion

After the Data Clean-Up stage, or concurrently, the process of converting the files and creating new files should begin. To do this, decisions must be made as to format, record length, content, codes, storage, processing frequencies and method of file arrangement.

Because of the many determinations which must be made concerning the data, its format, arrangements, etc., and because of the need for extreme care to assure that the file conversion will result in accurate and complete initial records, this project must be scheduled to allow for sufficient time to permit thoroughness and allow for review of the completed files to assure that they are correct.

The conversion team must insure that the planning schedule provides for expeditious action on file conversion and act promptly if delay occurs. In addition to assuring that a uniform format has been established and a sound schedule prepared, there must be certainty that official records have been used in creating the new files.

After the files have been prepared, a control must be maintained and procedures prescribed to keep the files current and accurate. This policing action is essential to successful processing of the initial production runs. Arranging for audit and approval by the department which will generate the information or use the product of the ADP system is an effective way to keep control of the converted files.

Site Requirements

The planning and preparation of the equipment site should not cause a great deal of difficulty in the installation of the ADP system. With well documented guidance made available by the manufacturers, precise requirements of underwriter associations, and the interest of other control and regulatory bodies, this should be one of the most disciplined phases of the conversion plan.

However, because there are so many items which must be correlated, it is necessary to prepare preliminary plans for the site reqiurements giving consideration to general locations, alternative sites, and area requirements and characteristics. The conversion team should be interested in seeing that a decision as to the site is then made promptly in order to permit development of positive plans. Such plans require preparation of specifications for all areas and involve considerable detail. Therefore any delay can be a deterrent to the activation of the system and can cause an appreciable loss in a short period of time.

One of the items which is frequently overlooked or given minor consideration, is the additional allowance for future expansion. The installation of computers often results in displacement of offices or other spaces and the natural reaction of management is to keep this disruption to an absolute minimum. But the conversion planners should take action to avoid precipitous management conclusions which may, at a later date, result in a major and expensive rearrangement.

Installation Schedule

The schedule of equipment installation, like the Site Requirements plan, is concerned with a variety of factors and requires careful dovetailing with the many items involved in the major considerations in conversion to ADP. If the computer arrives before any of the programs are completed, or before personnel are trained, then rental or depreciation loss will result. Conversely, if files have been converted, programs debugged, personnel trained and the equipment has not been installed or operative, management will be "champing at the bit" because the prospective payoff date will be delayed.

To avoid either of these contingencies requires a systematic plan, proceeding from designation of a physical installation coordinator to the preparation of an installation schedule and close monitoring of progress reporting. In order to permit timely installation of equipment, the plan should be synchronized with the site readiness plan. It must give consideration, not only to electronic data processing equipment, but also to auxiliary equipment, support equipment, supplies and rental and maintenance arrangements.

As the physical installation of an ADP system draws near, the adequacy or inadequacy of the conversion plans is brought sharply into focus. If all of the conversion elements, ranging from organizational adjustment to alternative processing plans, have been reviewed, evaluated and controlled on a continuing basis, the problems in establishing a realistic transition schedule will be diminished.

However, when the critical point of initial operation approaches, there may be a crescendo of confusion as the interests of the engineering, purchasing, administrative, systems, programming, operating, supervisory and management personnel converge. This is when the conversion planning team can clearly demonstrate its value, by acting promptly to see that problems are resolved. It is at this time that the value of controlled planning is most apparent.

Emergency Planning

The necessity to prepare for the contingency of partial or complete operational disruption must be recognized by all installation planners. The conversion team's interest in this item should be to ascertain that effective back-up procedures and plans have been specified and fully documented.

If arrangements have been made for use of alternative equipment and if duplicate files of instructions and basic records have been set up, when an emergency occurs the necessary services can be resumed with a minimum of delay. Caution must be exercised to be certain that the alternate files and records reflect current information; consequently, updating of the standby information must be an integral part of any procedural or related modification. In addition, close liaison with the organization with which emergency arrangements have been made is necessary, in order to insure continuing operative compatibility.

Also, establishment of specific job priorities, to be followed in the event of an emergency, should be completed before routine processing begins. Agreement as to the order of importance will, ordinarily, involve the heads of departments receiving the ADP service. Dependent upon management policy, the conversion team should decide, or see that a decision is made, as to the order of preference for emergency processing applications.

Readiness Review

The term "Readiness Review" is used, primarily in the Federal Government, to identify an on-site evaluation by a team from some higher echelon, for the purpose of determining the state of preparedness of the organization where the ADP system is to be installed.

Reviews of this nature are usually planned to take place 30 to 60 days before the equipment is scheduled to be delivered. They may be completed in a few days or take an entire week, depending upon the nature and complexity of the proposed system.

During the review, an appraisal is made of the attainment of the objectives which should have been reached, at this time, as compared with the conversion plan. All of the major items of conversion to the ADP system are evaluated. As a general rule, the review teams consider that 50 per cent of one operating shift should be ready for productive runs before the equipment will be certified for installation.

There is one feature of the appraisal just prior to equipment installation which is of special note. That is, a careful evaluation at this time will provide the opportunity to update the original objectives. Since a considerable period of time may have elapsed between the time of initiation of the feasibility study and the ultimate development of the ADP system, a revision of the objectives may be logical.

Public Relations

There are two aspects to the public relations phase of devising and installing an ADP system, i.e., the internal dissemination of information concerning the proposed system and the publicizing of the plans to outside sources.

Insofar as those who have experience in installing ADP systems are concerned, there is no doubt that the most important of these two elements is the furnishing of prompt and accurate information to all echelons within the organization. There are many reasons for the application of this Golden Rule.

First, there is a recognition by management of the importance of getting cooperation of all employees, whether they are concerned directly with the program or not. Another reason is that the ADP system usually involves many departments and cuts across organizational lines, thus the use of the new system may necessitate the creation of a new or revised personnel structure. Also, it is most desirable to dispel erroneous information on the deleterious effect of the computer installation on the employees.

If the potential value of the new system is made clear to the employees and they become convinced that the basic objective is to improve the enterprise through use of more economical or more efficient methods, then a climate will exist to enhance enthusiastic acceptance of the new tool. And finally, since the installation of equipment which may have a personal effect on employees insofar as their jobs, salaries, opportunities for advancement, prestige, authorities and responsibilities are concerned, they should be kept fully aware of their status so that their anxieties will be relieved.

The furnishing of information to outside sources, such as customers, suppliers and the general public is another matter which should be controlled. All well-managed companies desire to create a proper public image. In order to maintain that status, precaution must be taken to avoid the publication of erroneous or misleading information about the installation of an ADP system.

Before release of news items, a clearance with the conversion coordinator is desirable as there often is a tendency to divulge information prematurely, sometimes in exaggerated form, as a result of the decision to automate. In addition to screening releases for accuracy, a conservative approach should be taken on prognosticating the target date for commencing computer operations. That information should not be released until the Readiness Review team has expressed approval of the conversion progress.

Accrediting by Top Management

Earlier, the advantages incident to obtaining the unqualified support of the ADP installation project by top level management were reviewed in detail. Of course, it is possible to operate a data processing system without the avowed support of the highest echelon, but the opportunity for achieving all of the goals of a sophisticated system will be much greater when there is no question in anyone's mind that the data processing function is on the side of the angels!

When top management approved the justification for the installation of ADP equipment, that approval was based on the expectation that the basic objectives were susceptible to achievement within the confines of management's demands for information. However, the short range and long range goals, as envisioned at the time of the justification study will, almost invariably, require modification because the requirements of management do not remain static. Consequently, as the study progresses through the various stages, the information needs of management must be surveyed constantly to be certain that the demands will be satisfied.

When the study has reached the Readiness Review stage, i.e., 30 to 60 days prior to equipment installation, it is advisable to compare the current management information requirements with those which were in effect at the time the justification was prepared. The typical comparison will disclose many changes in management demands.

One of the principal reasons for this is that the information needs of management are subject to exhaustive investigation during the systems analysis and design phases of the study. This often results in recommendations to management for contraction, expansion, cancellation or replacement of the then current management intelligence. Consequently, the goals which were envisioned at the time of the justification stage may require modification when the systems development has been completed.

Unless this recognition is given to the need for reappraisal of the original objectives, a realistic guide for future evaluation of progress and performance will not be available. The revised objectives should be authenticated by the top level of management and used as the base for assessing the benefits and improvements resulting from installation and use of the ADP system.

As the installation date approaches, it is again necessary to apprise top management of the current plans for conversion to ADP. There are two prime reasons for doing this—first, there is the need to insure an understanding that the ADP equipment will be used for those things which the highest echelon considers to be most appropriate and which will serve the best interests of management. Secondly, with the acknowledgment and concurrence by the key officials of the plans for conversion, it is then possible to inform the entire organization of the final approval from the apogee authorities.

This notification may take a variety of forms, in order to allow for the widest possible dissemination of the information. Probably the best place to begin is at a meeting of the Board of Directors and the officers, or its equivalent. This should be followed by a statement from the principal official in one or more meetings with employees, in the house organ or in a special notice to all employees.

As indicated previously when considering Public Relations, internal coverage should precede release of information to public sources. This approach, which reflects management's concern for each employee of the organization, will reduce the possibility of erroneous interpretation of the objectives of the installation and prevent idle rumors from resulting in morale problems.

The positive support of the proposed ADP system by the top level of management will permit the project to proceed into the operating phase in an atmosphere of confidence and cooperation. In addition to being instrumental in activating this support, the conversion coordinator should be certain that top management's sanction is acknowledged by all key levels of the organization and that there are no obstacles to impede concerted collaboration in the transition to ADP operations.

Transition Schedule

The final item in this consideration of controlling the ADP conversion is one which is concerned with every significant event which has taken place in the devising of the ADP system—the transition. Before the transition from the design of the system to operational application, all of the conclusions, from organizational rearrangement to emergency planning, should have been made. This will permit complete concentration of time and effort on the many details which must be synthesized during the conversion.

If the coordinator has pursued vigorously his task of integrating the efforts of all those engaged in preparing for the initial operations, the problems encountered during the transition period can be resolved without the additional complication of necessitating major revisions of programs and procedures. These problems include preparation of test material; use of "live" data; communications requirements; collecting, recording, summarizing, processing and controlling source data; and preparation, distribution and analysis of the results of the ADP operation.

In addition to monitoring the entire transition, from parallel operations to routine operations, the conversion coordinator must maintain a rigorous surveillance of each application, as it is channeled into the ADP operation, to assure that all difficulties are promptly resolved and that the parallel cycles are kept to an absolute minimum. In some cases, it is more appropriate to bypass the parallel operation test and proceed directly to the production run; particularly after several production runs have proved to be satisfactory and external controls and audit trails, independent of the machine processing, are available to test the authenticity of the processing results.

Conclusion

Although it may appear that this outline of methods usable in controlling a conversion to automatic data processing can only be applied by those organizations which are installing large-scale data processing equipment, the fundamentals and principles are applicable to all installations, from the card wallopers to the tape twirlers!

In comparatively small installations there may not be any conversion teams, or committees, or even a "conversion coordinator" who is so designated. But there will be one or more members of the organization who have authority and responsibility to control the project. Whether or not there is a conversion manual, which contains guidelines, definitions, charts, schedules, a glossary of terms and other control measures, and a conversion coordinator with subordinate groups to organize and control the major transition, the conversion problem must always be given special attention and observed carefully.

There must be sound advance planning, if there is to be an acceptable degree of success in achieving the objectives. Without an intelligent and comprehensive guide for use in controlling the myriad facets of installing and using automatic data processing equipment, the problems of coordination and the pressures of time, together with the inevitable conflict of interests, would all serve to thwart the efforts to contribute to general management improvement.

Evaluating Proposals
from Computer Manufacturers

Kenneth C. Cole

To alleviate management's growing paperwork problem, computer manufacturers offer a large number of mechanized remedies in all shapes, colors, sizes and prices. These remedies promise great speed and accuracy in data handling and report preparation as well as dollar savings.

Such an abundance of sparkling computer prescriptions confronts the manager with a dilemma: "Which equipment should I choose?" "What is best for my company?" Thorough analysis of the dozens of computer systems on the market today is a difficult task. Conversely, the problem may be misleadingly easy to resolve by deciding to order the newest model announced by the supplier with which the company financial officer or president is acquainted through previous business dealings.

It is obvious, of course, that a decision to invest several hundred thousand dollars should be made only after thorough analysis of several types of available equipment. If properly used as part of the total computer study, one tool stands out as being particularly well suited for the manager's use in answering the question, "What is best for my company?" This tool is the equipment and systems proposals submitted by interested manufacturers. However, the contribution this tool will actually make to the overall computer

Reprinted by permission of the author and the publisher from *Management Services*, Vol. II, No. 6 (November–December, 1965), pp. 28–34.

study depends on several factors that are not always given sufficient emphasis in discussions of equipment selection. These factors are as follows:

1. the objectivity with which the overall system evaluation is conducted by the user company;
2. the extent to which appropriate company personnel participate in the study;
3. the type of data furnished by the company to the computer manufacturers;
4. the scope and depth of the manufacturers' studies;
5. the experience of the manufacturers' systems personnel;
6. the competence of company personnel to evaluate the proposals received and to reach a reasonable conclusion.

Objectivity

An important consideration in determining the value of manufacturers' proposals in the computer study is whether management personnel at all levels are truly objective and really want to choose the most suitable equipment regardless of supplier. If an advance decision has already been made to install a specific suppliers' system, only that supplier should be asked to submit a proposal as a part of the total computer study. It is unfair under these circumstances to ask other manufacturers for proposals. There is no justification for requiring them to devote substantial time to systems analysis and proposal preparation if the only purpose is to enable the user company to obtain free systems advice from a variety of qualified sources.

A decision to continue a longtime association with a particular supplier or to select a highly publicized system with minimum evaluation of competition is likely to be a questionable one. Admittedly, a company may have the highest possible regard for the quality of personnel, equipment, and service of one supplier. Management may be uncomfortably aware that, once the decision is made to "take a look at a few others," there will be a procession of EDP sales and systems personnel requesting appointments for equipment demonstrations and demanding equal time for orientation seminars.

Nevertheless, an EDP decision is one of major magnitude to most companies. A sound decision usually requires consideration of a variety of choices. Most business-oriented computer systems are classified as general purpose. Not one of them will exactly fit a company's needs. The problem is to find the general purpose equipment that comes closest to matching the specific current and future requirements of the user. This task warrants full consideration of more than a single course of action.

Company Personnel

The caliber of company personnel engaged in a computer study will affect the usefulness of the manufacturers' proposals. Too often important data processing decisions, committing a substantial portion of a company's budget, are made by lower-level management personnel because of top management's failure to concern itself with the problem. Many unsatisfactory experiences with computer ventures can be traced to general management's reluctance to accept responsibility and participate personally in the EDP program. Despite innumerable articles warning of just such pitfalls, some executives erroneously assume that their personnel are experienced enough to administer an electronic computer program. The job of analysis is delegated to persons who are not properly equipped by training or background to make an evaluation. Their work is not reviewed by higher management or by outside professionals.

Unless general management becomes directly involved, particularly in designating the management problems the computer is expected to solve and in selecting specific applications, it will find that decisions of considerable financial magnitude are being made by lower-level personnel who are not familiar with the company's longrange plans. Top management participation is important in the proposal-preparation and proposal-evaluation stages of the study. Executives can gain valuable insight into equipment capabilities, potential solutions to company problems, and the relationships of equipment costs and labor savings by discussing directly with the manufacturers' representatives the methods by which the company's data processing goals can best be attained. Management can and should find the time to get involved; indeed, it must find the time.

Specifications

A computer manufacturer can write and present a useful proposal only if the prospective customer gives him adequate specifications. He must have information about the applications to be converted to the equipment, the structure of the orginization in which the EDP function will operate, and the expected future growth. The illustration with this article, taken from a set of specifications actually used by a large company as the basis for obtaining manufacturers' proposals, outlines the sort of information that should be included.

Specifications must be prepared in such a way that all proposals will be directed toward the same goals and all of them will contain directly comparable information. A company seeking manufacturers' proposals that will give it maximum assistance in evaluating the available choices will also encourage the manufacturers to discuss the specifications further and to request more detailed information if necessary.

By this time, of course, the company should have conducted an extensive systems study of its own to identify those applications that are truly appropriate for computer processing. Existing clerical or punched card processing procedures should be examined thoroughly for possible simplification, or even elimination, before they are included in the computer plans. Even more important is the necessity to analyze other areas of company operations that may have been overlooked in previous mechanization studies. The objective of installing a computer should not be merely to convert existing punched card procedures but rather to obtain additional benefits— for example, in information flow and analysis for decision making—in other areas not yet explored.

Soliciting Proposals

In presenting specifications to equipment manufacturers it is a good idea to invite the manufacturers' representatives to an orientation meeting. At this meeting they should be told about the general data processing problems, the applications to be converted and the approximate volumes encountered. Then each manufacturer should be asked to indicate whether he wishes to submit a proposal. Those who do should be given written descriptions of the company organization, current personnel assignments in the departments affected, the cost of existing office equipment and detailed data about the file sizes, volumes and report formats of the major applications to be converted.

It is important for the customer company to specify precisely what the proposals should contain, defining the required scope and degree of detail, such as procedural flow charts, cost data and savings projections, so that all proposals will be comparable. The manufacturers will probably need additional information and assistance from the prospective customer as they progress with the preparation of their proposals. Usually one man in the customer company is designated to perform this consultation function in order to avoid disrupting the entire office.

If the manufacturers are properly familiarized with the company's problems, the recommendations made in their proposals should demonstrate accurately how the equipment of each will fit the customer's needs. If they lack definitive specifications, the computer manufacturers will be able to submit only proposals with standard information applicable to any and all potential customers. They cannot prepare proposals tailored specifically to a particular customer.

Manufacturer's Studies

Even if the company under study gives the manufacturers considerable information about its operations, there still may be a marked difference among the manufacturers in the extent to which these data are utilized. The customer company should note how much thought and analysis each manufacturer has put into his proposal.

Some proposals show clearly that the suppliers have given considerable study to the information provided them and have attempted to understand fully the interrelationships of various functions and data and their less obvious implications. Such proposals may include detailed schedules specifying not only how but also when each operation could be done.

Work scheduling is normally a critical part of a data processing operation. A supplier who has not thoroughly explored the scheduling problems may be recommending a system that is actually incapable of meeting processing and reporting-time requirements even though its overall utilization falls within the allowable percentage. To be useful, proposals should include provision for processing a peak day's work as well as that of an average day. Problems that arise should not be passed over with a remark such as, "No problem; it can be solved during implementation." In the end the "no problem" issues may prove to be among the most costly and time-consuming to resolve.

In short, the scope and depth of the analysis conducted by manufacturers' personnel and the amount of time and thought they have apparently given to the company's problems should be taken into consideration in weighing the content of proposals.

Manufacturer's Personnel

There is a decided shortage of experienced computer systems analysts, a shortage that can be expected to intensify as the number of computer installations grows. Equipment suppliers as well as users suffer from this shortage. As a result, relatively inexperienced personnel may be developing the details of a manufacturers' proposal.

A customer company should attempt to evaluate to some degree the technical competence of the persons who made the study, formed the conclusions and submitted the recommendations. The advice of these persons is reflected in the manufacturers' proposal. Whether their advice really represents a sound application of the manufacturer's equipment to the company's problems depends in large part on their background and experience. Since these same men are likely to be the ones most directly responsible for assisting user personnel in planning the computer system to be programed, they will be instrumental in realizing the anticipated benefits. If there is any doubt of their technical competence, this doubt should be extended to the contents of their proposal.

Training Burden

All the major computer manufacturers have invested heavily in programs for customer education and training. They realize that if the market for computer equipment is to expand, there must be an adequate supply of personnel capable of effectively utilizing the equipment offered. Since other possible facilities for training, such as public schools, colleges and private trade schools, have just begun to establish programs in this field, the burden until recently has fallen almost completely on the manufacturers.

The manufacturers employ large staffs of persons with the highest qualifications. These qualifications include intimate knowledge of the electronic components of the hardware, thorough familiarity with the techniques of programing applications for the equipment, outstanding reputations in teaching and research and valuable work experience in a number of major industries. This reservoir of talent is being used in the education of thousands of computer system users. Without this investment there would be few persons qualified to serve in the computer field today.

All the EDP manufacturers employ personnel who are capable of giving material assistance to a potential user during the competitive equipment evaluation and during the other stages of a total feasibility study. However, there are two problems. There are not enough experts to go around, and there often is not sufficient time to do a thorough job of analysis for every prospective user. The manufacturer must use the personnel who are available at the time and location concerned, and manufacturers' representatives vary in the scope and level of their competence.

Regardless of the vast storehouse of knowledge available in the manufacturer's entire staff, it is the local account representatives who are responsible for applying the portion of this knowledge most applicable to each user's problem. Some representatives are experts on how the equipment operates but are less familiar with specific industry applications. Others may have many years of experience in the use of magnetic tape systems but may be beginners in the field of random access. One person may be a recent college graduate who has just completed his company's orientation courses. Another may be a veteran systems man—but with years of experience in punched card accounting, not EDP systems.

There is no question that the manufacturers on the whole have done a praiseworthy job and are continuing to do so. They are continually improving their own staff training programs in order to give their personnel the

OUTLINE OF AN ACTUAL SET OF SPECIFICATIONS FOR MANUFACTURERS

I. Letter to computer manufacturers inquiring whether they are interested in submitting proposals

II. General description of the company, its activities and its organization

III. Outline of present data processing equipment and applications

IV. General description of the company's plans for data processing in the future:
  • Anticipated date of installation of new system
  • List of general applications to be processed on the new system
  • Major considerations to be used in analyzing and comparing competitive proposals
  • Statement of processing schedules within which the work must be completed
  • Deadline for submitting proposals
  • Anticipated decision date
  • Name of company employee with whom computer manufacturers should work

V. Flow charts of major applications:
  • Short description of the purpose of each run
  • Estimated number of input transactions
  • Estimated number of master file records
  • Estimated number of output records
  • Estimated number of print lines
  • Estimate of volume growth

VI. Description of the input, output, card formats and report layouts, and master files to be used in the computer runs:
  • Name of file, card or report
  • Number of records or lines
  • Length of file
  • Items within a file, card or report

VII. Statement of specific information relating to various subjects to be forwarded by each manufacturer:
  A. Number of hours within which all processing will be completed
    • Proposed schedule of processing
  B. Statement of the type of charts and degree of detail of work sheets required to be submitted to support the proposal
  C. Equipment hardware:
    • Computer system proposed
    • Monthly rental
    • Definition of rental shift
    • Alternate lease plans
    • Extra shift charge per hour
    • Purchase price
    • Purchase option plans
    • Cost per reel of magnetic tape and/or disk packs
    • Estimate of number of reels and/or disk packs required
  D. Estimated delivery schedule
  E. Order cancellation terms
  F. Installation requirements:
    • Electrical power
    • Flooring and enclosure
    • Space
    • Air conditioning and humidity control
  G. Amount of qualified systems and programing help furnished:
    • Type of programing classes available and locations thereof
    • On-site training classes?
    • Nearest testing and debugging facilities
    • Amount of machine time to be made available without charge for debugging purposes before and after system delivery
    • Description of utility programs and the assembler and/or compiler programs with stated availability dates
  H. Identification of installation of similar equipment in the area that would be available for operational support in case of emergency

knowledge that will be of greatest value to the computer user. Nevertheless, a company reviewing manufacturers' proposals should attempt to examine the backgrounds of the men assigned to the job at hand as one means of ascertaining how much reliance can be placed on their recommendations.

It is all-important that the proposals received by the company be reviewed by personnel who are qualified to make an intelligent analysis. If all the previously mentioned rules have been followed and the manufacturers have presented meaningful proposals, a valid evaluation of their content is necessary.

Analyzing manufacturers' proposals in such a manner that the important factors to be considered are set forth clearly and management has the data needed to make a wise decision is a difficult task. A number of articles have discussed the evaluation procedures themselves; there is no need to go into them here. Companies without systems staffs of their own often should seek outside assistance in making the evaluation. Even when qualified personnel are available within the company, it is sometimes advisable to retain private consultants to ensure objectivity and minimize any internal politics that may exist.

The importance of the proposal analysis can hardly be overemphasized. The entire proposal program can be a complete waste of time if the information presented is not properly interpreted and analyzed.

Conclusion

Manufacturers' proposals can be highly useful to a company engaged in studying various electronic data processing systems. Properly used, these proposals should serve as a basis for evaluating how well the available systems hardware will fulfill the company's data processing requirements. Full benefits from their utilization, however, will be realized only when the suggested guidelines have been fully considered. These guidelines may be summarized as follows:

1. Be sure that the true purpose of gathering proposals is to provide a basis for an objective analysis of competitive systems.

2. Get general management directly involved at an early stage—once the decision has been reached to make an extensive investigation of competitive systems.

3. Furnish the manufacturers with all pertinent data so that the content of the proposals can be of the greatest possible value. The investment of time in discussion and explanation should reap high returns through improvement of the proposals submitted.

4. Note the scope and depth of study the manufacturer has applied to the information furnished him. Has he fully understood the problems? Has he recommended a workable system?

5. Attempt to evaluate the qualifications of the manufacturers' systems personnel. What are the scope and level of their technical competence?

6. Determine whether company personnel are qualified to interpret and analyze the proposal data. If not, is outside consulting assistance desirable?

Computer Leasing Provides Future Flexibility

Roland Raver

Much has been written about the so-called "computer revolution" which has swept through American industry. Now there seems to be a smaller revolution within the larger one. More and more companies are discovering the advantages of acquiring computer equipment by leasing through a third party. Having seen the advantages within my own company, we look for the continued rapid growth of this kind of contract.

Let me cite our experience and the factors involved in our decision to pursue our present course. You may find many of the circumstances I describe here present within your own company.

Hamilton Watch Company has two divisions; one is engaged in the manufacture of consumer products (watches and silver tableware) and the other is involved with making military products. Our consumer product sales have been growing at a consistently steady rate for many years. On the other hand, for obvious reasons, there has been a tremendous recent growth in our military products division. It is the latter which caused us to look into a computer leasing program.

Meeting the demands of rapid build-up in Viet Nam has increased our need for capital in a tight money market. This dictates a close scrutiny of

Reprinted by permission of the author and the publisher from *Financial Executive*, Vol. XXXV, No. 5 (May, 1967), pp. 18–20.

each capital investment to guarantee the maximum return. We know that by increasing our working capital in the manufacture and sale of products, we can get a better return on capital employed than in the purchase of EDP equipment. For years we have employed this broad strategy by leasing special purpose and high-obsolescence risk production machinery.

Options To Consider

Last year we were faced with the necessity of acquiring third generation computer equipment. Up to this time we had been renting our second generation equipment from the manufacturer under its standard rental plan. At this point, the following options were open to us:

1. Outright purchase from the computer manufacturer.
2. Installment purchase.
3. Normal rental plan of the manufacturer.
4. Purchase lease-back arrangement with a third party.

Let's examine the assets and liabilities of each.

Outright Purchase from the Manufacturer

There is one favorable factor here: if you ignore risk (both obsolescence and changes in your EDP workload), the out-of-pocket cash investment is less than the alternative plans.

Basically, the liabilities are two. First, you are forced to use a fairly large amount of your capital which could probably be used for a greater return in some other phase of your business. (The quoted purchase price was over $800,000 in our situation. This is a sizeable investment to make in a piece of specialized equipment that in the past has had a high-obsolescence factor). Second, you are locked into a certain type and number of pieces of equipment—a "specific configuration," as it is called. Certainly, financial management does its best to foresee the needs of its business in the forthcoming years. However well this planning is done, dealing with the future involves elements of risk. Should the need for computer equipment expand or contract materially from a company's forecast, it is faced with the problem of disposal and replacement.

Installment Purchase

Of course, the major advantage here is that you are able to conserve your capital to a degree. You are only expanding so much over a four- or five-year period. Against this advantage is the fact that the total amount paid is more than it would be under an outright purchase agreement. And again you are locked in with the equipment you *think* will be needed in future years. Lastly, you lose the tax advantage offered by a leasing arrangement.

This method of acquiring equipment seems best suited to a company which does not have enough capital to purchase outright and which can gauge the future of its business volume very accurately.

Short-Term Rental with the Manufacturer

Very simply, this method offers the most flexibility of all of the plans. It is by far the most expensive, however.

Third Party Leasing Arrangement

Since this is the method which Hamilton chose, I would like to discuss it in the greatest depth.

When it became known that we were in the market to replace our second generation equipment with third generation equipment, we were contacted by two kinds of leasing agencies in addition to the manufacturer.

Money Men and Specialists

One type of company was the strictly financial institution whose business activities take it into leasing arrangements on all kinds of capital goods. Hamilton had dealt with these financial houses in previous years in connection with the lease of machinery and equipment. Now, when we discussed leasing computer equipment with them, we found they offered very little flexibility. As with other types of machinery and equipment, these financial institutions offered lease plans on computer equipment whereby they were to receive the full return on their investment from the first lessee. In most cases this meant we would have to commit ourselves to a seven- or eight-year lease to take maximum advantage of this plan. To terminate the lease at any time prior to the end of the seven- or eight-year period, we would have had to make up any difference between the depreciated value of the equipment and its market price at that time. Thus, we would become involved in a financial transaction, the success of which would not be guaranteed. The success of this type of transaction is based in great measure upon the resale value of the computer in the market place, a factor of which we could have no knowledge and over which we would have no control.

The second type of leasing companies from whom we received inquiries were those which specialized exclusively in computer and allied equipment. These firms offered a variety of leasing plans, some of which met our requirements for flexibility as well as provided significant annual rental savings. The following are key factors which characterize lease plans:

1. Short- to medium-term commitment (usually two to five years).
2. The greater the term, the greater the discount.

3. Opportunity in some plans to add additional input/output devices and to add additional core memory and features to the central processing unit within the framework of the original lease.

4. Upon completion of the original lease, the opportunity to discontinue the arrangement with no further financial obligation, or, under some plans, the opportunity to renew for short terms at a greater discount than the original lease.

5. In some plans, the opportunity exists to repurchase the equipment from the leasing company, which usually depreciates the equipment and, therefore, the repurchase price at a greater rate than the manufacturer. This can be significant for those firms who want to develop and establish their systems on a proven operational basis before committing capital funds.

Advantage of Flexibility

After thorough evaluation, we chose Continental Computer Associates, Incorporated, a leasing company specializing in computers, for several reasons. First, our basic requirement in acquiring the needed computer equipment was one of flexibility. Our director of systems and our EDP manager are constantly aware of the tremendous improvements being made all of the time within the EDP industry. They were, accordingly, extremely reluctant to have our company tied up with a certain configuration for too long a period. Over the last ten years their department has been able to reduce EDP expenditures while at the same time adding tremendously to the volume handled. During this period, personnel costs had risen considerably, so these favorable results had been attained by prudent usage of the right kind of equipment. We did not want to tie their hands for the future and wished to give them as much leverage as possible in using new equipment. So we definitely did not want a long-term leasing agreement. We were able to obtain a short-term contract, the terms and conditions of which suited the leasing company's future use of the equipment, and our present need for flexibility. This was a very major advantage to us.

Maintenance by Manufacturer

Maintenance was the second factor of importance to be considered. The maintenance contract offered by various leasing houses varied. One contract called for all maintenance to be the sole responsibility of Hamilton. Another contract offered to us would have included the services of the financial house's own maintenance crew. Still another stated that the cost of all engineering changes would be charged to Hamilton.

The company that we chose proposed that all maintenance would be supplied by the manufacturer. The cost of this maintenance, including all materials, engineering changes and preventive maintenance, was included in the rental fee. In this way, our maintenance coverage remained the same, and we were assured of getting the necessary engineering changes required to keep our newly installed computer current. Our initial reservations about the manufacturer's cooperation if we signed with a leasing group quickly disappeared. The manufacturer has performed willingly and completely on every facet of service from maintenance through supplies to schools for our people. We could not have had better service if we had signed directly with them.

Overtime and Tax Considerations

Another factor in our decision was the expensive premium which we would have had to pay the manufacturer for any usage over the standard 176 hours. With our present contract, we enjoy significant savings in this area of overtime use.

Still another consideration was the tax factor inasmuch as we secured a substantial credit when we signed this type of lease agreement.

In essence, though, the three factors which were most influential in our decision to sign our contract were length of contract, maintenance arrangements, and annual rental savings.

The reasons given here for our choosing this method of acquiring computer equipment were those which applied specifically to Hamilton. However, based upon our experience, we believe that there are some generalities which can be applied throughout the business community.

Be Prepared for
Technological Changes

Certainly any well-managed company must be thinking years ahead. So do not get tied into equipment which will restrict your future activities. The money you save initially on one kind of contract can be lost many times over by placing yourself in a position where you cannot take advantage of new technological changes. If you do find that the equipment you are using will satisfy your needs beyond the life of your lease, you can get a contract agreement to extend its life at reduced rates.

Next, rely heavily on your professional systems and data processing people. As financial managers, the final responsibility for the success or failure of this phase of business is often ours. In areas such as maintenance, however, it would be almost impossible to act knowledgeably without professional counsel. You probably have the brains available to you; take advantage of them. And, if you do not have this competence within your organization, it is worth retaining a consultant for a project like this.

Next, make the proposals given to you fit the situation, not the other way around. Consider, for instance, how much you are going to use the equipment. You should certainly try to operate on more than a one-shift basis. It is cheaper to add people than it is to add equipment. By the way, this points out again the importance of a thorough maintenance contract, which includes service both day and night.

Another point to consider is the interpretation of your contract for tax purposes. Be sure it will not be considered as an installment purchase.

Evaluate very carefully the company with which you are negotiating a lease. While this is important in any transaction, it is particularly so here because of the tremendous amount of money involved. Make sure you are dealing with a reputable company. Have all options and extensions clearly spelled out. Get as much flexibility as possible.

Work with Professionals

If at all possible, deal with professionals in the area of computers and punch-card equipment. It was so much easier for us to work with a company completely staffed with professional data processing personnel than it was to deal with companies staffed with strictly financial men. Working with professionals gives you confidence, helps to avoid mistakes, and perhaps, most important—it saves time.

There are professionals in the computer business. It's worth your time to seek them out.

8   EDP SYSTEMS AND MANAGEMENT CONCEPTS

Changes in Management Methods Resulting from Advanced EDP Systems

Richard F. Peirce

Management and administrative methods are being changed as a result of three major changes in data processing: (1) increasing capabilities of equipment, (2) sharply declining cost of equipment and (3) the experience gained from prior systems which leads to development of still more advanced new systems.

The purpose of this article is to discuss the factors which are significant to management due to these data processing changes, to evaluate the impact of these factors upon accountants as members of management and to consider the action which should be taken to recognize the changes in management and administrative methods resulting from data processing changes.

Factors Significant to Management

A number of factors that are significant to the relationship of the various functions of a business to data processing are apparent. These include:

Reprinted by permission of the author and the publisher from *Management Accounting*, Vol. XLVII, No. 8, Sec. 1 (April, 1966), pp. 9–15.

1. The increasingly close coordination and cooperation among functions of a business. Business problems are increasingly complex both in product requirements and in the operating environment. This requires greater and more effective interchange of data. For example, planning requires the exchange and processing of increasingly large amounts of reliable current data for personnel, facilities, research activities, etc.

2. Data processing systems process the same data for the various functions of a business. For example, the engineering, material, accounting and manufacturing functions all must have the same data pertaining to the raw material inventories of the company.

3. The difficulty of maintaining reliability of data when separate systems are used by each function to process common data. These differences may be due to the absence of regularly scheduled reconciliations, the absence of double-entry accounting and, in many cases, the lack of dollars as a control field. For example, when employee data are maintained by separate systems for payroll and personnel, differences may constantly exist between the files.

4. The increasingly close relations among businesses and between businesses and the government require that more data be assembled from divisions and functions of a business and transferred to other entities. For example, data on employee savings plans may be forwarded to a trustee in a form suitable for data processing.

5. The reduction in clerical groups within each function. The effective administration of data processing systems frequently requires a single function to control input and output for the whole system. For example, the input for new employees, terminations, etc., should come through one source. Accounting frequently is a logical source for both input and output for a system.

6. The increasing confidence in information prepared by data processing. Businesses now recognize that with a well-designed system which includes adequate internal controls the data prepared are extremely reliable. For example, management reports are prepared and used on an exception basis without detail listings of all activity related to the reports.

7. The data processing knowledge of business requirements has reached the level so that normal changes can be made without changing systems or programs. This means that systems can respond very quickly to change, and systems and programming effort can be utilized much more effectively than in the past. For example, financial systems are designed so that departments, cost centers, burden pools, etc., may be changed without changing the programs.

8. The increasing usefulness of on-line real time systems using large random access storage, which allow immediate access to current data. For example, material administration can do a better job if they can obtain the exact status of orders quickly and cheaply.

9. The recognition that data processing can provide information in a form from which decisions can be made or actions taken without further processing. Because the first systems developed were largely conversions from EAM systems it has taken time to improve the usefulness of the data processing reports.

10. The recognition that, excluding productive activities, most functions usually have two basic categories of work:
    a. Policy and planning decisions.
    b. Administrative or clerical duties.
    The additional recognition that the administrative duties can be delegated to data processing without the loss of the right to make policy decisions. However, when data originate or are subsequently processed by another function, the type of processing may change radically. For example, automatic pay-rate increases for employees may be issued automatically by a payroll-personnel system, thus entirely eliminating clerical activity.

These factors have created an unparalleled opportunity for accountants to strengthen their position as members of management. Data processing should serve as the nerve center for the business and the financial function may administer this nerve center, However, this opportunity is a double-edged sword. If accountants fail to pursue this opportunity, their status gradually will be substantially reduced. We are seeing this effect of data processing in other functions, such as material, at the present time. For example, the significance of the material requirements function has been significantly reduced in some companies as production control systems have been tied into engineering systems. The number of materials ordered based upon maximum-minimum quantities may become relatively insignificant under this condition. The same could happen to the financial function.

Recognizing that the most serious mistake that can be made is to operate with an outdated financial system, plans should be developed to revise a number of the administrative and management activities. Before substantially more effective management systems can be developed, advanced systems must be developed to handle the administrative activities. The accurate and up-to-date data developed by the administrative activities serve as a basis for making decisions.

The most efficient data processing for a business usually is by resource rather than by function. Functional lines may create artificial boundaries to efficient processing of data. Functional lines tend to require separate processing of input data and master files for each function. This repetitive processing of data increases costs, reduces reliability of data, and makes planning more difficult.

The principle resources which serve as the basis for major data processing systems include employees, customers, suppliers, plant and equipment, products being designed, raw material inventories, inventories being manufactured and finished goods inventories.

The basic systems that are needed include:

Personnel administration—to contain data and process all activities relating to employees.

The purposes of this system include:

a. Determine pay, taxes and deductions.
b. Determine retirement benefits and related contributions into the retirement fund.
c. Accumulate data for government and industry reports such as the monthly Bureau of Labor report.
d. Determine reports dependent upon time such as automatic progressions, service awards, vacation pay and benefits, and salary and job reviews.
e. Determine capabilities within the company by selection of employees with required education and experience or other skills.
f. Select employees to fill vacancies, serve as consultants, or otherwise serve the company.
g. Prepare address listings for mailing.
h. Provide reference and location data such as telephone directories and personnel listings.
i. Provide internal statistical data with respect to age, sex, experience, rates of pay, job classifications, etc.
j. Prepare revised rates of pay based on general increases.
k. Assist in transfer or relocation of personnel based on fluctuations or relocation of productions.

Property administration—to contain data and process all activities relating to the plant and equipment of the business.

The purposes of this system include:

a. Provide data required to prepare financial statements.
b. Provide the ability to analyze plant and equipment to forecast depreciation, establish reserve ratios, review replacement policies, and make other studies.
c. Provide data required for income tax returns.
d. Provide data required for property tax reports.
e. Provide data for determining insurable values of property.

f. Establish the capability within the corporation to perform effectively with available plant and equipment.
g. Improve utilization of property.
h. Provide data to specific functions such as maintenance and calibration for specialized purposes.
i. Assure that surplus property is disposed of promptly.

The objectives listed for the personnel and property administration systems illustrate the broad scope and multifunctional nature of major systems. Correspondingly broad objectives exist for other systems:

Material administration—to process all activities relating to raw material inventories.

Engineering administration—to process all activities relating to product development.

Manufacturing administration—to process all activities relating to products being produced.

Marketing and distribution administration—to process the activities relating to finished goods inventories.

Financial administration—to tie together the other administrative activities and perform miscellaneous functions. This includes a purchasing-payable-commitment application which ties purchasing to material administration, property administration and miscellaneous activities. It also includes the distribution of burdens, preparation of ledgers and the preparation of reports accumulating and comparing actual and planned costs.

The Summary of Information Flows of the Major Resources of a Company Within Data Processing shown in Figure 1 illustrates the relationship of the major resource systems to financial administration.

Several obvious objectives such as the reduction of costs, improvement of reliability, prompter reporting of data and increasing flexibility apply to all systems.

We need to understand the impact of these resource systems on our financial activities to recognize how dramatically clerical activities may be reduced. For example, a property administration system can prepare a journal entry to record additions to property based upon a receiving document. The system can automatically provide a journal entry each month recording depreciation and can substantially reduce clerical effort in making transfers of property.

The improvement of administrative activities is the first major objective.

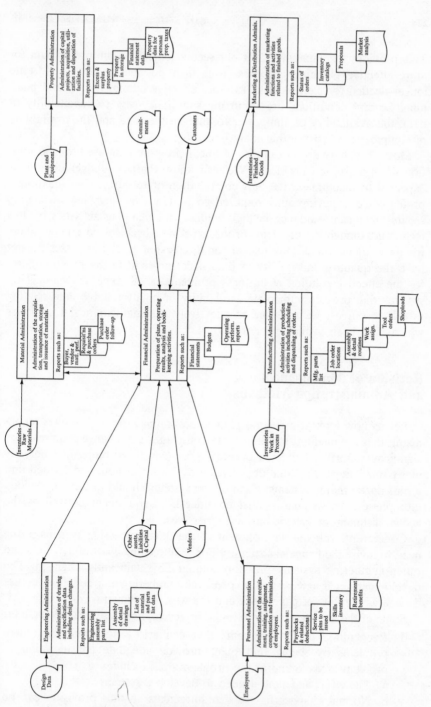

Figure 1. Summary of information flows of the major resources of a company within data processing.

This provides the capabilities for our second objective, the use of data for more effective planning purposes. It is then possible to direct effort no longer needed for clerical tasks to more effective administration and planning. Several conditions are occurring simultaneously, the availability of data, the availability of manpower to analyze the data and the availability of equipment to assist in this analysis.

Most of us have seen examples of linear programming used for the solution of optimization problems. We also know that the budget director is expected to recommend the best combination of resources that maximizes profits while achieving other required goals. However, very few businesses secure significant guidance in their budget and planning activities by this technique, though the problems of this type have been solved on computers for over fifteen years. One reason for this is that most businesses do not have the quantity and quality of data necessary and in the required form for the effective solution of business problems of this type. As we develop systems that provide immediate availability of highly reliable data relating to our resources, we are able to effectively use mathematical techniques which have been available for many years.

Revision of Management
and Administration Methods

Let us now look at a general plan to accomplish these objectives recognizing that for medium size and large companies any change requires very significant effort and that an eventual goal can be accomplished only by many small steps. The total objectives for a business should be divided into a half dozen major systems. Each of the systems should in turn be divided into phases. These phases must consider both equipment as well as the accomplishment of specific business objectives.

Concurrent with the development of the data processing systems is the need to revise the financial structure. For example, the chart of accounts and other numbering systems probably should be significantly changed. The development of a new system involves the numbering and coding structure as well as the flow of paperwork and the way programs process data.

Some of the key steps to be followed in developing these systems include:

1. Recognition of the problems that can arise and minimizing these problems by seeing that plans provide adequate consideration of problem areas. Some of the problem areas include:
   a. The effort and time needed to develop a system.
   b. Normal changes in users' requirements so that provision can be made to handle these changes without reprogramming.
   c. Cooperation with other functions.

    d. Recognition of the effort to supply input to the system. It may be better to have a system with very high reliability but lacking information of minor value than it is to have a system containing extremely extensive information but lacking reliability because of the effort required to create and maintain data in the system.

    e. Recognition that detailed reports may not be effective for control purposes because of the inability to read large amounts of data.

    f. Specific problems to be solved by the system. Frequently, these problems are not well defined.

    g. The extreme detail that must be considered in developing a system in making provision for every type and condition of input.

    h. Understanding of the capabilities of data processing by the user in order to derive the maximum benefits from the service.

    i. Recognition of effort required by the user to operate the system—the personnel training required to create input, maintain balancing controls and correct exception conditions.

    j. Consideration of cost of data processing.

2. Establish the general objectives of the overall financial system for the corporation prior to developing a specific system. Examples of general objectives are:

    a. The reporting structure which corresponds to the current organizational structure.

    b. Profit reporting by major groups within a division.

    c. The ability to analyze elements of cost for inventories—work in process and other accounts.

3. Establish the method or methods to accomplish each of the general objectives.

4. Form a task force with responsibility of establishing the specifications for a new system. The task force should have adequate representation of key employees from all functions and divisions.

5. For multi-divisional systems, identify specific areas of divisional and corporate responsibilities.

6. Determine the method for conversion.

7. Establish schedules for phases of the development.

The development of the new systems requires a corresponding management analysis function to use the data for more effective planning purposes. This function should include individuals knowledgeable in management tools such as linear programming and computer programming as well as financial analyses. The group should have access to a large time-shared computer which has data pertaining to the resources of the company on random access storage.

Summary

One of the most serious mistakes a financial function can make is to underestimate the significance of the management changes due to data processing. It is important to have plans for new administrative and decision making methods as it is to develop plans for new products and manufacturing methods.

Relatively few major data processing systems are needed by a company; one system for each of the basic resources of the company plus a financial system to link the other systems together. The scope of each system is very broad and encompasses several functions.

Management Information Technology in the Space Age

Michael R. Tyran

As one views the world's glowing accomplishments in outer space, it becomes apparent that the demonstrated successes to date are only the beginning to even greater human and equipment achievements in the space age exploration of the universe, ocean depths and the industrial technologies. These eventful conquests "whet the appetite" to make similar inroads of achievement in other fields of endeavor. The challenge is definitely here now—to accelerate our efforts in management information technology.

Although in some organizations, many applications have become mechanical, they are primarily concerned with the specific and detailed levels of information processing as, for example: accounts payable, the billing process, shop order control, payroll, labor distribution, etc. Still lacking is the emphasis on the overall management information concept and technology.

In this article, a plan will be outlined as to the why, what and how definitive direction can be established to achieve the desirable goals in management information technology. If the proper emphasis is placed on this effort, the results should be relatively comparable in scope and impact to those achieved in other fields.

Reprinted by permission of the publisher from *Management Accounting*, Vol. XLVIII, No. 8, Sec. 1 (April, 1967), pp. 3–13.

227

Today's Challenge

Inevitably, when any change is contemplated, questions always arise as to —"what's all the fuss about, we have been doing all right." Let us, however, review and inventory our position in information technology relative to some basic factors in our current environment as shown in Figure 1.

Neglect of any of the varied needs with respect to increasing information processing and reporting demands results in vendor and customer dissatisfaction, loss of discounts, late customer billings and larger working capital requirements, inadequate operation control, tardy or poor decision-making, renegotiation losses and so on. It is an accepted fact that everyone concerned with the direction and operation of any enterprise today must be "on his toes" if his organization is to survive in our complex way of life today. Effective, judicious and space-age oriented information processing is one important solution to the dilemma confronting us.

Information Processing Cycle

As a preliminary step to any decision involving a contemplated change to the space-age information processing philosophy, our present and future planning should be directed to the review and evaluation of the following pertinent considerations:

1. What is needed to accomplish the information processing task more effectively and expeditiously?
2. What tools are available to satisfy the requirements?
3. What planning is involved, what is its scope, and are the technically qualified personnel available?

Growth in Retail Volume
Equipment Availability
Changing Requirements
"State of the Art" Progress
Timeliness in Decision Making

Flexibility in Changing Plans (Budgets, Forecasts)
Greater Concentration on Analysis VS Manually Generated Reports
Growing Complexity in Customer Reporting

Competition from Competitors (Keeping up with the Joneses)

Improve Planning and Controls on
        Contract Status/Performance
        Cash Requirements
        Manpower Level
        Fixed Asset Budget
        Direct/Indirect Ratios
        Contractual Requirements

Figure 1. Today's challenge.

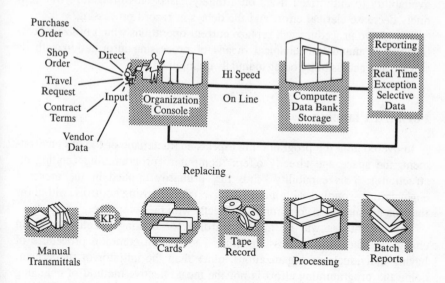

Figure 2. Information processing cycle.

4. Is management information technology really a need, a "must" or a "luxury" convenience to our organization's operation?

Figure 2 illustrates the direction that has occurred or will occur in many organizations if they are to achieve the maximum utilization or benefit from progressive information technology. The basic document data must be mechanically processed at its point of origin to achieve direct acquisition by the computer. The reasons are obvious from the standpoint of timely usage, control and data access by all concerned. Further, as related information is transmitted into the computer, the input can be manipulated and integrated for reporting significant and sequenced event data such as location status of the effort concerned (shop order control for example), fulfillment of specific contract requirements (in accordance with contract terms), etc.

The major objective of this process is timely flow and integration of the various related items of data so as to produce a composite set of facts rather than scattered "bits and pieces" of incomplete information. The latter result can only lead to improper evaluation of a given situation.

You will further note on this chart that the input and response transactions will be by wire communication between the station and the computer itself, with the urgency of need governing the timing of the input and retrieval requirements. Physical source-document movement will be minimal since the orginating paper will remain in the organization generating the paper-work with the information being transmitted to a central storage file for availability to authorized users on a timely basis. This procedure will definitely decrease clerical effort and the delays in record processing.

The above procedure will replace current operations which utilize a combination of manual/mechanical means of processing information with its storage and accessibility being manually maintained.

Forward Planning

In overcoming the programming aspects characteristic of today's environment, the space age already offers "computer" programming (coding instructions). This capability—thus far, primarily applied in the areas of engineering—coupled with more effective teleprocessing controls, will allow the systems analyst to communicate directly with the computer.

The advantages will be most rewarding for making effective program changes in the shortest possible time. The present common procedure of having individuals or organizations, other than the initiator of the system, doing the programming effort is not the most effective method of changing computer operation direction. The adoption of a single programming language (hopefully, universal and layman oriented) will certainly accommodate the concept of the systems analyst initiating and directly implementing the computer operation requirements.

The most neglected area in information processing to date has been the planning required in organizing for and determining management information needs. Valid and intelligible information is the result of a well-planned and organized system analysis and development effort—this is a "must" whether the procedure calls for manual or mechanical processing. Information is a most vital link or element of consideration in planning, managing, controlling and making decisions. It can be dynamic or dull and unmanageable. It can provide the guidance for improving your operation or misguide the user into inadequate or no decision-making. It can "make or break" you or your organization when one is involved with the planning effort concerned with sales, profits, expansion, employee morale, union difficulties, etc.

Figure 3 displays some of the more characteristic factors involved in past and current management information system development. The space-age concept requires techniques that must be exploited to obtain the desired results. A systematic approach, using scientific techniques with proper application and data integration, is the primary tool which will materially improve our information development and processing.

This procedure will allow you to simulate particular business conditions, test alternate plans and courses of action based on varied premises and eliminate much of the "guesswork" in the planning aspects of a business operation. There is no substitute for the "right information" on a timely basis

Past & Present

Space Age

Tape Storage Oriented
Unsophisticated Software
Expensive
Computer Usage Conflicts
Fear of Personnel Displacement

Third Generation of Equipment
Disc/Mass Storage
Time Sharing
Improved Cost Performance
On Line/Real Time
Video/Audio Response
Microfilming
Direct Access/Retrieval

Program "Patching"
Competition for Technicians
Multi Language Coding

Computer Programming
Single Language
Performed by Concerned
   Organization

Grew Out of Necessity
Improper Planning
Piecemeal

Systematic Analysis
Scientific Techniques
Data Integration
Clerical Effort Minimal
"State of Art" Sophistication

Figure 3. Forward planning.

for adequate planning and control. In other areas of endeavor, such as research and development, engineering, manufacturing, etc., these sophisticated techniques have been used for years, why not in organizations responsible for financial management information?

Changing Organization Relationship

The importance of the computer will have considerable influence and impact on space age organization relations. The computer and its related information technology advances have forced the need to cross all organization lines and functional activities.

Figure 4 indicates this overlapping relationships between organizations, and their dependence on the computer and its capabilities to fulfill their needs. As earlier discussed, the data from all organizations will be transmitted to a central computer for various processing activities such as sorting, updating, editing, integrating and storing. All organizations will be contributors to the processing of related information involved in any organizational activity. Each organization has its own contribution to the whole.

As operating activity occurs in each area, statistical information is pro-

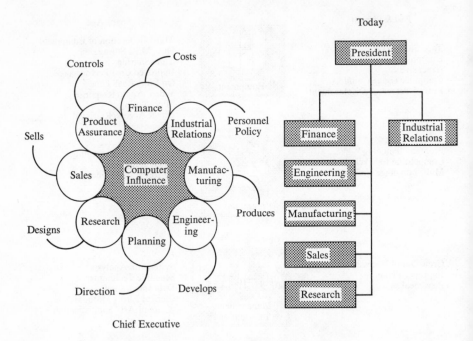

Figure 4. Changing organization relationship.

duced on costs, scheduling and performance. This data then becomes the basis for planning, controlling, scheduling, costing and monitoring the progress of the effort. As information develops from various transactions and activities, whether it be procuring supplies or performing direct or indirect functions, the data will be transmitted directly into the computer for file processing and storage. As organizations have a need to know in their planning, managing and controlling functions the overall or specific aspects of the activity's progress pertinent to their participation, they will be able to query and retrieve the appropriate information directly from the computer file.

All organizations will be originators as well as users of the data, thus making them interrelated and dependent on each other for information, with the computer being the processing controller and agent. Each organization will then be able to obtain and assimilate facts and figures for its operating needs in a timely manner. Information processed under this procedure will be complete and meaningful.

Figure 4 also illustrates the general organization structure of today. In many organizations much of the computer data is prepared for Finance and, in many instances, the reports relative to various activities are distributed to other organizations where they are interpreted, rearranged and reported for their particular and specific needs. This effort on their part necessitates many independent recordkeeping systems. Under the integrated data processing system, as discussed above, it is expected that collective requirements will be available in one general file from which can be extracted an organization's specific need in the form required, thus eliminating extensive record-keeping and reports.

Decision-Making Process

In our space-age environment, it will be a "way of life" to exploit the sciences for guidelines in establishing the bases for analyzing and projecting business operations, as shown in Figure 5.

The development of various statistical equations and models is a relatively simple task through the use of computer capability which accommodates mass storage or historical data that can be used in building appropriate and pertinent models. The major effort in this type activity will be the development of the procedure(s) or system necessary for instructing the computer in the process of manipulating the data to achieve the desired results.

Some simple examples of computer models that can be developed for planning and controlling purposes are (1) establishing fixed-variable relationships in overhead expense as related to direct labor hours or dollars,

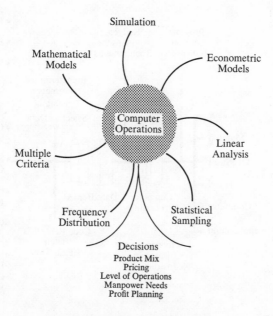

Figure 5. Decision making tools.

(2) volume-cost-profit correlations, (3) graphical breakeven point analyses, (4) sales volume versus capital required and the zone of profitability, (5) predicting future employment and price relationship, etc. Any manual technique used as a criteria for the decision-making process can undoubtedly be formalized into a computerized mathematical model. These models can then conceivably serve the purpose of testing the fallibility of estimates and conclusions through the probability methods.

Management Information Integration

In order to achieve the kind of information technology required to fulfill space age needs, the means must be established for integrating this data in a logical manner so that it can be manipulated, stored and retrieved readily on demand in the required form. As Figure 6 indicates, source detail, derived from purchase orders, receiving memos, travel requests, shop orders, etc. will be related to the common cost elements involved in the recordkeeping and reporting system. This information will be inputted into the system by direction of the "program action indicators." The information transmitted will be processed in accordance with the program instructions.

Additional data, in the form of budget detail, plans and requirements, will also be inputted into the program. Data banks will be updated and informa-

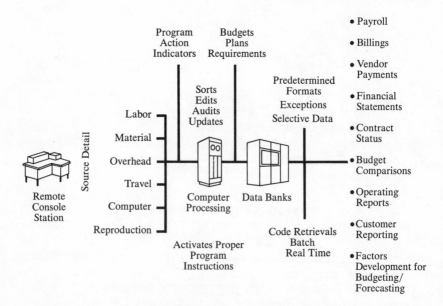

Figure 6. Data integration.

tion stored for retrieval on a selective, exception or batch process basis. If appropriate, predetermined formats will govern the output display.

The program will be constructed to provide in one report various elements of data. For example, the billing report will reflect labor, overhead, material, travel and computer costs, individually, for a given time period. Financial statements will reflect all of the elements currently contained therein starting with costs and fees to the sales buildup by contract and organization totals. Budget information will be appropriately entered on the reports requiring this data for comparative purposes.

In today's environment, information is stored on a number of magnetic tapes. To obtain a composite report of various elements of cost, the computer must extract this data from a number of tape records. A detailed instruction program must be written to make this type of extraction possible. The current practice is for information to be outputted "piecemeal" on many different reports and then manually consolidated in the form required.

The objective is to integrate data (all elements) into one central storage area in a manner conducive to ease of access, retrieval and reporting. This makes it possible to achieve various combinations of data reporting. It also reduces computer processing time and storage. The central file concept is the only efficient way to meet the data reporting demands in the future.

Integrated Record Processing

As discussed above, management information technology is dependent on the central file storage technique for reporting advantages. As noted in Figure 7, this procedure requires remote station input into a teleprocessing control system which, in essence, then governs the complete manipulation of the input, its control, storage and reporting. The teleprocessing controller is the monitor of the internal computer data processing activity.

This Figure shows that incremental data will be transmitted into your detailed data collection system where it will be screened as to its validity, edited and sorted. Invalid data will be rejected and transmitted back to the originating organization for correction. The valid increments of cost input will be entered into their properly classified files for the updating process. Listings of the computer-accepted input will be printed out for use in verification of submissions and as a reference tool by the concerned organizations. Internal computer records and instructions will associate certain other reference identifiers (charge and account numbers, etc.) to the data in order to update all of the appropriate files.

Data input may fall into various types of detail and summary files whose content depends on user needs. The incremental data inputted on a daily, weekly or monthly basis will update the basic or detail file records concerned with a specific journal voucher, account, work order, cost element, etc. This information is then further used in your cumulative system to update the summary files such as the cost and work in process ledger, project status file, etc. The organization and content of these files provide the basis for specific reporting needs. Other required information such as budgets, commitments and allocations will be included in your summary files to produce the proper comparisons and status reports as required.

The teleprocessing system will extract predetermined formats of data requirements and/or other specific information based on code inquiry need. The complete process of manipulating data and its storage will be a computer function. As soon as the data is released from its source and accepted by the teleprocessing control system, no further human intervention is necessary unless there is a need for specific changes or additions to the system. As discussed earlier, the vast storage of statistical data is available for other computer oriented activities such as the development of historical trend lines and statistical models for planning purposes.

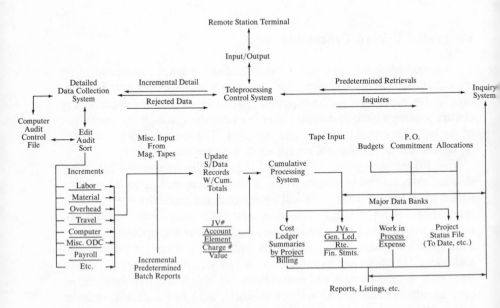

Figure 7. Integrated record processing.

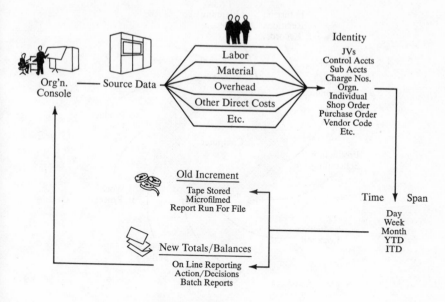

Figure 8. Record storage.

Record Storage

Figure 8 indicates the records contained in the computer file, as it shows the flow of source-document information into cost element categorization and then, classified, to its various subidentifiers. This is necessary in order that the information can be properly controlled, updated and reported to the various levels of need. The data must also be associated to a time span in order that the update process can be appropriately achieved.

In other words, the input can be submitted at any time of day (dependent on the schedule) and in the update process the daily, weekly, monthly, year-to-date and inception-to-date files will be simultaneously adjusted accordingly. The old incremental totals and balances can then be stored on tape or microfilmed whereas your new data will be available as an immediate source for "on line" or batch processing reporting.

Common Data Usage

Each element of information is used for a variety of purposes and reports. The reporting systems in today's environment have become voluminous with increased computer processing time in order to satisfy reporting demands.

Figure 9 indicates the usage made of labor distribution information. Most

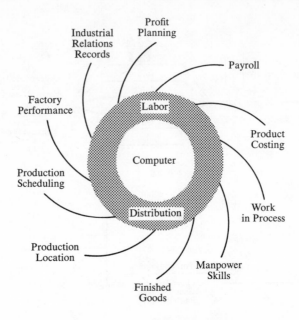

Figure 9. Common data usage.

everyone concerned with an organization's operation is involved with some facet of labor system. Labor data is needed for product costing, the location of the effort involved, workload scheduling, performance measurement, profit planning, etc.

Having information integrated and establishing its common usage, it is possible to produce composite reports which will greatly reduce and/or eliminate much of the single-purpose reporting. Common data usage also alows for satisfying the needs of a number of organizations for specific data from one central file.

Management Planning

In today's environment, the time span between establishing the premises of a plan and its mathematic construction for analysis and evaluation is quite lengthy. This situation does not afford management an opportunity to review the complete substance of the plan adequately nor the opportunity to make changes that can be readily reflected and adjusted results known on a timely basis.

In this computer age, it is expected that instructions reflecting initial premises, factors, decisions, etc., will be entered into the computer from remote station locations. Computer storage files of historical data, program control instructions and cost data banks are all absolute necessities for the management planning process. The computer controller, having received its input, will initiate the action required to produce preliminary data and guidelines for management evaluation relative to the development of a proposed plan and any required, subsequent deviation from the original premises will be quickly incorporated to indicate the effect of the change.

The kind of data that is planned for development by the computer is shown in Figure 10. It will be in terms of manpower trend, overhead rate predictions, projected dollar value of labor, material and other direct costs amounts, cash requirements, need for space expansion, etc. This information will be printed out in predetermined formats representing financial schedules or other specific and selective type report requirements. The initial output will be the basis for developing the projected formal plan of action.

It is planned that this data will be retrieved by the concerned management personnel through the media of audio, video or hardcopy communications. It will be reviewed by management who will decide what changes should be made in order to finalize the projected plan of action. Changes would be incorporated via wire transmission to the computer controller for data bank and management plan update and adjustment.

In a typical situation today, masses of detail have to be reviewed manually and factors and parameters established which can be used for application to

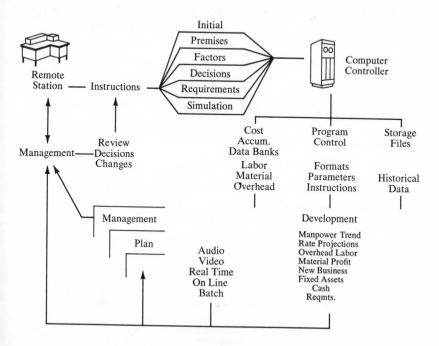

Figure 10. Management planning.

the anticipated conditions in the future. For example, orders booked on a firm basis would indicate a certain level of manpower. This manpower would be translated into hours of effort and priced. The need for space and working capital requirements would also be determinable through programmed criteria. Any change in the basic data has to be reflected throughout the complete plan detail. This is a major task to do manually; however, information technology through scientific techniques will make it possible for the computer to perform this activity in minimal time and greater detail than has ever before been possible.

Summary

Management information technology is a "must" in the space age. Business operations are increasing in complexity due to such factors as its changing role in relations with the U.S. and Foreign Governments, labor unions, communities, competition, reporting needs, etc. Intelligent and effective decisions will be even more important in the advancing space age.

The approach to meet this need for reliable and advanced information technology requires thorough, competent and complete planning through systematic analysis of what ·the requirements are and how they can best be achieved. The "total" information concept is a major factor in our review of what has to be done. This factor cannot be overemphasized.

- Here to stay

- Scientific technology application is a must

- A management tool for assistance in
    planning
    controlling
    decision process

- Must be thoroughly planned

- Must consider the "total" information aspect

- More emphasis on systems to reduce
  costs/disappointments on computer end

- Every good computerized information process results
  from good systems' techniques

- Computers are the means, systems are the way,
  meaningful information is the need!

- Must be oriented to space age philosophy and thinking

**Figure 11. Information technology
(summary).**

The increase in voluminous paper work makes it mandatory that steps be taken to achieve selective and exception reporting which also will eliminate the need for management's specific attention to routine activities. The question arises—"what are you doing about this situation before it becomes too late?"

The third generation of equipment is here now and its capabilities lend themselves to achieving the type technology required for space age information collection, processing and reporting. As Figure 11 indicates, the decision tools and technology are also available. Simplification and reduction in reporting volume will allow time for greater concentration on the planning aspect of a business operation. Video displays in the form of graphs, charts and selective reporting will enhance management's overall grasp of the organization's operating conditions which, in turn, can only result in more realistic and educated decision-making for managing and controlling an organization's activities successfully.

9   EDP AND BUSINESS ORGANIZATION

The Organizational Impact of Computers

Hak Chong Lee

From the earliest days of electronic data processing there has been general agreement that the new information technology would have a profound impact upon the structures and personnel of the organizations that adopted it. There has been much less agreement about the nature of that impact.

Predictions of widespread labor displacement, the elimination of middle management and increasing centralization of decision making have not yet come true. On the other hand, they have not yet been conclusively disproved. Despite more than a decade of rapid expansion of the use of computers and growing sophistication in their application, the patterns of change are not yet clear.

A number of research studies have supplemented the speculation and opinions about the impact of the computer on business organizations, but their results differ to such a degree that it is difficult to gain a clear understanding of exactly what is happening. The purpose of this article is to summarize and evaluate the present knowledge of how computers are affecting organizational structure, administrative decision making, employment and the skill content of employees' jobs; to determine the extent to which indi-

Reprinted by permission of the author and the publisher from *Management Services*, Vol. IV, No. 3 (May–June, 1967), pp. 39–43.

viduals agree on these effects; and, if conflict is found, to analyze the arguments.

The first question about which there has been a great deal of discussion is whether computers are going to centralize or decentralize the organizational structure and the process of administrative decision making. The best known and perhaps most controversial view on this question was expressed by Harold Leavitt and Thomas Whisler in their famous *Harvard Business Review* article, "Management in the 1980's."[1] In that article they made three important predictions.

First, they forecast that electronic computers would change the organizational structure drastically by forcing the regrouping of activities carried out in various functional divisions and at various levels of the organization. Because computers would make it possible to integrate on the basis of the organization as a whole a large volume of business information that was formerly segmented, a computer-using company would find it expedient to standardize operational procedures throughout the organization. This would lead to a great deal of consolidation of activities that had been functionally and geographically separate.

Secondly, Leavitt and Whisler predicted increased use of computers to process more and more of the routine management decisions. Assuming that the bulk of middle managers' work consisted of rather routine decisions, these authors concluded that middle management jobs would gradually be automated and taken over by computers. Thus, the magnitude of the computer's impact would be proportionately greater at the middle management level than at the clerical level.

They also foresaw a shift to top management of a larger proportion of innovating, planning, and creative functions, with concomitant centralization of the organization structure and the decision making process. All these changes would have a drastic effect on the shape of the organizational structure. Top management would "bulge" as middle management would "thin out." The overall organizational structure would change from the traditional pyramid shape to a shape looking something like a "football balanced upon the point of a church bell."

A number of actual research studies have tended to support the views of Leavitt and Whisler. Ida Hoos, for example, found in her study of nineteen business organizations[2] that computer applications in these companies had led to some radical changes in the organizational structure and in managerial decision making. Many jobs at middle management levels had been either

[1] Harold J. Leavitt and Thomas L. Whisler, "Management in the 1980's," *Harvard Business Review*, November–December, 1958, pp. 41–48.

[2] Ida R. Hoos, "When the Computer Takes Over the Office," *Harvard Business Review*, July–August, 1960, pp. 102–112.

combined or eliminated. Communication systems and decision making patterns in the organizations were undergoing changes, generally in the direction of centralization. As more and more operations were programed in the data processing department, the functions of operating departments were often undercut and the authority of many department managers truncated while the power and status of new computer personnel expanded.

Acceptance of Leavitt and Whisler's views is far from unanimous, however. Melvin Anshen,[3] for example, agrees with them about the increased use of computers in the areas of managerial decisions. But he takes issue with them on the question of how computers are going to affect the organizational structure and the locus of decision making.

Anshen believes that computers will be limited to repetitive decisions based on already quantified records of existing accounting, cost, and financial data and will leave relatively untouched such managerial decision areas as finding problems, setting objectives, implementing decisions and evaluating results, all of which require a great deal of management imagination and creative thinking. As a result, instead of gradually eliminating middle managers, computers will relieve them of repetitive decision making and related paperwork and thus give them more time to concentrate on creative and judgmental tasks. Instead of being shifted upward or absorbed completely into computers, the work of middle managers may become more like that of top managers.

Anshen denies that computers will necessarily lead to centralization of the organization structure or the decision making process. The trend toward decentralization may be slowed down, he says, but if this happens it will be caused by the geographic relocation of decision centers, not by abandonment of efforts to decentralize managerial responsibilities.

Anshen's views have also been supported by research studies. Donald Shaul,[4] for example, found in a number of companies that had installed electronic computers that middle managers had not been seriously threatened but rather that their roles in the organization had become more important than ever. The organization structure had not changed a great deal, offering little indication that greater centralization follows the installation of computers.

There is general agreement that computers, with their vast capacity to manipulate management information, will affect the process of managerial decision making. There is much less agreement, however, on the scope of the computer's potential in automating decisions and on the vulnerability of middle managers to displacement by computer programs. It is also recog-

---

[3] Melvin Anshen, "Manager and the Black Box," *Harvard Business Review*, November–December, 1960, pp. 85–92.

[4] Donald R. Shaul, "What's Really Ahead for Middle Management?" *Personnel*, November–December, 1964, pp. 8–16.

nized that the use of computers tends to require standardization of operating procedures and integration of data. Opinions differ, however, as to whether these changes necessarily mean more centralization of decision making and a change in the conventional pyramid form of organization structure. The evidence so far on all these points is inconclusive.

Manpower Displacement

Another hotly debated question is the effect of computers on employment. At issue are both the effect on total employment—in the company and in the economy—and the effect on the relative proportions of various types of employees, such as managers, technical personnel and clerical workers.

Technological employment has been a controversial subject since the time of the Industrial Revolution, but concern has heightened in recent years because of the growth of computer "automation." Reduction in the number of employees (usually clerical) in that part of the organization immediately and directly related to the computer operations has been widely anticipated. This anticipation has proved correct for the most part, as is shown by a number of research studies.[5] However, there has been no reduction in clerical employment in the economy as a whole and often none in the individual companies affected. The effect of the computer seems to have been to slow rather than reverse the rate of growth in clerical employment.

The computer's effect on the relative proportion of various types of employees is less clear-cut. As was previously discussed, Leavitt and Whisler expect that, since much of the work of middle managers can and will be programed into computers, manpower reduction will be greater at the management than at the clerical level. On the other hand, Anshen's belief that computerization will be limited to routine, repetitive decisions implies the reverse.

Actual research findings so far seem to support Anshen's view rather than that of Leavitt and Whisler. Indications are that manpower reductions have been greater in the clerical than in the managerial work force, both in absolute terms and in proportion to the total employment in the organization.[6] In some cases, indeed, the total number of managers in computer-affected departments has increased rather than decreased. Whether this trend may be expected to continue is far from certain at this time, particularly in view

[5] For example, see Hak Chong Lee *The Impact of Electronic Data Processing Upon the Patterns of Business Organization and Administration*, Shcool of Business, State University of New York at Albany, 1965, pp. 27–29.

[6] For example, see U.S. Bureau of Labor Statistics, *Adjustments to the Installation o, Office Automation*, Bulletin No. 1276, Department of Labor, Washington, D.C., May, 1960, and Edgar Weinberg, "Experiences with the Introduction of Office Automation," *The Monthly Labor Review*, April, 1960, pp. 367–380.

of the growing sophistication with which the computer is being applied to managerial decision making.

The only personnel change that seems to be more or less certain is that the installation of a computer increases the number of staff positions, mostly technical, directly associated with the computer operations. This increase is both absolute, in terms of total numbers, and relative, in proportion to the total employment.

Job Content

Another problem is how computers change the work content of those jobs that remain. The questions include how computers affect the overall skill level required in a job; how they affect specific work skill aspects of a job, such as mental, clerical, physical, etc.; and how they affect the distribution of work skill content among various types of jobs, such as clerical and managerial.

Because of the assumption that technology tends to mechanize unskilled and routine tasks, it is generally thought that computers tend to reduce the unskilled work component and increase the skilled task work component of affected jobs. There is considerable support for this view.

As was discussed earlier, Anshen believes that the jobs of computer-affected middle managers will be upgraded when computers take over the routine tasks, leaving the managers free for more creative and more analytical work.[7] Shaul's previously cited study also supports the idea of increased skills for managerial personnel.[8]

George Delehanty found in his study of several insurance companies[9] that the general skill level of clerks was shifted upward after computers began to be used. After the installation of computers in these organizations, as compared to before the computer, there were fewer clerical jobs distributed over low-grade classifications and more jobs over high-grade classifications. There also are other studies that generally support the existence of a tendency toward increased skill requirements in clerical jobs as well as managerial ones.[10]

Other studies, however, have indicated a different tendency. Some researchers, finding that computers upgraded some jobs while downgrading others, concluded that it was difficult to find a consistent pattern one way or

---

[7] Anshen, *op. cit.*

[8] Shaul, *op. cit.*

[9] George E. Delehanty, "Office Automation and the Occupation Structure: A Case Study of Five Insurance Companies," *Industrial Management Review*, Spring, 1966, pp. 99–110.

[10] For example, see Harold F. Craig, *Administrating a Conversion to Electronic Accounting*, Harvard Graduate School of Business Administration, Boston, 1955, pp. 68–70.

the other.[11] Other studies have found the skill level of the affected jobs largely unchanged; upgrading was limited to so small a number of jobs that there was practically no change in the overall work skill requirements after the computer installation.[12]

A study by James Bright,[13] however, showed a definite—and different— trend of change in work skills as a result of technological change. Through intensive analyses of different stages of computer-integrated manufacturing technology, he found that work became easier and less demanding at high stages of technology. Thus, he suggests a pattern of decrease rather than increase in the overall level of skill requirements.

Here again, the verdict must be "not proven." Much more research needs to be done on the computer's effect on skill requirements; existing observations on the subject are largely in generalities, lacking precise measurement of the magnitude of changes.

Special Problems

Why do opinions and research findings about the organizational impact of computers differ so sharply? One obvious problem is semantics. Frequently those whose opinions differ also differ in the meanings they attach to such key words as centralization, decentralization, decisions, work skills, managers, clerical workers and technical employees. This, of course, magnifies the differences among the opinions and also presents serious methodological problems in the conduct of research studies and the evaluation of their findings. It is crucial that a common understanding of these vital terms be attained by everybody.

Another, perhaps more important, problem is the discrepancy among evaluations of computer technology. "Experts" differ not only about future developments in computer science and the possibility of programing currently "unstructured" decisions but even about the current capability of computers in decision making.

Furthermore, the results of research studies in different organizations may differ because of differences in the way computers are used and the length of time they have been used in these organizations. For example, in companies that have been using computers primarily for accounting and financial purposes for a relatively short period of time the organizational changes may not be as drastic or as extensive as in companies where computers have

[11] C. Edward Weber "Impact of Electronic Data Processing on Clerical Skills," *Personnel Administration*, January–February, 1959, pp. 20–26.

[12] Jack Stieber, "Automation and the White-Collar Worker," *Personnel*, November– December, 1957, pp. 12–16.

[13] James R. Bright, *Automation and Management*, Harvard University, Boston, 1958, pp. 186–189.

been used for management decision making purposes and/or for a longer period of time.

A final source of conflicting opinions is the failure of researchers to recognize the importance of managerial philosophies, objectives and policies toward both the computer applications and the changes that these applications are expected to bring about in the organization. The managerial attitude toward initiating and accommodating the changes is also a major variable governing the nature and magnitude of changes in the organizational structure, in employment and in the work content of affected jobs.

Clearly, understanding of how computers affect the organization is essential to effective manpower and organizational planning. It is important, therefore, that the various opinions and research findings on the impact of computers be evaluated and interpreted with adequate cognizance of (1) the variations in the meaning given to key terminology used in describing the changing organizational patterns, (2) the nature and maturity of computer applications in an organization, and (3) the managerial attitude toward introduction and handling the changes in the organization. Recognition of the semantic problems and of the variables conditioning the organizational changes will promote better understanding of the nature of the computer's impact.

It is also important to realize that computer technology is always advancing, that computer applications are continually expanding, and that managerial philosophies and policies are continually adapting to changes in the technological environment.

Thus, the organizational impact of computers is changing all the time. As a result, continuing study is needed to clarify the issues and search for major organizational variables that may underlie the definite patterns of change that may be common to all computer applications.

Information Technology and the Accounting Organization

Sexton Adams
Doyle Z. Williams

In recent years many predictions have been made about the impact of "information technology" on the traditional accounting function. The consensus is that the accountant of the future will find himself swept into a new role. This role may be one that enhances the accountant's importance in the business organization, or it may be one in which he is subservient to a more broadly conceived organizational function.

One author recently wrote, "It is possible that future organization charts will show a 'director of [total] management information,' whose responsibilities will include the disciplines of statistics and operations research as well as accounting and its already related activities such as budgeting, cost accounting, electronic data processing, and systems analysis. . . . This function is beginning to evolve in some companies but in a somewhat disorganized and unidentified manner."* For a firm to realize its maximum potential, this author suggested, there must be a systematic, integrated approach to the realignment of the accounting organization in the wake of information technology advances.

Reprinted by permission of the authors and the publisher from *Management Services*, Vol. III, No. 5 (September–October, 1966), pp. 15–23.

*Harold W. Jasper, "Future Role of the Accountant," *Management Services*, January–February, 1966, pp. 51–56.

Case History

In any case, the advent of information technology in any firm has an immediate impact on the accounting organization and ultimately on the total organization structure. The exact nature of the changes wrought by information technology is rapidly becoming more clear-cut and more readily identifiable.

This article examines the impact of information technology upon the accounting organization of a large, progressive American corporation. This company, a leader in its field, has long been an advocate of continual modernization in all phases of its operations. The empirical evidence presented here concerning the reorganization of the accounting activities of this company indicates how the introduction of information technology may affect the location of the accounting function. In addition, an examination of the development of an actual integrated processing system, with the related organizational changes, may provide some hint as to the future nature of the accounting function in large industrial enterprises.

Punched Card Equipment

This company readily accepted a mechanized data processing system in the late 1930's, when it acquired an installation of IBM punched card equipment. This installation was located in, and operated by, the accounting division and was devoted entirely to accounting operations. Acquisition of new equipment continued over the years, particularly during the period immediately following World War II, as more and more of the accounting work was mechanized. The organization chart in Figure 1 reflects the location of the accounting division within the organizational structure in the mid-1940's. It should be noted that the head of the accounting department reported directly to the president's office.

By the early 1950's the original investment in punched card equipment had been substantially increased. In broadening the applications of this equipment, the company concentrated on the mechanization of accounting work as a means of cost reduction. As a result, the number of accounting division employees was reduced from 263 in 1946 to 174 in the early 1950's. As a result of plantwide interest, data processing activities were gradually expanded to other departments. By mid-1953 a considerable amount of nonaccounting work was being performed on IBM equipment.

Equipment Limitations

In the mid-1950's the systems staff in the accounting division became convinced that the limit in cost reductions and improved systems had been

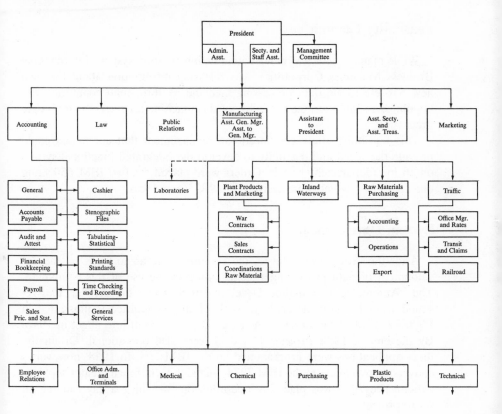

Note: To simplify this organization chart, the subordinate positions in some of the units
not directly related to the accounting and computer functions have been omitted.

**Figure 1. Organization chart before the
introduction of information system.**

reached with punched card equipment. The personnel directly involved with
the data processing activity were dissatisfied with the approach that had
been taken in developing the data processing system. Through a process
of evolution a system of small pieces had been developed. Mechanization
had taken place on a departmental basis rather than on an integrated functional basis. A study of the problem clearly indicated that maximum benefit
from mechanization could come only from development of an integrated
functional system crossing departmental lines. This study led to the development of a basic framework for an integrated data processing system. The
report of the study also pointed out that the conventional punched card
equipment lacked the speed and flexibility for fully implementing this broadly
conceived integrated system.

Feasibility Committee

While management was reevaluating its information system, International Business Machines Corporation was releasing information about the then new 650 electronic data processing machine. A three-man committee was appointed to look into the feasibility of this machine for the company's data processing.

This feasibility study convinced top management that computers could provide the speed and flexibility to develop the integrated functional system on an interdepartmental basis. Orders were placed for two IBM 650's and one IBM 705, which were delivered in 1955 and 1956.

System Development

After the orders were placed, the committee began to work on the development of data processing systems suited to the use of this equipment. The "Automated Information Development System," or "AIDS," that resulted from the systems analysis work of this committee is illustrated in Figure 2. Five of the projects, A, B, C, D and E, went into effect in 1956. By the end of 1958 Projects F and G were also operational. Originally, these applications were programmed on the IBM 705. In 1958, however, a conversion was made to the IBM 7074—a machine of much greater sophistication. The 7074 was placed in operation on two shifts a day running all seven projects.

Organization of EDP

Originally the computer was placed under the responsibility of the company's chief accountant. The decision, which was practically automatic, was considered sound. The computer was thought of as an ultra-high-speed version of the conventional tabulating machine. Its principal advantage was thought to be more rapid and more accurate processing of the same data that had been prepared in the past.

There was another reason for locating computers in the accounting division—the chief accountant's leading role in the feasibility study preceding the installation. This study was, generally speaking, chiefly concerned with drawing a comparison between the expenditures for the new equipment and the anticipated clerical cost reductions. In addition, this study indicated that maximum benefit from mechanization could come only from development of an integrated data processing system. This kind of analysis was a proper function of the financial officer, and most of the cost elements and savings were within his own field of responsibility.

Project A—Materials and Stores

1. Storehouses issues and receipts
2. Stock level control
3. Central tool control
4. Domestic Research Co. inventory control
5. Automatic purchase ordering
6. Purchase follow-up
7. Invoice verification
8. Payable checks
9. Material distribution
10. Analyses and reports

Project B—Payroll and Personnel

1. Manpower scheduling
2. Timekeeping
3. Payroll administration
4. Payroll deductions and checks
   (incl. thrift, annuity, and tax reports)
5. Employee benefit plan administration
6. Service records and seniority
7. Education records
8. Personnel statistics
9. Medical records
10. Safety and training records
11. Labor distribution
12. Locker identification records
13. Retirement income computations

Project C—Fixed Assets

1. Appropriation control
2. Construction records and reports
3. Construction close-outs
4. Plant records
5. Retirements and transfers
6. Plant ledger
7. Depreciation calculation

8. Plant catalog
9. Annual reports

Project D—Financial and Cost

1. Cost distribution entries
2. Code checking and translation
3. Cost allocation
4. Voucher register
5. General ledger
6. Cost and financial reports and analysis

Project E—Secondary Reports

1. Short and off-sequence reports
2. Multi-project reports and analyses
3. Off-frequency reports

Project F—Sales and Shipping

1. Order record
2. Package inventory reports
3. Shipping schedule
4. Shipping papers
5. Bills of lading
6. Invoices
7. Sales statistics

Project G—Operations Analysis

1. Operating data
2. Inventories
3. Meter and gauge calculations
4. Laboratory data
5. Material balances
6. Miscellaneous statistics
7. Utilities and chemical distribution

Figure 2. Automated information development system projects.

Computing Centralized

With the initial installation of the computers, a group was set up to handle the technical computations on the IBM 650 and 705. As time went by, it became evident that all computing should be centralized in one department and that the programing for business and technical computations should be performed by one group. Consequently, a methods development and programing department was formed for this purpose and remained under the supervision of the chief accountant as noted in Figure 3. Thus data processing, although now a separate section, continued to operate within the accounting division, with responsibility for operation of the computer and the maintenance of all operational programs.

As the AIDS program became more complex and as other phases of information technology developed, the placement of data processing in the

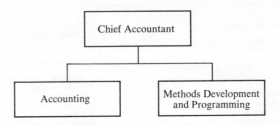

Figure 3. Accounting division.

accounting division was questioned. The range of computer applications far exceeded the limits of the traditionally structured accounting process. The growth of this management information system extended the organizational impact of electronic data processing from the machine room to other departments.

AIDS

An examination of the Automated Information Development System program provides some insight into the developments that led up to what may have been the most significant reorganization in the company's corporate history.

Project A: Materials and Stores. The company's storehouse contains some 25,000 items of maintenance and operating supplies. In addition to controlling this inventory, the IBM 7074 is utilized for reordering, follow-up, checking and paying invoices on these 25,000 stock items. This not only makes the function of inventory control easier and the entire system of record keeping more accurate, but it also makes important information for decision making more easily obtainable by several levels of management. For instance, information heretofore difficult to compile is being obtained for use in value analysis, appraisal of vendor performance, reports to management, and studies of stock obsolescence.

Project B: Payroll and Personnel. There were two major goals for the payroll and personnel project: (1) to reduce the tremendous duplication of personnel records and (2) to assist management in employee job scheduling. The first objective has been accomplished with the expected success. In general, the reduction in clerical work has greatly aided supervision and management personnel by permitting them to concentrate on their primary task—supervising. But the attainment of the second objective has proved to be of greater importance. Planning personnel in particular now can do a more effective job of forecasting construction and maintenance projects and scheduling the manpower necessary to carry out these projects. One scheduler states that thanks to this phase of the AIDS program he now receives ten times as much pertinent information as before to assist him in fulfilling his function.

Project C: Fixed Assets. This project involved maximum mechanization of fixed asset reports and records, formerly prepared manually. Until July, 1956, when this project became operational, the company accounting records were maintained on approximately 30,000 manually posted cards .These records have now been converted to master tapes and are updated on the 7074. This tape serves as one of the subsidiary ledgers underlying the general ledger, which is maintained as part of Project D.

Project D: Financial and Cost. Project D covers the general accounting, financial and cost report preparation. It involves the accumulation of a general ledger history tape and the preparation of general and subsidiary ledger entries, including the voucher register. Each of the other projects provides basic accounting data to this project for processing. Output consists of a variety of reports including labor and material cost distribution reports, material issues by classes and accounts and cost reports by processing units.

Project E: Secondary Reports. This project provided for collecting and organizing data for the preparation of reports that could be conveniently produced directly in the other projects. It also provided for the collection and organization of this information and the subsequent preparation of these reports. Since its conception in July, 1956, many additional reports have been initiated. Not only has this project eliminated the manual effort formerly involved in such report preparation, but it also has provided faster, more accurate information to all levels of management.

Project F: Sales and Shipping. Through the use of the IBM 7074, customer data and shipping data are processed for maximum mechanization of the sales and shipping function. Two departments of the chemical operations division, the packaging and shipping department and the chemical movement department, work closely on this project. The 7074 also produces shipping papers, package inventory reports, customer invoices, sales statistical reports and the necessary accounting entries to reflect customer sales. Moreover, the program determines the most economical number of packages of various styles that should be carried, based on prior shipping experience. This program has resulted in some reduction of inventory items and also provides optimum use of floor space. Finally, the optimum scheduling of the manufacture of various products is a major function of Project F.

Project G: Operations Analysis. This project is designed to maximize mechanical preparation of operating, raw materials inventory and laboratory data. As a result of the operation of Project G, control of the manufacturing output is accomplished more quickly. This project also provides valuable information for the plant simulation program, for the checking of errors in measuring instruments and for use in determining the design of future chemical processing units.

Integrated System

The seven major systems provide essentially an integrated system. Each has an output that enters directly into daily plant operations. In addition to this direct output, there are various accounting entries that are fed into a financial project for the preparation of the profit and loss statement and balance sheet. These seven projects also provide a variety of statistical data. Thus, this single Automated Information Development System furnishes top and middle management personnel with valuable information to increase the profitability of operations.

Organizational Changes

During the first stages of the AIDS program the methods development and programing department performed many of the clerical functions formerly carried out in the affected operating departments. When the AIDS Program became fully operational, there was evidence of an increased need for greater coordination and communication among the affected operating departments. Consequently, there were signs of pressure building up in such a way as to challenge the efficacy of the departments that communicated with one another through the projects of the AIDS program.

The development of the integrated information system resulted in the organizational structure presented in Figure 4. This corporate structure was established in 1962 and has remained basically unchanged at this writing. In comparing this organization chart with that of the mid-1940's (Figure 1), it is readily apparent that there has been a revolutionary change centering around the location and function of the accounting division.

Accounting Division

The accounting division has been reduced in status in the organizational hierarchy and is now called the accounting department. In mid-1964 it included 72 people. It reports to a new division, the administrative services division. Whereas the chief accountant formerly reported directly to the

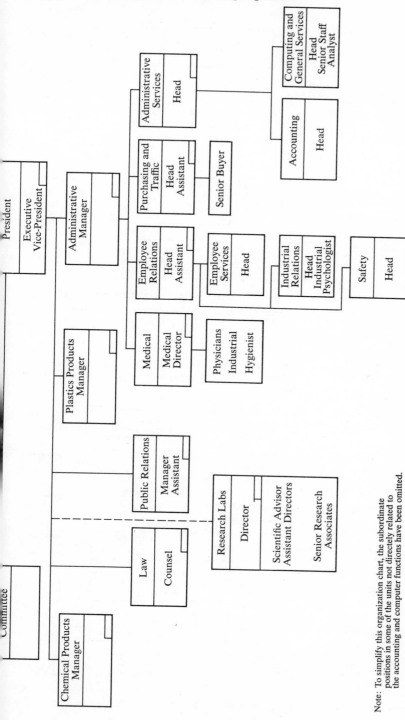

Figure 4. Organization chart after the introduction of information system.

Note: To simplify this organization chart, the subordinate positions in some of the units not directly related to the accounting and computer functions have been omitted.

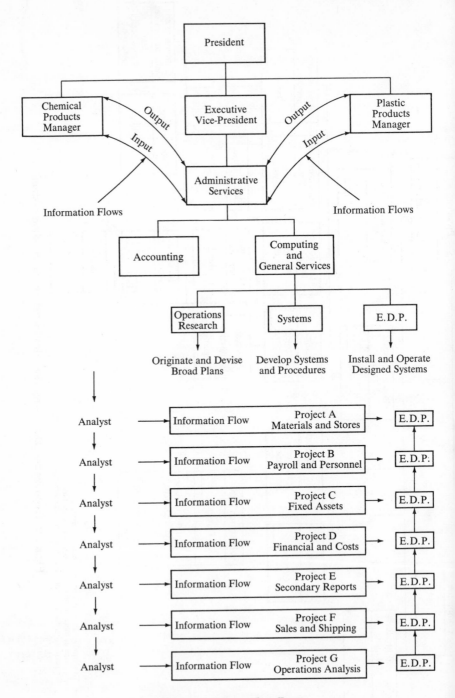

Figure 5. Information flows.

president, he now has two intermediaries between himself and the president's office.

On the same organizational level with the accounting department is the computing and general services department, formerly styled methods development and programing department (Figure 3). The operation of the AIDS program is the primary function of the computing and general services department. For operational purposes, this department is divided into three sections—business systems, operations research and data processing. This department, like the accounting department, reports to the head of the administrative services division. The functional operation of the computing and general services department is illustrated in Figure 5.

The creation of the administrative services division was the primary result of the advent of information technology through the operation of the AIDS program. It developed out of a real need to plan and manage more effectively the flow of information—the lifeblood of the company. In this connection, it should be noted parenthetically that the administrative services division "charges" the other divisions for services rendered much as a service bureau charges its clients. In evaluating the performance of the operating divisions, top management is conscious of the cost of the information to them. As a result, the operating departments must evaluate the usefulness of information against the cost of that information as charged to their operations. Thus, information is not generated for information's sake.

Conclusions

Through a series of events over a period of time this company learned an important lesson: If maximum benefit is to be derived from data processing equipment, the computer must be utilized as something more than merely a large accounting machine. A vast quantity of information becomes available. With the reorganization that is almost always necessary to obtain and effectively utilize this information, the traditional accounting department becomes ancillary to the primary information process. Whether the nature of organizational development will be similar in other companies as they, too, reorganize for an integrated information system remains to be seen. The developments described in this paper, however, make it abundantly clear that accounting departments of the future will not be able to remain in their *status quo*.

The company discussed in this article has found it impossible to proceed without a director of management information, the administrative services director. The day has already dawned when his responsibilities include the disciplines of statistics and operations research as well as accounting and such related activities as budgeting, cost accounting, electronic data processing and systems analysis.

Organizing, Staffing, and Operating the Information Services Function

Robert W. Shopoff
William R. Jack

There is an ever increasing demand for accurate timely information in modern business today. With the increased demand, there is an increased responsibility placed on business management to ensure the information system meets these demands.

The most important areas which bear on the effectiveness of an information services group are—organization, staffing and method of operation.

Each of these areas is discussed in the following sections. In this discussion, we have aimed to develop the basic or fundamental points involved, rather than attempt to detail a solution for each individual situation or condition.

Defining Information Systems. In the following discussions, we will consider information systems from a broad viewpoint. They are defined to include the collection, edit, storage, transfer, calculation, combination and dissemination of data or business information. This includes manual, me-

Reprinted by permission of the authors and the publisher from *Management Accounting*, Vol. XLIX, No. 2, Sec. 1 (October, 1967), pp. 3–8.

chanical or electronic methods meeting the information needs of all phases of a business organization.

Defining the Scope of Information Services. The information services function has the following responsibilities in the area of information systems:

1. To review, analyze and document existing systems in all areas of the company.
2. To develop and install an integrated information system serving the needs of all phases of management.
3. To prepare computer programs, plug boards and other necessary adjuncts to process data on punched cards and/or electronic equipment.
4. To provide and operate the necessary equipment to ensure efficient information systems.

Organization

The key to the success of the total information services activities is a clear definition of functions to be performed and the responsibility of each function. The principal functions should include: Systems and Procedures, Data Processing.

These activities should be organized under a common manager responsible for total information services. Typically, the title of this position might be manager or director of administrative services or of information services.

Before discussing the function and responsibility of each of these activities or departments, it would be well to question where the total activity should be placed in the overall business organization.

Typically, this activity has reported to the controller or chief financial officer. In the long-term planning, as the scope of data processing broadens to a total business information concept, consideration should be given to elevating this activity to the higher corporate level, with the manager of administrative services reporting directly to the general manager or chief corporate officer. This can have two advantages. First, it will allow the manager of administrative services to know management's goals; to be aware of changes in the goals as they occur; and to build the system around these goals. It also allows the administrative services department to meet the broad demand for information for all phases of management.

The important point is that the manager of administrative services must recognize he has a total business to serve—whether it be marketing statistics, production data, engineering theory or financial reports. He must break from the traditional accounting approach and view the problem broadly—quite the same as the chief executive officer—satisfying each area's needs in order to attain all of the company's goals.

Let us look at the division of activities and responsibilities within the administrative services group and examine the reasons behind the suggested organization.

The most important point is the separation of the data processing and the systems and procedures activities. The systems manager has the responsibility to lay out the long-range and intermediate plans in the data processing and systems area and then develop the detailed procedures. This is a creative-thinking-analysis type work, which should not be burdened with hourly or daily deadlines. His counterpart, the data processing manager, must direct his attention to developing a coordinated group to provide timely, accurate information, reports or documents. This is a "doing" operation—one which faces daily pressures for output and demands keen administrative as well as technical ability. While it is agreed that there must be a good exchange of information between these two functions, and the department managers must work closely together, we feel the clean split of responsibilities is critical to the progress and degree of excellence achieved in the area of developing a modern information system.

Not only does such an organization separate these two different types of activities which require different talents, but it provides a clean interface between the data processing department and the other departments that are requesting or using the data processing services. It relieves the data processing manager of interruption or diversion caused by questions or new requests which should be directed to the systems manager.

Systems and Procedures

This department includes the design of the proper systems or work procedure to complete the required business activity or information needed as well as the analysis of the information flow or result required, the detailed procedure, forms design, and equipment selection (if alternatives are available). It also includes programming the procedure if electronic processing is involved. The systems development logically includes manual procedures or those utilizing other business machines.

One function coming under the systems and procedures would be the evaluation as to whether a given information service should be performed in-house or by an outside source. This might arise particularly with special requests or the initial stage of a new program. In this case, the systems manager should be able to evaluate the outside cost to ensure an economic source.

The personnel consists of a department manager and systems analysts or engineers. In larger organizations, you normally find a project leader or senior analyst directing the work of several analysts.

Data Processing

This department would include the function of processing all computer and/or punched card applications, responsibility for teleprocessing communications systems and maintenance of all data processing files.

The department normally consists of three sections under the direction of the department manager: input, control and operations. The input section consists of key punching and verifying, and other input methods. The operations section includes console and machine operators, tape and disk handlers, and programmers required for program maintenance of current applications. (An alternate approach is to put all the programming under the direction of the systems department.) The control section works with both the input and operations sections to maintain proper data control in terms of input and output. In a large operation, it may be best to have two control groups; one within the input section and one in the operations section.

Staffing the Information Services Function

In terms of numbers, we know of no criteria to establish an absolute minimum or maximum quantity of personnel required to develop, design, install, operate and maintain a management information system. In discussions with other companies, we find wide ranges in the number of personnel engaged in the effort. For example, one large machine tool manuufacturer anticipates expending 86 man years in developing and installing a management information system in a two or three year period, this effort to be about evenly divided between systems development and programming. A large pharmaceutical firm, however, expects to invest between 250 and 300 man years over a five year period with the number of people so engaged (excluding data processing operations personnel) ranging from a low of 22 in the fifth year to a high of 78 in the second and third years. Both companies have had computers on-site for at least five years, and cannot be considered novices in the art and science of computer usage.

Certain rules of thumb regarding personnel costs have been developed based on surveys of large companies using computers. One such study ("Managing to Manage the Computer," by James W. Taylor and Neal J. Dean, both of Booz, Allen and Hamilton, *Harvard Business Review*, September-October, 1966) indicated that of the 33 large successful companies included in the survey, those spending up to $1 million annually on information services spent 17 per cent of these expenditures on systems and programming, 42 per cent to 47 per cent on operating expenses and 36 per cent to 41 per cent on machine rental. However, these ratios would certainly be different for companies desirous of establishing a total information system within a reasonably short time. The most that can be said is that personnel costs will vary directly with management's desire to have installed an efficient total information system, and inversely with the amount of time allocated to complete its implementation.

Although it is a truism, the old saying "Quality rather than quantity" could never be more valid than it is today in the data processing personnel area. With the mushrooming growth in computer installations over the past fifteen years, available and experienced or talented people are scarce. But unless and until company managements recognize the need for highly qualified individuals to man the key positions in the information services organizational structure, systems "effectiveness" will continue to rank relatively low. Data processing in this respect is the same as any other critical function within the company.

The fact that such a severe personnel shortage exists in this area has forced many companies into internal recruiting to fill the key positions. Certainly there are several advantages to this approach, including detailed knowledge of company operations, organization, policies, problems and personnel. Many companies are firm in their belief that it is far simpler to train a company employee in systems and computer techniques than it is to educate a newcomer in the intricacies of company operations. On the other hand, if the entire systems development group is recruited internally, the danger exists that possible new innovations will not be considered and that sacred cows will, without question, continue to be sacred. Hence, the computerized system will be performing only the same old functions, albeit considerably faster and more accurately.

Perhaps the ideal system group is one consisting of newly recruited systems personnel from outside the company with a generous sprinkling of seasoned employees with knowledge of company operations. In this atmosphere, each individual can absorb the others' knowledge quite rapidly.

An alternative is to staff the systems group with experienced systems analysts while assigning within each functional area a "systems liaison" man responsible to the manager of that area for the development of computerized systems relating to that function. This approach has the advantage of fostering a greater feeling of participation in and acceptance of any new systems developed. Care must be taken, however, to ensure that the liaison man is relieved of all his other duties so that he may devote himself fully to systems task. Further, this method of operation could tend to discourage beneficial organizational changes which might otherwise arise implementing a total information system.

Qualifications

Qualifications generally considered necessary at the higher levels of the information services personnel include the following: •

1. Ability to think in terms of total corporate requirements, rather than along more narrow functional lines.
2. Understanding of corporate organization and objectives.
3. Knowledge and understanding of computers and their potential uses, in both the commercial application areas and the scientific and technical areas.
4. Ability to get along with all levels of management.
5. Ability to work well under pressure.
6. Imagination, enthusiasm and creativity while remaining a realist.
7. Ability to inspire subordinates to high levels of performance.

These same qualifications, perhaps in lesser degree, should be sought in the systems analyst, systems liaison man and programmers. The Programmer's Aptitude Test prepared by IBM is useful as a guide in determining the aptitudes of individuals toward the detailed logical type thinking required in each of these positions.

Despite the critical shortage of experienced personnel, management should insist on developing a high-quality systems and programming group even though it may take longer to fill all the available positions. In light of the dependence on the information system by all major areas of the business, this would appear to be the least costly approach to take.

Operating the Information Services Department

Systems Development

In the early days of punched card equipment and during the 1950's, most companies making use of data processing equipment developed their systems on an application-by-application basis. These applications were, generally speaking, of the "bread and butter" variety—that is, the mechanization of routine clerical type operations, cost justification for which was based almost solely on the number of clerks made available for other work. The applications were generally servicing only one functional area of the company, usually the controller's area. Too little thought was given to making multiple uses of the data to help satisfy the information needs of all the functional areas of the company.

Today's thinking in terms of systems development has been radically altered from that of the 1950's as a result of the development of low-cost, mass-memory devices with tremendously increased internal computing speeds, plus a growing reservoir of experience in computer usage and better software and programming aids. The current trend is toward development of "data banks" of selected information and usage of this data in multiple ways to build up integrated management information systems useful to all levels of a management in all functional areas of the company.

Needless to say, the planning and administration of systems development have also become more complex with these developments. What is now needed is the planning and design of a "master framework," in effect, representing the entire information requirements at all levels of management within the company.

Unless such a framework is developed in rather fine detail beforehand, the systems manager can never be certain that sections or subsections of the management information system will fit into the overall systems complex. If they do not fit, many additional man months of systems development and programming can be expected, and many months of delay will occur before the full benefits of the total systems approach can be realized.

In summary, systems managers should plan their long-range systems goals before attempting to implement new systems on a piecemeal basis. Obviously, a complete simultaneous installation of all phases of a management information system is not possible. The framework must be sectionalized, priorities assigned to the different sections and available manpower assigned to the task of analyzing and developing those areas having the highest priorities.

Throughout the development and implementation of the various sections of the management information system framework, analysts should attempt insofar as possible to design flexibility into the system and to provide for a reasonable degree of expansion. Further, company management should keep the systems manager fully informed as to plans and expectations for the company's growth and diversification (product and geographical as well as market) in order that provision can be made in the overall framework to include the necessary information systems to support this growth.

Systems Standards and Programming Standards

At a very early stage in the development of management information system framework, and certainly before any section or subsection is assigned for development and implementation, the systems manager should establish certain standards to which all analysts and programmers must adhere.

The degree and depth to which these standards should be detailed is, of course, a matter of judgment and depends on local situations, but should include at least the following items:

1. Standard methods of flow charting and block-diagramming.
2. Standard section of punched card (or punched paper tape layout, or direct teleprocessing input) for transaction, system or division codes.
3. Standard methods of tape and/or disk labelling.

4. Standard programming language(s).

5. Requirement for balancing and editing routines and provision for audit trails.

6. Standard report sizes.

7. Degree of program and procedural documentation.

Program "Straight-line Modules" vs. Complex Logic.   In the more complex programs, it is frequently possible to develop lengthy main lines of logic and through the use of switches, indicators, etc., to develop a compact but complex program to accomplish the desired results. This conserves internal memory and may initially save some programming time. However, this approach may also result in greater than normal difficulties in de-bugging the program and, if program maintenance is later required, may consume as much programming and de-bugging time to modify the routine as it did to write the program initially. The opposite approach, which might be called "straight-line modular logic," calls for repeating sections of the program where required while developing the entire program in modules. This approach is generally easier to de-bug (de-bugging of certain of the modules can be done even before the entire program is completely written) and results in a program which is considerably easier to modify. It is suggested that systems managers give some consideration toward which approach (or at what middle ground) their block diagramming, logic layout, and programming should be directed.

Data Processing Operations Standards

As with systems and programming, certain minimum standards should exist in the data processing operations area. The following items should be among these minimum standards:

1. Scheduling of routine work.

2. Job numbering.

3. Well defined operating procedures.

4. Housekeeping.

"Closed Shop" vs. "Open Shop" Operations.   Many companies today run a "closed shop" in their DP operations, by providing a program de-bugging service for the programming group. This generally provides a more efficient machine room operation by preventing programmers from trying to de-bug their programs while sitting at the machine. This approach has the additional advantage of forcing much of the necessary operating documentation to be prepared before de-bugging can begin. Managers should determine which mode of operation is the better one for their respective operations.

Summary

In the installation and operation of an effective management information system, many problems can be expected. The degree of success achieved will depend on:

—Establishing the proper system and processing organization within the corporate framework.

—Proper definition of responsibilities within the systems and processing organization.

—Selection of personnel.

—Establishing standard methods of planning and operation.

Recognition of these factors will provide a solid foundation to develop a system that will meet the demands and requirements of modern management.

10 APPLICATIONS

Computers Used as Accounting Tools

Guy W. Lambers

Over the past decade, the primary function of the accounting department at the Instrument Division of Lear Siegler, Inc. has changed.[1] In times past the emphasis was on accuracy often at the expense of speed; the accountants did not take a very active part in the day-to-day management of the business.

Today, with our electronic data processing system, we have speed plus the ability to process masses of data in many diverse and imaginative ways; accounting at the Instrument Division is now a "management tool" which furnishes *all* levels of management with data (daily, weekly, monthly) whereby management can effectively utilize the resources it has available.

Our electronic data processing center has the following equipment:

IBM 14 10 System:
1411 central processing unit—40K positions of core
Two 1414 input-output synchronizers

Reprinted by permission of the author and the publisher from *Management Accounting*, Vol. XLVII, No. 5, Sec. 1 (January, 1966), pp. 29–37.

[1] Lear Siegler, Inc., is listed by *Fortune* magazine among one of the top 500 corporations in the United States; annual sales approach $200,000,000. The Instrument Division, located at Grand Rapids, is the largest single division of the corporation and accounts for approximately one-third of the total sales. It manufacturers aircraft and missile instruments primarily for military use.

Two 1405 disc files with dual arms
Six 729 Model IV tape drives
1415 console
1402 card read punch
1403 printer

IBM 14 01 System:
1401 central processing unit plus 1406 auxiliary unit—12K positions of core
7155 switching control console allowing use of four of the 729 Model IV tape drives attached to the 1410 system
1402 card read punch
1403 printer

IBM 14 01 System:
1401 central processing unit—4K positions of core
1402 card read punch
1403 printer
Peripheral equipment such as key punching and card sorting machines.

The Computer as a Tabulating Tool

Prior to getting our computers we had tabulating equipment which could only process cards. Therefore, we were limited as to the amount of data which could be processed into a system. The printers (IBM Model 407's) could print only at the rate of 150 lines per minute.

With our present system we are able to process data into cards, magnetic tapes and magnetic discs. The present printers print at the rate of 600 lines per minute.

The following books of original entry are processed through our electronic data processing center:

1. Sales journal.
2. Cash receipts.
3. Voucher register.
4. Accounts payable check register.
5. Payroll register and labor distribution.

Sales Journal

Every month 1,500 invoices are key punched into the data system to produce our monthly sales journal. This journal shows detail such as customer, part, project and sales order numbers; quantity; and selling price.

The sales journal is printed in several different ways such as: invoice number, product code, type of contract and customer sequence.

Cash Receipts

All cash receipts are identified to specific invoices. The information is then key punched into the system. A journal of total daily cash receipts is maintained manually.

Voucher Register

Approximately 2,000 vouchers are processed weekly. A weekly voucher register is issued every morning for the previous week. It shows, among other items, the classifications of costs into over 10,000 different accounts. These weekly registers are summarized every four weeks, including a register for a partial week when necessary.

The vouchers processed are also sorted by payment date and a "pre-check run" is issued showing amounts due vendors by date. This run is used to determine cash requirements on a "close-in basis."

Accounts Payable Check Register

Approximately 3,000 checks are paid monthly to vendors. They are issued twice each week. A stub attached to each check shows the invoice being paid and the cash discounts taken. All the accounting department needs to do is inform the data processing center to pay invoices through a certain due date based upon the "pre-check run" mentioned above. A monthly check register is made from the checks issued.

Payroll Register and Labor Distribution

Approximately 2,600 employees are paid weekly. The data processing system performs the complete function of computing gross pay, withholding tax deductions, F.I.C.A. and other miscellaneous deductions. It also computes the net pay and issues a payroll check. All employees who are paid on a weekly basis must fill out a prepunched time card on either a daily or weekly basis.

Direct labor personnel fill out *daily* time cards on both sides. One side is used to compute the payroll. The opposite side of the card shows hours worked by job number and type of labor performed such as standard labor, rework labor, set-up labor, etc. Key punched, this information forms the basis of our direct labor distribution.

Indirect labor personnel fill out weekly time cards on only one side. This side is the basis for both payroll and distribution of cost to the departments.

The Computer as a Tool
for Application of Data

It is really through the manipulation or application of the source data discussed above which has given us the ability to perform a function useful to the day-by-day management of the business. This use might also be called using the computer "in depth." Most of the data to perform this function are stored either on punched cards or magnetic tape and are readily available for further applications, as illustrated in the following paragraphs.

Standard Product Cost and Labor Analysis

For each part of the production hardware a standard cost has been determined. It consists of standard material expressed in dollars and standard direct labor expressed in hours.

The material standards, established by our cost accounting, are based upon purchase history by part number stored within the data processing system. Standard hours, as established by our production engineering, are converted to dollars of labor and burden by application of a standard labor and burden rate.

Standard material costs are compared with actual material costs obtained from the voucher register, and purchase price variances are calculated. Standard labor hours are compared with actual direct labor hours in many ways, as discussed below.

Input data from the daily time cards, mentioned previously, enables us to furnish each department every morning with a report of the previous day's performance in terms of earned, off standard, line rework, set-up, salvage rework and inspection hours. Likewise, a set of weekly reports is furnished for the previous week's performance. One of these reports shows variances from standard labor by department in terms of hours per earned hour, grouped by department and by groups of like parts called component codes.

Figure 1 is a reproduction of one of these reports. Figure 2 shows the very same report in terms of dollar costs per earned hour.

Another weekly report (labor part history) shows the same information by individual part number for the previous week and also in eight-week totals. Operating managers use this information to pinpoint problems and take corrective action where necessary. It is the foundation for their cost control. All of this data is supplied by our electronic data processing center on ditto masters without any manual calculations or printing. Accounting uses this data on a monthly basis to calculate the monthly cost of sales for hardware production.

The relief of inventory to cost of sales is accomplished each month by

Direct Labor Hours Analysis

							Production						Variance Hours Per Earned Hour					
Week Ending																		
Dept. no.	Prod. hours	Earn. hours	Off std. hours	Line rework	Set up	Total contl.	Lost time	Total	Salvage rework	Scrap	Var. hours	Non-std. hours	Off std.	Line rework	Set up	Lost time	Total variance
F113																	
F114																	
F116																	

Figure 1.

Direct Labor Dollars Analysis
Departmental Labor Variances
Cost Per Earned Hour

Week Ending 11-07-65

Dept. no.	Earned hours	Total contl. var. dollars	Scrap dollars	Total var. dollars	Lost time dollars	Cost Per Earned Hour						% of earn. to total	% of var. to total
						Total dollars	Total contl.	Scrap	Total var.	Lost time	Total		
F113													
F114													
F116													

Figure 2.

comparing the numbers of parts sold with the standard costs for these parts. Variances to be written off are calculated by furnishing the computer with a set of variance rates which are applied against the standard cost. The only manual labor involved is the calculation of the rates applied.

Engineering Project Cost Accounting and Control

We have an engineering facility which employs approximately 400 people. The costs incurred by this facility are collected and controlled by means of numbered project authorizations. These project authorizations are further split into items identified to "work tasks." A total estimated expenditure is authorized for each project item.

Each month our engineering department prepares a forecast to complete of anticipated expenditures for each project item by month for six months. Anticipated expenditures beyond six months are shown in one total.

Input costs for each project and item come from the voucher register, direct labor time cards, and transfers from production. The first two types of input costs mentioned come directly from source data already within the computer. The last type must be key punched.

Every Wednesday morning an "IBM run" is made of the month-to-date cost as of the end of the previous week. Actual and forecast costs of current month's input are compared by project and item number. These reports— issued in two formats: by project and by department—give the engineering operating managers a "close in look" at the current status of each project and department.

A monthly project item status report is also issued by the electronic data processing center for operating managers. It shows the very same detail (except on the monthly basis) plus cost to date, estimated cost to complete,

Project Item Status				

Engineer Item		Hours	Labor & Burden	Material	Total
Proj. No.	Est. Input this Mo.				
Description	Actual Input this Mo.				
	Cost to Date				
Start Date	Est. to Complete				
Finish Date—Orig.	Total Est. Cost				
Est.	Total Est. Cost Last Mo.				
C/1 M MS	Authorized				

Engineer Item		Hours	Labor & Burden	Material	Total
Proj. No.	Est. Input this Mo.				
Description	Actual Input this Mo.				
	Cost to Date				
Start Date	Est. to Complete				
Finish Date—Orig.	Total Est. Cost				
Est.	Total Est. Cost Last Mo.				
C/1 M MS	Authorized				

Engineer Item		Hours	Labor & Burden	Material	Total
Proj. No.	Est. Input this Mo.				
Description	Actual Input this Mo.				
	Cost to Date				
Start Date	Est. to Complete				
Finish Date—Orig.	Total Est. Cost				
Est.	Total Est. Cost Last Mo.				
C/1 M MS	Authorized				

Engineer Item		Hours	Labor & Burden	Material	Total
Proj. No.	Est. Input this Mo.				
Description	Actual Input this Mo.				
	Cost to Date				
Start Date	Est. to Complete				
Finish Date—Orig.	Total Est. Cost				
Est.	Total Est. Cost Last Mo.				
C/1 M MS	Authorized				

Engineer Item		Hours	Labor & Burden	Material	Total
Proj. No.	Est. Input this Mo.				
Description	Actual Input this Mo.				
	Cost to Date				
Start Date	Est. to Complete				
Finish Date—Orig.	Total Est. Cost				
Est.	Total Est. Cost Last Mo.				
C/1 M MS	Authorized				

Figure 3.

total estimated cost, total estimated cost last month, and amount of expenditure authorized. Figure 3 is an example of this report. Another report which summarizes this information by project is given to a higher level of management.

In the foregoing reports we have used engineering's current month's forecast for one report and their forecast to complete for another report. In addition, these forecasts are used for a monthly report which shows anticipated expenditures for each of six months in two ways: by project and by department. The information by project is used to forecast the engineering's financial activities and the information by department is used by the engineering management as a manpower planning tool.

Project costs are transferred from inventory to cost of sales when they are billed to customers. This operation is accomplished within the computers by matching projects billed, as shown by the sales journal, with the project cost incurred.

Control of Perishable Tools and Supplies

All perishable tools and supplies are purchased and distributed to the using department by the tool crib service. Prior to this year (1965 the Instrument Division had problems in controlling these items. Because of the high-volume, low-cost (individual items) transactions (withdrawals from and return to the crib), it was not economical to maintain a detailed manual inventory control system. Consequently, the tool crib service had problems in maintaining adequate supplies on hand and the accounting department had problems with cost distribution as there was no adequate way of determining the users and frequency of use.

In the early part of this year the electronic data processing center established a system which has helped us solve most of our problems.

In our new system, all purchase orders as well as receivers are key punched. A filled out requisition card in duplicate is required for each withdrawal from the tool crib and return to it. This card shows requisition number, perishable tool and supply number, description, location (department number and foreman group), unit of measure, authorization, etc. The original is kept by the tool crib and the duplicate is kept by the withdrawer. When the item is returned to the tool crib, it must be accompanied by the duplicate copy so that the withdrawing foreman may receive credit. All the data are transferred from the cards to magnetic tape for storage. These data form the basis of the tool crib's inventory control. A reorder point formula has been established to determine when to order more items.

The system issues weekly a report on purchase orders overdue and the information on overdue shelf life. (Certain items such as paint, epoxy and adhesives must be used by a certain date after which they are not usable.)

The monthly report shows withdrawals and returns by foreman group within each department. One copy goes to the accounting department which uses it for distribution of costs to the using departments. Other copies are sent to the tool crib service, department heads and foremen, for their information and use. Figure 4 shows a flow chart of this system.

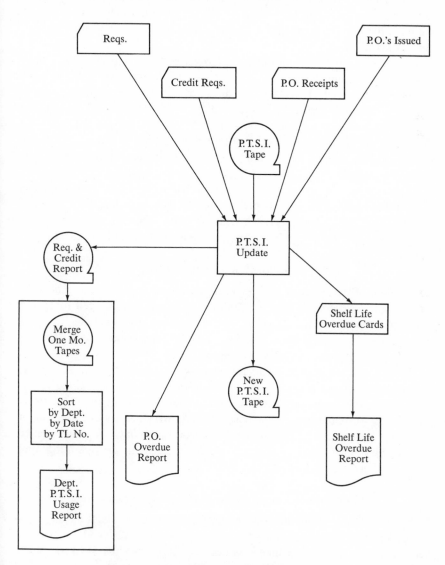

Figure 4. Flow chart of perishable tools and supply items (PTSI).

Fixed Asset Ledger

Approximately 25,000 items of machinery, office equipment, test equipment and permanent tools are located in 135 departments. At the time of acquisition, an asset number is established and attached to each item, and the description, year of acquisition, and cost are entered into the system and stores on magnetic tape. The yearly depreciation charge is calculated for each item on the basis of a set of depreciation rates determined for each year of acquisition.

Whenever an item of equipment is moved between departments, a move ticket is issued and the information is entered into the system. Periodically a report is made which shows cost, the current year's depreciation and the total depreciation reserve accumulated to date. This report is made in department number sequence allowing us to spread the current year's depreciation by department. The monthly depreciation is calculated merely by dividing by twelve. This report will be used in the future to take cycle inventory counts.

Currently we are in the process of establishing category codes for each item. When this information is processed into the computer, we will be able to determine the quantity of each item on hand. This information is especially important for determining future acquisitions of tools and test equipment.

Departmental Expense Ledger

Portions of the voucher register and payroll are merged to make up the departmental expense ledger. All indirect expenses are charged to specific departments and further classified within department by cost element, such as supervisory salaries, office salaries, vacation pay, holiday pay, overtime, supplies, maintenance, travel, depreciation, etc.

Each month we receive a run for each department which shows indirect cost by cost element for the current month, the prior month and the year to date. These departmental costs are summarized into cost centers for use in calculating burden rates. Total costs balance with control accounts in the general ledger. Each is also summarized according to operating management responsibilities, and copies of the summary are sent to the operating managers for their information and use.

Elimination of Annual Physical Inventory of Stockroom

The stockroom maintains a perpetual inventory of all parts by using our electronic data processing facilities. The accuracy is checked by periodic cycle accounts which are made without closing down the stockroom and halting production.

The accuracy is such that the accounting department uses these quantities in place of the annual physical inventory. They are priced with standard cost already stored on tape and the total is compared with the general ledger control account.

Customer Reports

Certain contracts require that we prepare monthly reports to customers according to their format. Since all of our source data are stored in the electronic data processing center, it is relatively easy to prepare. For one such contract we are required to show: cost this month, cost to date and forecast of cost to complete by càlendar quarter. This data must be further detailed by area of expenditure such as production, engineering, tooling, test equipment, technical data and quality control. Within each area costs are shown by cost element as follows: hours, labor and burden, material, material handling, consultants, general and administrative expense and profit.

Sales Forecasts

Every month we prepare a forecast of sales by month for one year forward. It is made up of two basic parts: firm billings and anticipated billings. Every month the electronic data processing center issues a build schedule and a ship schedule showing quantities and prices for all hardware for which we have a firm contract or purchase order. This information is used by the production control in determining material and manpower requirements, and in scheduling of production. The ship schedule is used by the accounting department for forecasting firm billings.

Anticipated billings are estimated by contracts people who have a knowledge of customer requirements and expected customer buys. Each anticipated order is given a probability rating from 1.0 down to 0.1. These probability ratings, key punched together with dollar estimates, result in a tabulation of anticipated billings which is merged with the firm billings described above to make our sales forecast.

Other Subsidiary Registers and Reports

Several reports are used only by the accounting department:

Bank Reconciliations. Two of our bank accounts, the accounts payable and payroll accounts, are reconciled by electronic data processing. The payroll account is reconciled weekly and accounts payable is reconciled monthly. The only additional input required in order to complete the reconciliation is the key punching of the checks returned from the bank. They are key punched in the same order as received. When the resulting cards are matched with the applicable check register, the unmatched cards constitute the outstanding checks.

Accounts Receivable Ledger and Customer Statements. A merger of the sales journal and cash receipts input produces the accounts receivable ledger which shows in detail all charges and credits and the current balance of the individual customer accounts. The total of these balances agrees with a control account total in the general ledger. At the end of every month, statements to customers are printed from this ledger.

Accounts Payable Ledger. A merger of the voucher register and check register produces the accounts payable ledger. The total of the open balances agrees with a control account in the general ledger. A trial balance is made every month, the total of which agrees with a control account in the general ledger.

Payroll Tax Reports. All reports for Federal income tax withholding, F.I.C.A. and unemployment taxes are made upon the basis of information furnished through the payroll system. Employee W–2 forms are also printed by the computer.

Future Applications of the Computers

Each application of the computer suggests new ideas for further integration. Currently studies are being conducted in several areas. Two of these areas, not previously mentioned, are the elimination of vendor invoices as a necessary prerequisite to payment of a liability and the distribution of service department costs to the other service departments prior to distribution to production and administrative departments. The latter proposal is discussed briefly below.

One of the perennial problems of all manufacturing business is the accurate distribution of service department costs, which may be stated as the problem of defining "true service costs" after reciprocal transfers between service departments have been made.

At the Instrument Division we have made only a partial attempt to distribute "service on service." The cost of our occupancy and maintenance departments are distributed to other service departments in addition to distribution to the production and administrative departments. All others are distributed directly to the production and administration departments.

We have investigated the solving of simultaneous linear equations by the computer, which, because of its speed, makes distribution of "service on service" economically feasible. There are, of course, "canned programs," already written for solving such equations. However, they involve matrices of a different size. We therefore started writing our own program. It is not yet completed and is being held in abeyance pending delivery of our IBM System 360, scheduled for delivery sometime in the latter part of 1965.

Conclusion

Our experience has emphasized two attributes which every accountant must possess—imagination and ability to communicate—in order to fully utilize the electronic data processing facilities.

Use of EDP and Teletype in Monthly Financial Closings

Maurice W. Beichley
Harvey L. Poppel

Last June, when the Westinghouse Electric Corporation Board of Directors received their May corporate financial statements, the following explanation was included:

The enclosed Income Statement and Balance Sheet were generated by the Univac 490 Computer. This completes another of the initial objectives for the Tele-Computer Center. The raw data was transmitted from the various profit centers directly into the computer through the corporate teletype network. The computer performed the consolidating functions, including intercompany eliminations and tax calculations, and printed the statements without manual intervention.

This marked the end of an historical closing procedure that required nearly 100 geographically scattered corporate profit centers to manually prepare voluminous accounting workpapers and statements necessary to report monthly financial data to the central accounting office in Pittsburgh. Monthly financial closing reports required two days to reach Pittsburgh from the more remote locations. When this monthly closing information was

Reprinted by permission of the authors and the publisher from *NAA Bulletin* (now *Management Accounting*), Vol. XLVI, No. 5, Sec. 1 (January, 1965), pp. 27–32.

not received early enough on the scheduled closing day for consolidation, telephone calls—some exceeding an hour— had to be made to obtain this information. A staff of fifteen clerical people then spent an additional 100 man-hours to summarize and consolidate Westinghouse and subsidiary companies' results, develop intercompany eliminations and redistributions, generate entries based on profit-center figures, compute federal and state income taxes, and prepare abbreviated statements for management review.

By using the Westinghouse teletype network in combination with the UNIVAC 490 computer facilities located at the tele-computer center in Pittsburgh, headquarter's accounting now receives a transcript of each profit center's trial balance at month-end. Figures are transmitted directly into the computer over the teletype network. The computer performs all consolidation functions previously done manually, including the computation of federal and state income taxes, and generates the desired corporate statements.

Preliminary Study

Many skills are required to solve a project of this complexity; therefore, a task force of representatives from the accounting, communications, technical operations and systems departments was appointed to examine the problem and come up with a recommended solution. Obviously, the development of this complex program necessitated detailed communications between accounting people and the technical staff responsible for the computer operation. This resulted in a complete systems analysis of existing procedures which not only produced numerous beneficial changes in accounting practices, but also simplified programming.

When a study is undertaken for mechanization, inefficiencies in existing methods and procedures are frequently uncovered. One of the results of such a systems study at Westinghouse was the conversion of subsidiary companies reporting to agree with Westinghouse chart of acounts. This has yielded an improvement in financial analysis, as well as simplified intercorporate communications.

A PERT (Program Evaluation and Review Technique) network was developed to show the most critical path of events and to enable the most effective scheduling of the project. By analyzing the project in this way, logic and reason called for a two-phase attack:

Phase I provided the means to obtain the required financial data from the reporting profit centers via the communications network and accumulate the results.

Phase II provided the means to complete the complex consolidating functions performed at headquarters, generate entries based on profit-center figures, compute federal and state taxes, develop inter-company eliminations, and prepare statements.

As a result of the PERT analysis, the mailing to headquarters and manual summarization of reports was discontinued four months in advance of the final completion of the project.

Communications Procedures

In planning for a simplified reporting-by-wire communications, the need was evident for complete and detailed instructions in profit centers. As a result, a Wired Book Closing Communications Manual was written and distributed to members of the accounting and communications departments at each reporting location several weeks before the communications system was put to use.

The transmission format is discussed in detail in the key section of this manual. This discussion covers:

A—Opening format instruction.

B—Data-message, main body format instruction.

C—Closing format.

Strict format requirements must be followed to ensure correct data communication. An example of the standardized format, together with explanatory notes, is shown in Figure 1.

Opening Format Instruction

The opening format of the "data-message" consists of a set of 40 characters. The first 20 characters represent the standard opening format for any corporate teletype, multiple-address message. The second 20 characters form the specific information necessary for wired book closing processing to interpret and verify the content and identity of the data-message.

Column 26 (numerical or correction code) prescribes a *zero* to be punched if it is to be the first transmission from the reporting location in the current month. A reporting location is defined for this purpose as being a unique, two-digit, alphabetical code.

If corrections or additions to previously transmitted figures under the same two-digit alphabetical code are to be made, a *one* is punched in column 26. Code *one* will insert or substitute for those acounts specified in the latest message.

Any data-message from a single location may be sent in segments of any size as long as each segment has the proper opening and closing formats. For example, if the data-message has been broken up into several parts, the first section to be transmitted must have a *zero* and all succeeding segments a *one* punched in the numerical correction code.

Columns 29-33 indicate the reporting location's accounting identifying number. This number has been assigned for verification purposes only.

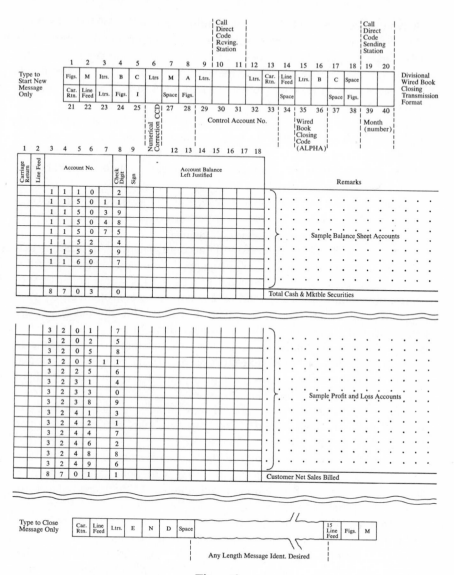

Figure 1.

Columns 35-36 are filled in with the reporting location's alphabetic code. The month is shown in columns 39-40.

Data-Message Main Body Format Instruction

After the opening format has been completed, the data portion of the message follows without any intervening characters. When filled in, each line of the format will represent one account number and balance.

A typical account and balance will require the indexing of 10 to 18 keys. The first five data characters represent the account number. For some totals and all operating statistics, artificial numbers are assigned. Some artificial totals are created to aid in the verification of balances transmitted. All balances have at least one cross-checking total in processing. Accounts having a zero balance are omitted.

Column 8 (check digit) is an additional numerical digit mathematically assigned to each account to reduce to a statistical minimum the possibility of a misassignment by the over-all system of any intended balance. This digit must be punched correctly or the entire line (account number and balance) will be rejected.

Column 9 is the algebraic sign. Because of the absence of a plus ($+$) sign on standard teletype equipment, a period (.) is used for all debit balances. A minus ($-$) is used for all credit balances.

Columns 10-18 are available for the account balance. All account balances are transmitted as whole-dollar figures. The pennies excluded by this procedure are accumulated for account groups and the whole-dollar total of this accumulation is then reported as a separate account number.

The account balance is "left justified" to column 10, and the line is terminated at the conclusion of the unit-dollar digit. "Left justification" is a method of placing a number in a specified area so that the first significant non-zero digit be placed in the left-most position of the number. All remaining digits of the number follow in sequence, a total maximum of 9 digits (up to $999,999,999) allowable.

Although accounts are prenumbered on transmission forms, sequence of punching accounts is not critical. Therefore, accounts accidentally omitted or overlooked can be inserted at any time following a completed line. If a mispunched balance is found before the closing format is begun, the corrected balance can be repeated with the proper account designation in the same data-message, as the computer will retain only the latest balance for each valid account.

If a mistyped account number, or check digit or both, is found before the closing format is punched, the correct account and balance can be included in the same data-message. In addition, if the mispunching results in another valid account number, that account must also be repeated with its correct balance.

Closing Format

After all accounts and balances have been typed and visually checked for alignment, obvious errors, etc., the closing format must be punched.

The first seven characters must be as follows: carriage return, line feed, letters, E, N, D, space. Following these seven characters, any variable identification which the reporting location designates, can be punched. This includes such things as time, date, name of reporting location and individual responsible, etc. The variable identification should be followed by the standard message closing characters.

Preparation

The required five-channel paper tape necessary for wire transmission can be prepared on one of several devices, such as a standard teletype transmitter, flexowriter, bookkeeping machine with paper-tape attachments, a punched-card-to-tape converter, or by using direct computer punched paper-tape output hardware. However, the format as outlined above must be maintained regardless of the device used.

Computer Processing

Input

The input system is designed to satisfy three basic objectives of information collection: completeness, accuracy and conciseness. The real-time accumulation and verification of closing figures is made possible by the capability of the UNIVAC 490 computer to receive, process and transmit teletype mesages directly through its main memory.

The computer programs which process and interpret the incoming financial data are controlled by parameter specifications which are maintained by the accounting department. These specifications are structured in tabular form for the program's reference and are entered into the random-access storage of the UNIVAC 490 prior to closing day.

Two days prior to closing, certain statistical figures are relayed to the profit centers from Westinghouse Electric International Company and Canadian Westinghouse, Limited. This communication is handled and verified through a separate UNIVAC 490 programming system which retains selected data from this transmission in random storage.

To ensure the accuracy of the incoming messages, two separate sets of internal checks are made. As the message is received, the opening format is inspected to determine the nature of the message (original or correction) and the reporting location. Each line of the data portion of the message is reviewed for validity of format, account number, check digit and balance. All correct lines are restructured in random-access storage. Immediately after this first pass, any errors found are automatically sent back by the program to the reporting location in the form of a teletype message.

Approximately every hour, the restructured closing figures and stored International and Canadian information are reviewed by a second program. All amounts are cross-balanced against transmitted subtotals and grand totals. Each account and balance is compared with predetermined dollar limits and special restriction parameters. In addition, the data is checked for the inclusion or exclusion of major account groups as specified by the controlling tables.

As a result of this second audit, one of three possible teletypes is automatically generated and sent back to the reporting locations:

1. If all tests have been satisfied, an acknowledgement message is sent.
2. Whenever the data fail to pass all checks, an error message is created that details incorrect information.
3. If the reporting location has not sent their figures by a preset time, a late message is generated.

A final match of each profit center's transmission against an overall predetermined control maintained at headquarters accounting is made before the real-time collection is considered complete and accurate.

Each time the second phase of real-time audit is performed, a copy of all information held in random storage is written on magnetic tape. When the financial data accumulation is completed, this tape is used as one of the direct inputs into the final batch-type processing and report generation programs. This allows a second UNIVAC 490 computer to work these final complex memory and time-consuming operations while the real-time assigned computer can continue efficiently performing its other functions.

Output

There are three primary functions that are performed subsequent to the collection of closing detail.

The first function consists of the completion of the corporate ledger information by the generation of headquarters' accounting ledger entries; development of intergroup, intercompany and intercorporate eliminations; calculation of income taxes; special accrual calculations; and the redistribution of special income, sales and orders. Complete worksheet printouts are produced to provide a manual "audit trail." New balances are posted to a historical master file and prior months' figures are extracted for statement preparation.

The second function, performed on the second UNIVAC 490 computer, is the production of a series of reports showing all transmitted and internally generated financial data in a concise, complete and workable format. The content, sequence and layout of these reports, as well as the development of the calculations, are controlled by the predetermined tabular specifications maintained by the accounting department. This allows a high degree of program-independent flexibility in systems modification.

The last function is the production of corporate statements (profit and loss statement, balance sheet, etc.) directly on the computer's high-speed printer. The closing figures are printed on blank white paper. These are subsequently over-laid by clear plastic mats and then photographed. This final step completes the fully automated, financial-closing cycle. From the time that the real-time information has been collected and verified, less than two hours of elapsed time are necessary to prepare the reproduced statements.

Conclusion

The successful operation of this wired book closing program has clearly indicated the unlimited potential of transmission of accounting data from reporting locations on a real-time basis to a centralized computer for processing. Wire communications have been established, tested and proved as a successful method of receiving financial data from each reporting location. The availability of profit center and corporate financial information on an immediate-inquiry, random-access basis assures faster, more accurate data for management decision-making. This wired book closing program is a major step toward a total management information system on a real-time basis.

11 SERVICE BUREAUS

The Three Levels of EDP Practice

Victor E. Millar

At the present time, more than 26,000 computers are installed in the United States. Current estimates indicate that this number will have increased by about 30 per cent at the end of 1966.

Every new installation adds to the demand for men experienced in the design and installation of computer systems. The demand for such people in major business centers throughout the country has reached such proportions that many users are unable to attract qualified EDP personnel for their installations. Sometimes the computer manufacturer is able to provide technical assistance in these areas. However, the manufacturer's ability to provide adequate technical assistance has been strained for several years. He has exactly the same problem as the typical user in attracting, training and keeping qualified personnel. As thousands of new computers are sold each year during the next decade, it is expected that the assistance of the manufacturers in designing and installing computer systems may have to be even further curtailed.

Demand for Qualified Professional Assistance

As a result of the shortage of qualified personnel, many of the 26,000 computers were installed by systems men who did not have the necessary

Reprinted by permission of the author and the publisher from *The Journal of Accountancy*, Vol. 123, No. 2 (February, 1967), pp. 41–44.

background and experience for their assignments. One of the direct results of this practice has been an apparent increase in the number of computer installations which are judged by their own management to fall short of their original objectives. The shortcomings take many forms. It is frequently found that the expected savings are not achieved or that the other proposed systems advantages are never realized. Sometimes the conversions to the new system is not made on schedule or, when it is made, the machinery is found to be inadequate to process all of the work in the available time, or there is no time remaining for the "other" applications which were part of the original justification for the computer.

On the other hand, the one thing that can be counted on in connection with the installation of a computer is that the computer will stay and the installation will expand in spite of any deficiences in the initial installation. The companies which have experienced difficulty in achieving their objectives in the use of computers and which are now planning to broaden their bases of mechanization or perhaps convert to more sophisticated systems are contributing as much to the demand for reliable personnel as are the companies which are installing their first computers.

As a consequence of the limited supply of qualified EDP personnel, there has been a significant increase in the demand for professional assistance in the design and installation of computer systems. This need is currently being met by service organizations—CPAs and others—that have demonstrated their ability to provide technical competence in the EDP field. In recognition of the increased demand for this type of service, some of the major CPA firms are already committed to developing and expanding their EDP competence. The results of a research study financed by the American Institute of CPAs and published in February 1966 indicate that about one quarter of the CPA firms are now engaged in some phase of EDP work.[1]

Arguments Against Expanding the Scope of a CPA Practice into the EDP Field

However, many other CPAs have apparently surveyed the field to try to evaluate the potential for such a practice and have concluded that the cost of branching off into a new area is not justified by the benefits. It is argued that the training of a CPA offers no technical preparation or background for an EDP practice and that an entry into that field requires one of two alternative approaches—both unsatisfactory. The firm must either adopt a training program for audit personnel which will require a long and costly period of nonchargeable time or it will be necessary to bring "outsiders" into the organization.

[1] *Computer Survey Results—Voluntary Comments*, Computer Research Studies No. 1, February 1966, AICPA, New York City.

It has also been argued that work in this field is unrelated to auditing and should be left to the technicians or the engineers. After all, the CPA doesn't get involved in other equipment installations such as a new punch press or molding machine. Furthermore, any expansion in the present scope of a CPA's practice represents a dilution of manpower which would otherwise be used to expand the basic auditing practice. Finally, many CPA firms are simply too small or, for other reasons, have no potential EDP users among their clientele.

These are all sound arguments on which many practitioners will make a decision not to expand their practices into the EDP field. However, this field is not one which must be accepted in its entirety or not at all. One of the conclusions apparent to the reader of recent AICPA publications is that many of the practitioners have not recognized that there are several levels of practice in the EDP field. Some of the reasons given for not developing an EDP practice seem to be related only to the broadest level of practice and may have no bearing on another level.

Three Levels of EDP Practice

There are three levels of EDP practice and each should be considered on its own merit: (1) reviewing computer proposals, (2) performing computer feasibility studies or (3) supervising computer installation projects. A fourth level of practice might be based on the use of a computer by the CPA in connection with his write-up work. However, this level is more closely related to a service bureau operation and should not be considered in the same category as the other three levels of professional practice.

Each of these three levels is a logical area of practice for the CPA firm. The second and third levels, however, require a commitment in manpower and time that far exceeds that required by the first. Accordingly, the first level is probably of interest to the greatest number of practitioners at this time.

Before concentrating on the first level of practice, a brief description of these three levels may help to better define the scope of practice associated with each one. The first level of practice is based on the review of a proposal for the installation of a computer. The proposal generally results from a study performed by the manufacturer or the client. The analysis of the proposal includes a review of the proposed savings to be realized and of the one-time costs of designing and installing the new system, and an impartial evaluation of the other advantages to verify that they can be realized and are directly related to the installation of the computer system. It also includes a review of the work that has been done to select the equipment which best meets the requirements of the proposed system.

The second level involves the actual performance of computer feasibility studies as opposed to reviewing the work done by others. The results of a feasibility study are expected to be as described above—an appraisal of the economics, a summary of the other advantages and a proposed installation schedule and equipment recommendation. There is a good reason for the CPA to expand his practice into this area. From the viewpoint of the client, it is certainly more efficient to do the job right the first time than to have to repeat portions of the work as a result of a subsequent review. From the viewpoint of the CPA, this service offers an improved basis for the development of a reputation in the EDP field and, along with it, an increased fee potential.

However, this level of practice generally requires a more significant commitment to the development of an EDP practice. It requires either several years of experience in reviewing the work of others, an expensive training program or the direct hiring of qualified personnel from outside sources. Even then, the firm of certified public accountants cannot be expected to make a significant contribution in this level of practice unless it also participates in computer installation projects.

It is only through this third level of service—installation work—that the firm is able to develop the experience, in depth, that makes it possible to conduct feasibility studies which are based on an independent evaluation of the facts. Installation work provides the firm with firsthand experience in the basic concepts of good systems design; in effectively evaluating both equipment and software; in hiring, training and supervising qualified personnel; in realistically estimating the time required for detailed design, programing and conversion of a computer system; and in identifying the costs, the savings and other advantages related to the installation of the computer.

This third level of practice, even more than the second, requires a complete commitment to the development of an EDP practice. One or more men may be assigned full time to an installation project which may extend over a period of one to two years. When a firm has only a few men and all are assigned to installation work for a long period of time, the firm's ability to promote new work is often seriously curtailed. It is evident then that a successful installation practice requires a sizable base of qualified personnel.

The CPA in the First Level of EDP Practice

Until an installation practice has been developed, however, it is difficult to establish a base for the training of new men. It has been our experience that the best approach to the training of EDP personnel is to follow the same pattern used in the training of audit personnel. A man with an aptitude for working with computers should be assigned to work for an experienced man on an installation project. Having been through an installation, he can then be assigned to feasibility studies, still under the direct supervision of experienced personnel. He can then be expected to train another generation of men by supervising installation projects. It is the installation practice, and not the feasibility studies or review of proposals, that provides the most effective basic training ground for new men.

From the foregoing, it can be seen that the easiest way to start an EDP practice is by reviewing proposals which have been prepared by others— client personnel or the manufacturer. In spite of all the arguments for staying out of this field, there are several important reasons for the CPA's becoming involved in the EDP activities of his clients, at least at this first level of practice.

First, the CPA has a responsibility to determine the effect of the proposed system on his audit program and to verify that the requirement for internal control has been satisfied.

Second, even though he is without experience in EDP work and has no technical background, he can bring to the engagement a thoroughly independent appraisal of the documentation and support for the claims. As a result of the mystery assigned to the EDP area by some companies, management frequently relies on computer manufacturers or on personnel in their own organization who may not be in a position to make an independent evaluation of the facts.

Many of the common oversights are readily apparent to the independent observer—even without technical training. Some are as common as the failure to add fringe costs to salaries or to add overtime rental to computer costs. Sometimes, the installation plan provides for adding programers before there has been time to design and document the proposed system, or for eliminating clerical personnel before the conversion to the new system has reached a point where those positions can realistically be eliminated. These are examples of common oversights which can be found by the observer who brings nothing but independence and common sense to the engagement.

In addition, the CPA is uniquely qualified in terms of background and training to practice at this level. He has developed an analytical ability which puts him in a good position to independently evaluate a proposal in terms of the projected savings or other advantages attributed to the proposed system. He also understands the importance of documentation and support as well as the value of a detailed installation schedule or work program. If the necessary documents are available for review, he is capable of reviewing them for reasonableness and completeness. If they are not available, he can explain their importance and recommend that they be developed.

Finally, the review of work performed by others represents the easiest place to begin an EDP practice. Yet it offers a significant opportunity to be of service to the client, and it is a good way to begin developing an EDP practice.

Accelerating the Development of an EDP Practice

If, after evaluating the three levels of practice, the CPA decides that he would like to develop a practice at the first level, he will take the first opportunity to assign one of his men to review a computer proposal, even though the man may be relatively inexperienced in EDP work. When this man is assigned to his first engagement involving the review of a computer proposal, it is probable that a detailed review of the documentation, some intelligent questions and an independent critique will be adequate to provide a significant service to the client. On this and on each subsequent engagement, the CPA's base of experience will, of course, be expanded. He will develop guidelines and standards related to each phase of his review and, over a period of time, will be able to evaluate some of the technical considerations included in the proposal.

However, as in any other field, his development would be more rapid if he were able to benefit from the experience of others and not rely solely on his own practice. Unfortunately, the literature to date has been aimed primarily at the programer, and it has not been directed toward the subjects which would be of interest to the practitioner starting an EDP practice.

One of the major contributions of the recent AICPA computer survey was that it demonstrated that a large share of the profession has little knowledge of the requirements or rewards of an EDP practice. A worthwhile next step for the profession would be the preparation of a technical EDP manual containing standards and guidelines which have been found to be useful by the firms of certified public accountants who have developed a successful EDP practice.

The subject matter of such a manual should include descriptions of the approaches to computer studies which have been found to be successful in the past and a description of some of the technical considerations related to the evaluation of computer plans. The manual would include at least the following areas:

1. *Principles of computer system design.* This section would describe the basic principles of good system design for batch systems—both cycle and daily—and for on line systems.

2. *Techniques of evaluating and selecting equipment.* This part would explain the techniques for matching the machine to the system requirements, estimating computer timing, determining the requirement for expandability and configurating and pricing equipment. It would also outline the general approaches to negotiating contracts with the manufacturers.

3. *Basis for estimating savings related to a computer installation.* This portion would cover the basis for estimating personnel eliminations, equipment replacement and other indirect savings.

4. *Basis for developing a detailed installation schedule and estimating the one-time costs.* This section would discuss the basis for estimating the time required for the design and installation of the computer system and estimating the personnel costs, the site preparation costs, the one-time equipment costs for test time and duplicate rental, the cost of tapes and disks and the other estimated costs.

5. *A technical checklist and description of the requirements of an installation.* This section would include a technical checklist describing such areas as the software functions, standard conventions, design and documentation standards, systems controls, testing techniques, conversion techniques and the operating standards.

Even though this is a fast-changing field, many of the techniques of good systems design, equipment evaluation and job administration are so basic that they change little over the years. We have found that a great number of the principles developed in connection with our first computer installation are as valid today as they were 12 years ago.

The EDP Practice of the Future

The arguments for developing an EDP practice may, of course, be academic. Ten years ago, great concern was expressed about the effect of computers on our audit practice. There have been some changes in scope and technique; however, as we all know, the changes have been far less than was feared. However, there are now being planned vast automation projects in most major U.S. industries. Service bureau operations are expanding. Large-scale time-sharing computers are being made available to small users. Integrated computer systems are being designed to bypass hundreds of clerical steps, and listings once used by clerical personnel are being replaced by machines that can communicate directly with computer-stored data.

We may yet find that the concern of a decade ago was valid. If so, only the smallest CPA firms will be able to avoid becoming directly involved in EDP work.

If more practitioners decide to take the first step—where by aptitude and experience they are qualified to practice—the resulting demand for information will, perhaps, result in the development of a more significant educational program. However, until more interest has developed within the public accounting profession, it will be left to those CPAs who have already developed a significant base of EDP experience to assist the others through the technical meetings or through the publications of the profession.

Use of a Data Processing Service Bureau—A Case Study

Paul W. Hedges

The "X" Electrical Contractors has been a respected name in electrical contracting in Southern California for twenty years—known for quality work. In a business where many small operators work out of their garage and do no job costing, the company has developed into a business with a large fleet of trucks and two warehouses with at least one hundred jobs in progress at one time. It specializes in large commercial and industrial work and is thus forced to maintain fairly complex job cost records.

The processing of payroll, accounts payable and job cost by hand proved to be inaccurate and time consuming:

—Clerk #1 spent three days a week on payroll, complicated by the requirements of various unions. The balance of her time was spent posting job ledger cards.

—The time of clerk #2 was consumed almost entirely by pricing requisitions from the trade book and matching documents for accounts payable.

—Clerk #3 spent half her time extending requisitions and the balance adding costs and summarizing jobs for billing.

Reprinted by permission of the author and the publisher from *Management Accounting*, Vol. XLVIII, No. 12 (August, 1967), pp. 23–26.

—Clerk #4 handled all typing and correspondence, answered the phones, and helped with dispatching and emergencies.

The Initial Steps

A study was made by the controller to determine whether to buy book-keeping machines, an in-house computer or use a data processing service bureau. The bookkeeping machines and computers which would be required for the type of output needed, were too expensive. The monthly cost, including an operator, would be higher than a service bureau and would not be as flexible. Furthermore, it was undesirable to incur such a large capital invest-ment in an area which was largely experimental for this type of business. This report was submitted to the Board of Directors which approved a further study of the use of service bureaus.

The study of service bureaus and construction of a system took about one and one half years. It was necessary to devise many new forms in order to communicate with the field and the service bureau. A material code book with over 6,000 items was prepared. Before contacting any service bureaus, the controller took a night course in basic computer programming and sys-tems, to familiarize himself with the terminology.

Choosing the Service Bureau

After the necessary groundwork, format sketches were prepared of how the runs would appear. Five different service bureaus were contacted: two large national bureaus (A and B), a fairly large bureau (C) covering the Southern California area, and small local bureaus (D and E).

Bureau A was eliminated immediately since it was primarily interested in selling its packaged programs. Bureau B prepared a satisfactory set of specifications for the proposed system, but would only accept an annual contract for a figure ten percent higher than the estimates from other bu-reaus. Bureau C was mainly interested in expanding its installation by use of satellite bureaus connected to a central computer. Its interest in the pro-posed system was only as a prospective package which could be sold to other contractors. Dun and Bradstreet reports were drawn on bureaus D and E to establish their financial stability. References were checked to verify the quality of their work, and the principals were questioned regarding their background and ability in the field.

Bureau D was chosen since it seemed to be the most stable and was willing to give a creative approach to the system. The following information was provided to bureau D in order to start processing:

1. Job to date figures on all jobs broken down to hours, labor, material, overhead, and direct expense.
2. Estimates on all large open jobs, to be set up as a comparison with actual.
3. A list of employees showing name, address, social security number, marital status, gross pay and various federal and state tax deductions.
4. A physical inventory coded by product, for extension from the material list book.

The following sequence of events illustrates the type of problems encountered:

November 10th, 1964—The first payroll was processed but the program had not been completely "de-bugged." It was necessary to write the checks by hand since the only good figures provided were for gross pay.

December 22nd, 1964—The payroll went smoothly for the first time this week. There were still problems with the job report programs. Some items in the cards would not print out and others came out as a series of nines.

January 15th, 1965—The first job reports were received on this date, including labor and material detail, and the summary comparing actual with estimates and computing overhead.

April 25th, 1965—The basic package was going smoothly and since all purchases had been fed in, disbursements and beginning balances were added to arrive at an accounts payable trial balance.

June 15th, 1965—Accounts payable was finally printed out in good order and balanced to general ledger. Between April and June there were problems in communicating to the programmer what the final result should be. The next step was to feed in data on closed jobs and costs used on progressive billings for a work in process run.

August 10th, 1965—The concept of costs flowing into work in process and cost of sales was difficult to explain to the programmer; however, on this date the first work in process run was received and it balanced to the general ledger.

August 10th, 1965 thru January 31st, 1966—Entire system was operating smoothly. There were other details to add, but it was necessary for company personnel to learn the full use of the reports.

February 15th, 1966—Service bureau D informed the "X" Electrical Contractors that they had received a good offer from service bureau C and was selling out to them. Service bureau C contacted the company and advised that they had a very competent programming staff and would give them the same personalized service which service bureau D had given.

April 10th, 1966—The computer was released and all of the work was being sent to Los Angeles. All personnel from service bureau D had been terminated.

April 25th, 1966—The payroll was coming through on time and the other runs were either late or out of balance. The man running the work was on the night shift and could not be reached. Other bureaus were contacted and they informed "X" Electrical Contractors that it was not a simple, overnight transition from one bureau to another, even with prepared programs and procedures. They must obtain copies and familiarize themselves with the system.

June 25th, 1966—Service bureau C changed local managers four times and key-punch supervisors three times. There was an almost complete breakdown in communications. Service bureau F, a small local bureau, was investigated. They had been in business for over twelve years, had good references and appeared stable financially. The programs and procedures were withdrawn from service bureau C and turned over to service bureau F.

August 30th, 1966—Service bureau F was having some problems with several of the programs which were converted to a larger computer and with procedures which were not up-dated. However, the reports were coming through on time and in balance.

Questions

1. Was a data processing service bureau the best solution?
2. Should the service bureaus have been changed immediately when bureau D was sold?
3. What are the problems peculiar to data processing bureaus and what factors need be solved for small business operations?

Actual Solution and Recommendations

In the case of "X" Electrical Contractors, a service bureau proved to be the best solution. This was the case of a comparatively small company with a small office staff and with paperwork requirements out of proportion to its size.

The EDP processing cut payroll time down to one day a week and eliminated hand posting and extending. It saved one full clerk's time besides providing a great deal more information.

The detailed up-to-date job costing enabled the company to bid closer and more competitively and thereby increase their sales volume. Without additional expense, an automatic monthly control, by job, was established over work in process.

A run of purchases, by account number, eliminated the hand posted check disbursement record and invoice record. Product coding of purchase invoices enabled the purchasing agent to check the accuracy of supplier's pricing periodically.

Runs by product code at the end of the year were constructed to provide a run similar to a perpetual inventory, to balance with the actual physical. The department heads and general foremen in the field learned to use the runs to check the progress of jobs.

Experience proved that it was wise to insist on copies of the programs and procedures and see that they were continually up-dated. A change should have been made as soon as possible when service bureau D was sold to service bureau C, which had been investigated previously.

A service bureau must be chosen the same as a key employee. Their stability, interests, abilities, education, and the tools they have to work with must be checked out. Communications are a major problem. The controller of "X" Electrical Contractors minimized this by taking a course in programming and systems but still had some problems. Service bureau personnel are technicians trained in the use of machines to process large volumes of paperwork. They do not understand accounting terminology.

One approach is to attempt to locate a bureau which has been established by CPA firms to process their clients' paperwork. This problem has been recognized and recent attempts have been made to correct it by using accounting personnel in the bureau.

The basic approach of "X" Electrical Contractors of using a small bureau was sound. The large bureaus depend on a fixed program with very few changes, for efficiency. A customized system needs personal attention.

Patience and continuous selling of the system to yourself and your management is required. A service bureau can give a smaller company a good job and an invaluable tool for much less than owning the equipment.

12   SIMULATION

Essentials of Computer Simulation

James C. T. Mao

With the development of modern electronic computers, simulation promises to be an important tool for decision making under conditions of uncertainty. Because of its technical nature, simulation in most business is generally carried out by specialists in the operations research group. Moreover, since much of the literature on simulation is directed towards these specialists, business executives more often than not find it difficult to get an informed opinion of simulation as a decision-making tool. The purpose of this article, therefore, is to explain the essentials of simulation in less technical language, making it more broadly accessible. The article contains a simple example showing how simulation can be used to determine a firm's risk of cash insolvency.

Nature of Simulation Studies

Simulation may be defined as the technique of evaluating the merits of alternative courses of action through experimentation performed on a math-

Reprinted by permission of the author and the publisher from *Financial Executive*, Vol. XXXV, No. 10 (October, 1967), pp. 55–62.

ematical model representing the actual decision-making situation.[1] There are two aspects of this definition that require special emphasis. First, every simulation study starts with the construction of a mathematical model designed to capture the essence of the relevant features of the real world, thereby revealing the functional relationships among the variables being investigated. The familiar breakeven analysis, the economic lot-size formula, and the various capital budgeting models for investment decisions are all examples of this type of mathematical abstraction.

Second, the phrase "through experimentation performed on a mathematical model" describes how the mathematical model is used in any simulation study.[2] The mathematical model serves as a medium of statistical experimentation. This usage of a mathematical model in simulation is what distinguishes simulation from optimization, since in optimization studies the mathematical models are solved analytically rather than experimentally. It would be ideal, of course, if we could readily derive analytical solutions from all of our mathematical models. Unfortunately, this is sometimes impossible, since a problem may be so complex that either it has no analytical solution or it has an analytical solution which is too costly to derive. In both of these situations, mathematical models can still be useful in serving as the basis of computer simulation.

Since mathematical models in simulation studies serve as the bases of experimentation, the focus in their construction is on specifying the inter-relationships between the individual elements making up the problem and on describing the randomness in these elements. These mathematical models, when activated with actual data, enable the analyst to forecast the kind of results that one might expect under actual conditions. By repeating the experiment many times for each alternative policy and by comparing outcomes, one can pick out that policy which produces the best simulation results. On the presumption that statistical errors tend to average out in the

[1] The following references contain excellent discussions of computer simulation as a tool for improving business decisions: Frederick S. Hillier and Gerald J. Lieberman, *Introduction to the Techniques of Operations Research* (Stanford, Cal.: Department of Industrial Engineering, Stanford University, 1966), ch. 16; Dimitris N. Chorafas, *Systems and Simulation* (New York, N. Y.: Academic Press, 1965), T. H. Naylor, J. L. Balintfy, D. S. Burdick, and K. Chu, *Computer Simulation Techniques* (New York, N. Y.: John Wiley & Sons, Inc., 1966). For special applications of simulation to financial decision making, the reader may also wish to consult the following: Alexander A. Robicheck, "The Use of Computer Simulation in Financial Planning," in Robicheck (ed.), *Financial Research and Its Implications for Management* (Stanford, Cal.: Graduate School of Buisness, Stanford University, 1966); and David B. Hertz, "Risk Analysis in Capital Investment," *Harvard Business Review* 42 (January–February, 1964), pp. 95–106.

[2] The idea of viewing computer simulation as a statistical experiment received much emphasis in the writing of Hillier and Lieberman. See their work cited in the preceding footnote.

long run, that policy which produces the best simulation results may in fact be the best policy when implemented under actual conditions.

Three Steps of Simulation

It will be useful to outline in reasonable detail the steps in planning and conducting a simulation study. Dimitris N. Chorafas has presented such an outline in graphic form reproduced in Figure 1 with minor extensions.[3] Notice that three separate steps are clearly delineated in this graphic outline: (1) mathematical model construction, (2) experimentation performed on the mathematical model, and (3) evaluation of the experimental findings. In what follows, we shall describe each of these three steps with special emphasis on the type of questions which are likely to confront financial executives who use simulation as a decision-making tool.

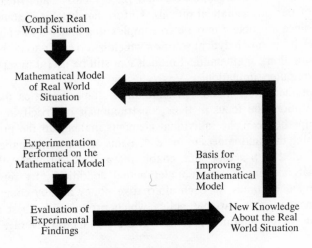

Figure 1. Planning and conducting a simulation study. Source: Adapted from a figure appearing in Dimitris N. Chorafas, *Systems and Simulation* (New York, N. Y.: Academic Press, 1965) p. 29.

Mathematical Model Construction

Perhaps the most critical step in any simulation study is the construction of a mathematical model which is simple enough to permit easy experimentation and yet complete enough to capture the relevant aspects of the business situation being simulated. It is clear that such a model is not likely to

---

[3] Chorafas, *op. cit.*, p. 29. See also Robicheck, "The Use of Computer Simulation in Financial Planning," *op. cit.*

be constructed unless the analyst is thoroughly clear in his own mind as to what he wishes to learn through the simulation experiment. A prerequisite for model construction, therefore, is a clear definition of the objective of simulation.

Given the objective of simulation, the analyst is then in a position to pick out from a business situation those variables which have an especially direct bearing on the particular business decisions being simulated. For example, if the purpose of simulation is to compare the net present values of two competing investment projects, the key variables in such a study would include sales revenue, cost of sales, rate of taxation, and the cost of capital. On the other hand, if the purpose of simulation is to determine the optimal cash balance, then the key factors to consider are cash receipts, cash disbursements, the opportunity cost of holding cash balances, the penalty of cash shortage, and perhaps some measure of the management's attitude toward the risk of cash insolvency. The list of key variables is thus seen to depend directly on the objective for which the simulation is intended.

Once the list of variables is compiled, the variables are linked together through a system of equations. Some of the equations in the system will be economic relationships, the validity of which can be empirically verified. Other equations in the system will be accounting identities which are true relationships by definition. An example of the first type of equation is the relationship between the volume of sales, the cash discount, and the amount of outstanding accounts receivable. An example of the second type of equation is the accounting identity: ending inventory = beginning inventory + purchases — withdrawals. It should be noted that, since management simulation studies are undertaken for the purpose of evaluating alternative courses of action, the analyst should construct his model in such a way that the controllable and uncontrollable variables can be easily separated. The fact that simulation itself may uncover additional alternatives not previously envisaged makes this suggestion all the more important.

Since the real world is characterized by uncertainty, the variables in a simulation study are sometimes viewed not as constants, but as random variables with probability distributions.[4] To keep the model simple, however, the randomization process should be restricted to those variables which are deemed critical in the decision process. In general, realism in model construction should not be carried too far. An overly realistic model is not only difficult to construct but also costly in terms of the time and the resources needed to operate it. Moreover, unnecessary details in a simulation model tend to distract the management's attention from the important to the trivial considerations. Thus, in the words of Hillier and Lieberman, "The overly

---

[4] A random variable may be defined as a numerical quantity whose value is dependent on the outcome of an experiment. The possible values, together with their respective probabilities of occurring, are referred to as the probability distribution of the random variable.

realistic model easily degenerates into a mass of trivia and meandering details, so that a great deal of programming and computer time is required to obtain a small amount of information. Furthermore, failing to strip away trivial factors to get down to the core of the system may obscure the significance of those results that are obtained."[5] In short,the test of a good model is not its ability to reproduce reality, but its ability to capture the essence of reality with a minimum of details.

Simulation as a Statistical Experiment

Implementing a simulation model containing random variables requires the generation of random observations from the probability distributions used to characterize these random variables. Consider, for instance, a mathematical model for the purpose of simulating random fluctuations in the cash balance of a firm. If sales volume is the source of this random fluctuation, we will need random observations on sales as input to the simulation experiment. Assuming the probability distribution of sales to be known, the procedure for generating random observations consists of two steps. First, generate a sequence of random numbers from the interval 0 to 1.[6] Second, use the random numbers to induce a corresponding sequence of random sales from the known probability distribution of sales. The reader is perhaps aware that library tables are available for generating random numbers.[7] But how exactly does one go about using random numbers to induce random observations from known probability distributions? The answer to this latter question constitutes an important part of one's understanding of how simulation can help to improve decision making under uncertainty. Because of its importance, the answer to this question will be deferred until the next section of the article, where a more thorough discussion will be made.

Let us assume that a set of random sales figures has been obtained. For each of the sales figures in this set, the mathematical model will produce a corresponding figure for the cash drain (or surplus) during the period under study. The resulting set of random cash flow figures will enable management to evaluate the effect of sales fluctuations on its cash balance position. Owing to the random nature of the experiment, the management will not be able

---

[5] Hillier and Lieberman, *op. cit.*

[6] If we pick numbers from a population in a way such that each number in the population has the same chance of being selected, then the numbers actually selected are described as random.

[7] Random numbers can be generated by tossing coins, rolling dice, etc., or by reference to library tables such as the Rand Corporation's, *A Million Random Digits with 100,000 Normal Deviates* (Glencoe, Ill.: The Free Press, 1955). Most computers today are equipped with random number generators which could be thought of as built-in coin-tossing or dice-rolling devices.

to predict with complete certainty what its cash balance will be at the end of the period being simulated. What the management will obtain from the experiment is the probability distribution of its cash balance position resulting from the random fluctuations in its sales.

Evaluation of Experimental Outcome

Simulation is a useful analytical tool because it provides management with the necessary data for evaluating the optimality of alternative business decisions. Any such evaluation presupposes the existence of a clearly defined criterion for measuring the degree of optimality associated with each policy. The concept of optimality, therefore, is a function of the criterion by which an outcome is evaluated. Depending on the criterion chosen by management, a given set of experimental outcomes could conceivably lead to more than one optimal policy. For purposes of illustration, we shall present in this section one simple criterion for determining the optimal cash balance of a firm.

Consider a simulation experiment which studies the effect of random sales fluctuations on the cash position of a firm. The output of this particular experiment consists of various possible values for the cash drainage during the period being simulated, along with the corresponding probability of each value being realized. Given this probability distribution of cash drainage, the question logically arises: In what way can this information be of value to the management in formulating its financial decisions?

To answer this question, let us say that financial management uses the simulation findings to help determine the optimal cash balance at the beginning of its planning period. One possible strategy is to set the beginning cash balance at a level such that the probability of a cash shortage during the period is equal to some acceptably low value α. As an example, suppose the management sets α at 0.05, and suppose the simulation experiment reveals that the probability distribution of cash drainage is as given in Table 1. The optimal initial cash balance is therefore $600, since if the firm does maintain an initial cash balance of this size, the probability of a cash shortage during the period is exactly equal to .05.

Generating Random Observations
with Random Numbers

An important phase in the implementation of any simulation study is the generation of observations on those variables in the model which are designated as random. As stated earlier, this phase is carried out by first generating a sequence of random numbers and then translating these random numbers into observations on the random variable. The purpose of this section is to explain and illustrate this procedure.[8]

Let us suppose that the sales variable in a simulation example has a probability distribution as given in Table 2. To generate observations from this probability distribution of sales, one must first establish a table of correspondence between all possible values of sales and all possible values of a random number between 0 and 1. The particular correspondence should reflect the probabilities with which different sales levels may occur. To illustrate, suppose the interval between 0 and 1 is divided into one-hundredths and each of these 100 two-digit numbers has an equal chance of being chosen in a random experiment. Then we might assign the ten numbers {.01, .02, . . ., .10} to a sales of $630, the twenty-five numbers {.11, .12, . . ., .35} to a sales of $640, and so on until the one number {1} is assigned to a sales of $700. (See Table 3.) Next, from the set of one hundred two-digit numbers between 0 and 1, generate a sequence of random observations in such a way that the probability of any number being chosen

Table 1
Probability Distribution of Cash Drain During the Period Being Simulated

Cash Drainage	$400	$450	$500	$550	$600
Probability	.05	.20	.50	.20	.05

Table 2
A Hypothetical Probability Distribution of a Firm's Sales

Sales X	$630	$640	$650	$660	$670	$680	$690	$700
P(X = x)	.10	.25	.30	.25	.05	.02	.02	.01

Table 3
Correspondence Between Sales and the Values of Random Numbers

Sales	$630	$640	$650	$660	$670	$680	$690	$700
Random Number	.01-.10	.11-.35	.36-.65	.66-.90	.91-.95	.96-.97	.98-.99	1.00

[8] The procedure for generating observations on random variables is explained in somewhat more analytic terms in the following references: Herbert P. Galliher, "Simulation of Random Processes," in *Notes on Operations Research* (Cambridge, Mass.: The M.I.T. Press, 1959), pp. 231–51; Hillier and Lieberman, *op. cit.*, pp. 13–20.

is equal to $\frac{1}{100}$. The sequence of random decimal numbers so generated, let us say, happens to be .90, .52, .83, .29, .65, .38, etc. Then, according to Table 3, the corresponding observations on sales are $660, $650, $660, $640, $650, $650, etc.

It should be especially noted that since ten of the 100 two-digit numbers between 0 and 1 are assigned to a sales of $630, this level of sales will be observed with a probability of exactly .1 ($\frac{1}{100} \times 10$). Similarly, a sales of $640 will be observed with a probability of .25, a sales of $650 with a probability of .30, and so on. What one has provided through the correspondence between sales and random numbers is a procedure for generating observations on sales in accordance with the probability distributions given in Table 2.

Simulating the Risk of Cash Insolvency

We now present a simple example of how simulation can be used to determine a firm's risk of cash insolvency during a recession. The risk of cash insolvency is simply defined as the probability that cash balance at the end of recession falls below zero.

Underlying Model

The following model was first constructed by Gordon Donaldson to determine a firm's risk of cash insolvency in the event that the economy is hit by a recession.[9] The extent to which sales of the firm will decline was uncertain, but the management was assumed to be able to specify the probability distribution of its sales during a recession. Interest expenses, tax liabilities, operating, selling and administrative expenses were regarded as optional for purposes of maintaining solvency. Moreover, the level of sales and the average collection period on receivables were assumed to be independent with known probability distributions.

On the assumption that the firm's outstanding debt can be successfully refunded at maturity, the firm's cash balance at the end of recession, K_1, is given by the expression:

$$\widetilde{K}_1 = K_0 + \widetilde{C} - \widetilde{V} - F - I - \widetilde{T}$$

where K_0 stands for cash balance at the onset of recession, C stands for collections on accounts receivable during recession, V stands for total variable cash expenses during recession (excluding taxes), F stands for total fixed cash expenses (excluding interest) during recession, I stands for total

---

[9] Gordon Donaldson, *Corporate Debt Capacity* (Boston, Mass.: Harvard Business School, 1961), Ch. 7 and Appendix B.

interest payment during recession, and T for total tax payments during recession. Notice that since sales volume is a random variable, so are C, V, T and K_1. The sign $\sim$ is used to distinguish random variables from constants.

If the probability distributions of recession sales and recession collection period are known, then this equation can be used to determine the firm's risk of cash insolvency, which is simply the probability that the firm's ending cash balance, K_1, is negative.

Data for the Simulation Experiment

A simple numerical example will be used to illustrate how the model could be used as a basis of simulation. The firm is assumed to have a normal daily sales of $1, a normal collection period of 30 days, a ratio of .3 between variable cash expenses and sales, daily fixed cash expenses of 40 cents, daily fixed noncash expenses of 4.17 cents, and an initial cash balance of $35. In a recession, the probabilities are .1, .4, .4, and .1 that daily sales will equal 80 cents, 70 cents, 60 cents, and 50 cents respectively. (See Table 4.)

Table 4
Probability Distribution of Daily Sales
During Recession

Sales	Probability
80¢	.10
70¢	.40
60¢	.40
50¢	.10

Given daily sales of 80 cents in a recession, the probabilities are .5, .2, .2, and .1 that the average collection period will lengthen by 10, 20, 30, and 40 days respectively. The corresponding probabilities are .4, .3, .2, and .1 if daily sales equal 70 cents; .1, .2, .3, and .4 if daily sales equal 60 cents; and .1, .2, .2, and .5 if daily sales equal 50 cents. (See Table 5.) Moreover, the firm is assumed to have $197 of debt in its capital structure, with interest payable at the rate of .07328 per day. Finally, the tax on net corporate income is assumed to be 50 per cent. If the firm is hit by a recession lasting 360 days, what is the probability that the firm will become insolvent?

Actual Simulation

To start the simulation, the first step is to generate random observations on the level of recession sales in accordance with the probability distribution in Table 4. We accomplish this step by generating random decimal numbers and attaching to these numbers the following meanings: any random number

Table 5
Probability Distribution of Increment in
Collection Period During Recession

(S = *daily sales during recession*)

Increment in Collection Period	Probability			
	S = 80¢	S = 70¢	S = 60¢	S = 50¢
10 days	.5	.4	.1	.1
20 days	.2	.3	.2	.2
30 days	.2	.2	.3	.2
40 days	.1	.1	.4	.5

between 0 and .10 means daily sales of 80 cents; any random number between .11 and .50 means daily sales of 70 cents; any random number between .51 and .90 means daily sales of 60 cents; and any random number between .91 and 1.00 means daily sales of 50 cents. After the sales level is observed, one needs to generate random observations on the increase in collection period in accordance with previously assigned probabilities. This latter step is accomplished again by generating random numbers and assigning to these numbers the appropriate meanings in accordance with Table 5.

Corresponding to any set of observed values for sales and collection period, the equation enables us to compute the firm's ending cash balance, K_1. Repeated runs of this experiment will produce a probability distribution of the value of K_1. The firm's risk of insolvency is simply the percentage of times when the value of K_1 is less than zero. In the present case, the results show that if the firm is hit now by a recession lasting 360 days, there is a probability of .085 that the firm will become insolvent.

Finally, the computer can be made to test the sensitivity of the risk of insolvency to changes in the length of recession, the size of the initial cash balance, the size of the initial debt and the ratio of cash variable expenses to sales.[10]

Further Applications

This has been a brief introduction into simulation as a tool for decision making under conditions of uncertainty. Although the example here dealt with risk of insolvency, simulation has also been used to formulate financial decisions in areas of dividend policy, capital structure, short-term financing, and capital expenditures. Readers interested in learning more about these other applications ought to consult the specific references given in the bibliography.

[10] The computer program for implementing this simulation experiment is available upon request from the author at The University of British Columbia, Vancouver 8, Canada.

Bibliography

1. Elwood S. Buffa, *Models for Production and Operations Management* (New York, N. Y.: John Wiley & Sons, 1963).
2. Dimitris N. Chorafas, *Systems and Simulation* (New York, N. Y.: Academic Press, 1965).
3. Herbert P. Galliher, "Simulation of Random Processes," in *Notes on Operations Research* (Cambridge, Mass.: The M.I.T. Press, 1959).
4. Fred Hanssmann, *Operations Research in Production and Inventory Control* (New York, N. Y.: John Wiley & Sons, Inc., 1962).
5. David B. Hertz, "Risk Analysis in Capital Investment," *Harvard Business Review* 42 (January-February, 1964).
6. Frederick S. Hillier and Geral J. Lieberman, *Introduction to the Techniques of Operations Research* (Stanford, Cal.: Department of Industrial Engineering, Stanford University, 1966).
7. T. E. Hull, *Introduction to Computing* (Englewood Cliffs, N. J.: Prentice-Hall, Inc., 1966).
8. T. H. Naylor, J. L. Balintfy, D. S. Burdick, and K. Chu, *Computer Simulation Techniques* (New York, N. Y.: John Wiley & Sons, Inc., 1966).
9. Rand Corporation, *A Million Random Digits with 100,000 Normal Deviates* (Glencoe, Ill.: The Free Press, 1965).
10. Alexander A. Robicheck, "The Use of Computer Simulation in Financial Planning," in Robicheck (ed) *Financial Research and Its Implications for Management* (Stanford, Cal.: Graduate School of Business, Stanford University, 1966).
11. Thomas J. Schriber, *Notes on Precharting Fundamentals* (Ann Arbor, Mich.: The University of Michigan, 1966).
12. Henri Theil, John C. G. Boot, and Teun Kloek, *Operations Research and Quantitative Economics* (New York, N. Y.: McGraw-Hill Book Company, 1965).

Using Simulation to Design a Management Information System

Adolph F. Moravec

Designing a new management information system is at least as difficult a task as designing a new production machine. Typically it takes as much— if not more—time, effort, and attention from specialists and management alike.

Yet there is no comparison between the two design jobs in terms of the predictability of the results. New equipment, after a normal shakedown period, usually performs pretty much as expected. New management systems, on the other hand, all too often require so much debugging that they never reach a stage when they can be considered final.

Some of this unpredictability is inevitable, of course. Because information systems involve human beings, they can never be designed in as scientific a manner as equipment can. Yet if management systems could be pretested, as machines are, many post-installation headaches could be avoided.

A method of pretesting that is now receiving increased attention from systems men is simulation, that is, experimenting with a simulated model of the information system. This article attempts to provide some basic guidelines for using simulation in the design of a management information system. A specific model and simulator are developed step by step to illustrate

Reprinted by permission of the author and the publisher from *Management Services*, Vol. III, No. 3 (May–June, 1966), pp. 50–58.

the methodology. The example used is taken from a defense industry both because the bulk of the experimentation with simulation thus far has been in defense industries and because that is the area in which the author's principal experience lies. The basic principles, however, are applicable to any kind of industry.

Since a management information system must meet the complete—and ever changing—needs of a company, it must by its very nature be the product of a research and development effort. Since the system will be used—and in part designed—by individual managers, it must to some degree represent their personal viewpoints. Therefore, the system must have the flexibility to permit change as new managers or new managerial ideas create the need for redesign.

Changes will be required both because of changes in managerial personnel and thinking and because of changes in the character of the business. For this reason the system design must be open-ended, that is, amenable to change in a simple and relatively effortless manner. To do this requires a sort of R&D approach to the systems design effort. Manual simulation, as is explained in this article, offers an economical and effective R&D tool.

Basic Design Methods

There are three basic methods by which an information system can be designed.[1] They are as follows:

1. Experiment with real facilities, machines and men.

2. Use formal mathematical analysis, that is, construct equations describing the various alternatives.

3. Conduct simulated experiments, by computer or manual means.

With the first method, which is, of course, by far the most common, a plan is suggested and approved and is simply put into effect. If the plan proves to be inadequate, it is modified. Thus, the company ends up experimenting with its own men, machines and facilities. In some cases this is the only method available—and it does get action—but it is confusing and costly to operate inefficiently for a long period of time while "testing" alternatives. This cost and confusion can be avoided by the use of more formal analyses.

The second method is a desirable and powerful approach. However, since it requires writing equations that completely describe the system under study, it is often too complicated to use effectively. Furthermore, the technique presents often insuperable communications problems for the systems

[1] Donald G. Malcolm, "System Simulation—A Fundamental Tool for Industrial Engineering," *The Journal of Industrial Engineering*, May–June, 1958.

analyst. It is usually difficult to convince management that a formula has the complete answer.

The third method is that of experimenting by using a simulation model. Simulation adds a new dimension to management's analytical powers by breaking involved situations down into logical steps and trying them out. In this way it is possible to eliminate costly trial-and-error operations.

Simulation

As was explained in an earlier issue of *Management Services*,[2] simulation is a technique that permits experimentation with and testing of certain management policies and procedures in much the same way an aeronautical engineer tests his design ideas in a laboratory or wind tunnel. The model of information system must be completely defined. However, the simulation activity takes place by varying the computation, output anlysis, and management decision making. Thus, the program, input control, and information system data networks are flexible and can be revised after each simulation cycle. These elements are not tied down until the simulation has been completed.

Two terms should be defined at this point. The model is defined as including the basic systems flow, the major function and operations to be performed, and the essential data elements to be put into the system or received from it. The simulator is defined as the program of instructions or procedural actions necessary to receive, process, and report data. The simulator, the mechanism that runs the model, produces the end product as a result of simulating the model and its logic.

The simulation process frequently uncovers problems that otherwise would not have been recognized until too much design water had gone over the dam. The differences between the systems requirements and the results actually achieved by the model and simulator show the system designer where changes need to be made in the system.

Sometimes problems can be alleviated or eliminated simply by changing one systems requirement for another. Sometimes requirements must be dropped altogether; they begin to look like frosting on the cake when examined in the light of design difficulties. Occasionally results more than satisfy requirements, indicating that requirements can be increased or that the system can be simplified.

The basic objective of simulating an information system is, of course, to test and improve the system. The process is useful for these purposes:

[2] E. N. Khoury and H. Wayne Nelson, "Simulation in Financial Planning," *Management Services*, March-April, 1965.

1. Developing the basic (operational) information flow logic and determining the essential data needs and their dependencies
2. Determining the action and interaction requirements necessary for the decision making process
3. Ascertaining the changing needs of the firm in order to provide guidelines for future program flexibility.

However, it has subsidiary benefits as well. The simulator is designed to permit the operating manager as well as the systems analyst to try out his ideas. This involvement of management in the simulation process is highly desirable since it enhances management understanding and eventual acceptance of the system.

Although the simulation process itself aids in understanding the information system, the model-building techniques that were devised to achieve the simulation are even more helpful. The very process of creating, in a quantitative way, a complete information system with all its variables and parameters helps to give both systems men and management a clearer understanding of the basic structure and logic of the management modus operandi.

Manual vs. Computer

Simulation can be either manual or computerized. The example described in this article is manual. Each type has its advantages. A computer model can be recycled rapidly. However, a manual model displays the fundamental logic of the system without the interference of huge files and data records. It can be constructed with minimum cost and time resources. It bypasses the computer programing step and the intricacies associated therewith. It can, if need be, provide the pilot methodology for later construction of a computer simulation program.

Both computer and manual models, however, are designed, developed, and tested with actual data. Either provides a miniature of all the essential functions and actions needed to operate and monitor a business.

Basic Prerequisites

Constructing a simulation model of a company is part of the investigation phase of the overall plan for designing an information system. It is performed by operations analysts who are capable of determining the important things that must be managed and defining the kinds of data that will be required to enable management to monitor a program, project, or operation. Like any other model-building project it must be staffed by individuals skilled in model building, and it must be actively supported with management time, interest and guidance.

Before construction of the model can begin, management must determine its basic data processing philosophy. For example, it must decide whether the system to be designed should be based upon the total systems (input-oriented) concept or the single information flow (output-oriented) concept.[3] It also should have a basic plan for designing an information system.[4]

And it must have a definite list of objectives spelling out just what the information system is intended to do. It is possible that not all of the objectives will apply to the manual simulation model at this point in time; however, they should all be listed so that the model can be continually evaluated.

The information system objectives that are to be applied to the particular model being constructed in our example are as follows:

1. To provide each level and position of management with the fundamental information that can be used in the conduct of each manager's job.

2. To filter the information so that each level and position of management receives only the information it can and should act on.

3. To provide information to the manager only when action is possible and appropriate.

4. To provide the analysis, data or information in any form requested.

5. Always to provide information that is up to date.

6. To provide information in a form that the manager can understand and digest easily.

Other information systems can, of course, have other objectives. These are the ones selected for the example that is illustrated in this article.

In order to simulate a possible information system and test whether it meets these objectives, it is advisable to select a specific operation or project and try out a possible information flow for that operation or project. The project used as an example in our case illustration is the construction of a military boat.

The ingredients or specifications needed to design the model include goals, functions, condition elements, and decision making alternatives. The specifications given for this example are those that were selected for this particular model. A construction company or financial institution might have quite different goals. The goals, however, whatever they are, must be clearly stated and understood.

The goals of our model are as follows: (1) to provide an information system cycle that is to include both planning and control functions and activities, (2) to base it upon recent defense procurement concepts, and

[3] A. F. Moravec, "Basic Concepts for Planning Advanced EDP Systems," *Management Services*, May-June, 1965.

[4] A. F. Moravec, "Basic Concepts for Designing a Fundamental Information System," *Management Services*, July-August, 1965.

(3) to make provisions for trade-offs of resource alternatives as part of the decision making operations in the model.

Condition Elements

The major condition elements of the model in our example are to be the following: time and schedules, cost and cost/effectiveness, and performance and performance/effectiveness. The decision making resource trade-off alternatives are to consist of dollars, man-hours, time, and technical performance. The functions to be included are project or program planning, authorized in-work operations (actual), and control between planning and actual authorized in-work operations.

After the specifications are complete, the model and its simulator can be constructed. This should be done in three phases. In the first phase the information system cycle and its scope are defined. In the second phase the planning model and simulator are developed, and in the final phase the control model and simulator are developed.

Cycle Definition

In the first—and perhaps the most difficult—phase of model design we must define the conceptual model in words and in terms of network flow diagrams. Here we identify the key operations that the enterprise must accomplish in order to function properly.

Since the hypothetical company in our example concentrates its marketing and sales efforts in the defense industry, it was decided to establish a single information system keyed to to the armed services' needs for proposal submission and for progress reporting after a contract has been awarded. The same system is to provide the necessary reports for successful management of projects within the company. These reports are to include performance measurements of schedules, costs, and technical performance.

Because success or failure in this industry is now so much affected by new defense procurement philosophies (fixed-price incentive contracting), this particular information system is to be designed so as to provide management with data on decision making alternatives during the planning phase as well as during the operational phase. The system must provide data for planning and estimating and for comparison of approved plans against actual accomplishments. The system must provide for visibility and predictability of impact (the meaning of results achieved). Planning, contracting, and operational control must be tied together for "early warning" visibility —early warning in the sense that planning and contracting data can be tied to performance information for forecasting purposes.

The greatest problem in model building is in determining the company's true operational requirements—both data and actions—and in sequencing these operational requirements for proper decision making. For example, in the defense industry we are using as an example, proposal actions and data precede contractual actions and data, which in turn precede operational performance actions and data; costs, schedules and performance measurements cut across all of these action operations, and decision making points appear all along them.

A review of our hypothetical company's requirements for its operating and decision making needs results in the information system cycle indicated in Figure 1. This system cycle provides the fundamental framework of the information system that is to be designed. Broadly, it is broken down into a planning function and a control function.

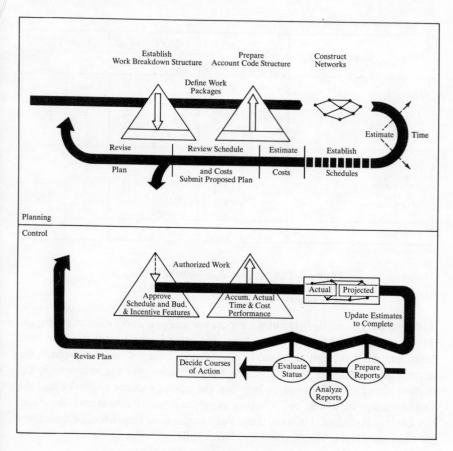

Figure 1. Information system cycle.

Planning Simulation

The top half of Figure 1 indicates the essential operations in the planning area of the model. The first step is to establish a work breakdown structure for the project, define its work packages, and set up an account and responsibility code structure. Then PERT-type networks and flow charts showing the sequence of work packages and the flow of data are prepared, and time/cost curves for the pertinent skills utilized on the project are established.

In the fourth step times required for all skills on each task are estimated and associated with the appropriate costs. Times for simulation purposes are estimated in a semi-random manner by rolling a die. For each task an optimistic, most likely, and pessimisitic time is estimated, and an expected time estimate is calculated from the standard PERT/Time formula.[5]

Time and Cost Estimates:

Tasks	Initial		Least Cost		Least Time	
	Elapsed Time	Cost	Elapsed Time	Cost	Elapsed Time	Cost
Motor:						
A – Parts Const.	3	3.00	4	2.00	1	4.00
C – Assembly & Test	3	.50	3	.50	1	2.50
Total	*6	3.50	7	2.50	2	6.50
Hull:						
B – Design	2	3.50	4	2.00	1	4.00
D – Fab	2	2.00	2	2.00	1	3.00
E – Assembly & Test	1	2.50	3	.50	1	2.50
Total	5	8.00	*9	4.50	*3	9.50
Cost Total		11.50		7.00		16.00

*Indicates Critical Path

Figure 2. Project planning—phase II. Step 5: Project multi-evaluations (min.-max.) planning report B.

Step 5 produces the first output report for analysis and evaluation (Figure 2). It presents a range of time (and associated cost) estimates for each task, including the initial estimate developed in Step 4, the least-time estimate, and the least-cost estimate. Its purpose is to give the manager information about the relationships between the costs of doing the tasks and the various times in which (by altering combinations of resources) the tasks can be accomplished. He uses these data in the next step when he considers the risks involved in various cost-time trade-offs.

$$\frac{^5a + 4m + b}{6}$$

Risk Evaluation

Figure 3 is a plotted output that represents the information in Figure 2 pictorially. It depicts the variable risk evaluation anlysis. (Figure 3, rather than Figure 2, illustrates the form in which management should receive such information for decision making purposes, in my opinion.) This report presents management with its first major decision making point requiring action. Management must accept the plan offered (the initial or medium-point time/cost estimates) as representing an acceptable risk, or the preceding steps must be recycled.

Depending on the importance of this program and the number and resource commitments of in-house projects, management might call for another iteration run in an attempt to refine the risk evaluation analysis. After

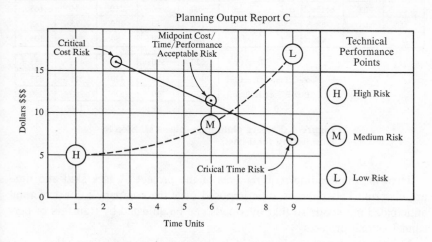

Figure 3. Project planning—phase II. Step 6:
Variable risk evaluation analysis. First major
decision-making required action: a plan must
be acceptable or steps 1 thru 6 recycled.

various plans are developed through simulation, they are evaluated and the "best" plan selected. (The "best" plan is determined by the relative weights given to cost, time, and performance risks as a part of the overall marketing strategy.)

New Condition Element

In this case the initial plan (with its mid-point risk condition) is acceptable. It now becomes a management decision making condition for the final information system.

Table A	
Tables Skill/ Code	Hr. Wage Rate $/Hr.
5	2.00
6	1.00
7	1.50
8	1.50

Note: Indirect Cost is 50% of
Total Direct Cost

Table B		
Activity	Direct Material Cost $	Material Lead Time
A	100	3 Time Units
B	100	3 Time Units
C	50	2 Time Units
D	70	2 Time Units
E	30	2 Time Units

Planning Output Report C

Activity	Resp. Code	Time Hours	Cost Code	Wage $/Hr.	Direct Labor	Direct Mat'l.	Total Direct	Indirect 50%	Total
A	01	120	5	2.00	240	100	340	170	510
B	02	80	5	2.00	160	100	260	130	390
C	03	120	6	.50	60	50	110	55	165
D	04	80	7-8	1.50	120	70	190	95	285
E	05	40	6	1.00	40	30	70	35	105

	Direct Labor	Direct Mat'l.	Total Direct	Indirect 50%	Total
Total Cost	620	350	970	485	1455
A-C Total Motor Cost	300	150	450	225	675
B-D-E Total Hull Cost	320	200	520	260	780

**Figure 4. Project planning—phase II. Step 8:
Computing total cost.**

Then the manloading requirements of the project by task skill and time
are charted. This chart is superimposed over the company's chart of total
anticipated manloads so that overloads can be adjusted by transfers of personnel among projects.

The result is another planning output report (Figure 4) demanding a decision. Figure 4 shows tables of constant cost factors and a summary of total
dollars by activity and work break-down structure. Management now must
decide whether to accept or reject its data. If the decision is negative, all
the preceding steps must be simulated again with different data. If the decision is affirmative—as it is in the case of our example—the simulation
can continue into the prenegotiation phase of the project.

Prenegotiation simulation is an attempt by the company to prepare a sort
of "value analysis" of a set of contract conditions that will come close to
optimizing the company's operations and yet leave room for contract ne-
gotiations with the customer. The simulation is intended to reveal the various
possible profit alternatives and the trade-off possibilities among them.

For the defense contractor this is a critical part of the simulation, since
the decisions involved here are key ones in terms of submitting an attractive
proposal to the customer. However, since defense procurement is such a

highly specialized field and the various incentive factors to be considered are so different from the profit and loss considerations important in nondefense business, this phase of the simulation will only be summarized briefly rather than being described in detail.

The purpose of this part of the simulation is to vary the elements for which incentive profits may be earned (cost, systems performance and time schedule) to see which incentive rewards the company wishes to aim for. This choice depends chiefly on the company's estimate of its ability to qualify for each of the various incentive rewards.

Target profit and cost are set, either subjectively or as part of the bid request. Then various combinations of minimum, maximum and target performances on each of the three incentive elements that will meet the profit goal are calculated.

Simulation Runs

For example, one simulation run determines the cost control performance required if high incentive fees are to be earned for this element, with lower incentive fees for systems performance and delivery schedule compliance. Another simulation varies the incentive weights to determine the technical product performance standards that must be met to earn high incentive fees for that category. After reviewing the results of the simulation, management selects the incentive mix it prefers.

In this particular case management feels that it has the greatest control over product technical performance and believes the customer will want to provide greater incentives for this element (representing in this case the speed of the vehicle). It decides, therefore, to assign the greatest weight in its bid to technical performance.

Since rewarding conditions are now tied to the contract, the planning data must be recalculated to allow for these incentives. The steps that led to Figure 4 must now be repeated to incorporate this new factor. Figure 5 shows the new total dollar costs.

Control Simulation

At this stage of the simulation the contract has been negotiated and approved by both customer and contractor, and the control portion of the information system cycle now to be set up and tested. Provisions must be made for accumulating actual time and cost data and for preparing reports for analysis and evaluation. The planning and control functions must be tied together so that control operations will be geared to the planned performance targets and cost budgets.

Table A	
Tables Skill/ Code	Hr. Wage Rate $/Hr.
5	2.00
6	1.00
7	1.50
8	1.50

Note: Indirect Cost is 50% of Total Direct Cost

Table B		
Activity	Direct Material Cost $	Material Lead Time
A	100	3 Time Units
B	100	3 Time Units
C	50	2 Time Units
D	70	2 Time Units
E	30	2 Time Units

Planning Output Report

Activity	Resp. Code	Time Hours	Cost Code	Wage $/Hr.	Direct Labor	Direct Mat'l.	Total Direct	Indirect 50%	Total
A	01	140	5	2.00	280	100	380	190	570
B	02	91	5	2.00	182	100	282	141	423
C	03	240	6	.50	120	50	170	85	255
D	04	80	7-8	1.50	120	70	190	95	285
E	05	40	6	1.00	40	30	70	35	105
Total Cost					742	350	1092	546	1638
A-C Total Motor Cost					400	150	550	275	825
B-D-E Total Hull Cost					342	200	542	271	813

Figure 5. Reward operating data.

Control Reports

First the activities to be completed (called events in PERT terminology) and their time schedules for the complete system and for its major components must be listed in display report form. This was already done, of course, during the planning phase of the project, but only after the completion of customer negotiation are these controls ready to be put into final form. Figure 6 illustrates a breakdown of technical performance events by major components, in this case motor components. A technical performance index (in this case simply the percentage of events completed on time) is used to monitor progress.

The second step in setting up the control portion of the model is to provide for monitoring of cost/time performance. The report form and display panel used for this purpose are shown in Figure 7. The display panel at the top of Figure 7 is used to record actual costs versus planned costs and reward (with incentives) costs; Control Report A at the bottom of Figure 7 is used to record actual completion times as compared to planned and reward (incentive) completion times.

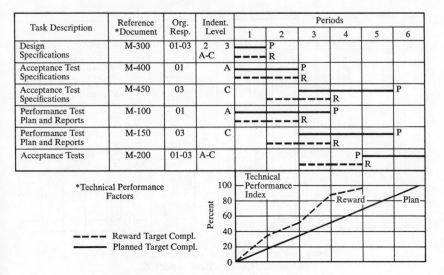

Task Description	Reference *Document	Org. Resp.	Indent. Level	Periods					
				1	2	3	4	5	6
Design Specifications	M-300	01-03	2 3 A-C	P R					
Acceptance Test Specifications	M-400	01	A	P R					
Acceptance Test Specifications	M-450	03	C		R			P	
Performance Test Plan and Reports	M-100	01	A	P R					
Performance Test Plan and Reports	M-150	03	C		R			P	
Acceptance Tests	M-200	01-03	A-C				P R		

*Technical Performance Factors

– – – – Reward Target Compl.
——— Planned Target Compl.

Figure 6. System performance tasks: motor detail.

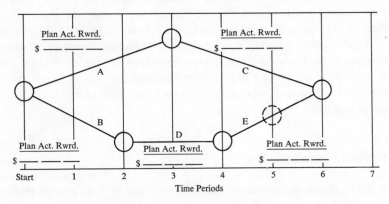

Control Report A—By Period

	Paths	Planned		Actual .		Variance		Reward		Variance	
Time Period		Sch	$	Sch	$	Sch	$	Sch	$	Sch	$
	A										
———	B										
	C										
Completed	D										
	E										
	Total	/////		/////		/////		/////		/////	

Figure 7. Project control—phase III. Step 2: Management display panel.

Time Units	Activity Resp. and Skill Codes	Plan Target Hrs.	Plan Target Cum.	Reward Target Hrs.	Reward Target Cum.	Actual Hrs.	Actual Cum.
1	A 01 5	40	170	70	285		
	B 02 5	40	195	91	423		
	Total	80	365	161	708		
2	A 01 5	80	340	140	570		
	B 02 5	80	390	91	423		
	D 04 7-8	–	–	40	142		
	Total	160	730	271	1135		
3	A 01 5	120	510	140	570		
	B 02 5	80	390	91	423		
	C 03 6	–	–	120	127		
	D 04 7-8	40	142	80	285		
	Total	240	1042	431	1405		

Time Units	Activity Resp. and Skill Codes	Plan Target Hrs.	Plan Target Cum.	Reward Target Hrs.	Reward Target Cum.	Actual Hrs.	Actual Cum.
4	A 01 5	120	510	140	570		
	B 02 5	80	390	91	423		
	C 03 6	50	55	240	255		
	D 04 7-8	80	285	80	285		
	E 05 6	–	–	40	105		
	Total	320	1240	591	1638		
5	A 01 5	120	510				
	B 02 5	80	390				
	C 03 6	80	110				
	D 04 7-8	80	285	Sub-	Sub-		
	E 05 6	20	52	Max	Max		
	Total	380	1347	477	1546		
6	A 01 5	120	510				
	B 02 5	80	390				
	C 03 6	120	165				
	D 04 7-8	80	285				
	E 05 6	40	105				
	Total	440	1455				

Figure 8. Project control—phase III. Step 3:
Schedule/Cost control report B.

Control Report B (Figure 8) is used to record cumulative dollars and man-hours (actual versus the various plans) during the project. Control Report C (Figure 9) displays the cost overruns or underruns by period.

At this point a highly unsophisticated model of a particular company's operation has been designed. Many variations on the model are possible; only by repeated cycling and recycling through the various functions of planning and control can management settle on its view of what an ideal model should contain.

Project Simulator Kit

To facilitate such repeated simulations a sort of management game might be played. A project simulator kit was designed especially for the model described in this article. A similar kit—consisting essentially of visual aids for the display of simulation results—could be designed for any model; it would, of course, display other reports suited to the particular information system being designed.

This kit consists of five display panels for operational control. Actual operations are simulated by making decisions, calculating the results, and recording the data thus generated on the four monitor panels. (The fifth panel is used to record the alternative decisions that are available and the choices made.) On the panels are the reports shown in Figures 6, 7, 8 and 9.

The operational cycle starts when the first period target dollar amounts (from Control Report B, Figure 8) are placed on the first display panel,

Management Display—Cost Progress Chart

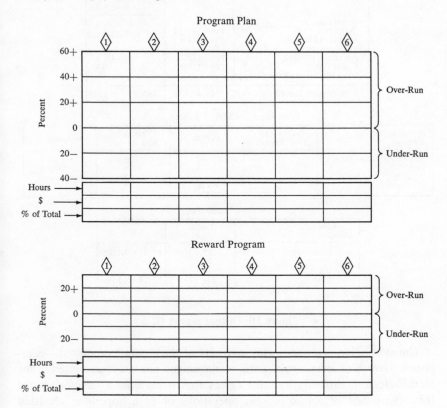

Figure 9. Phase III control. Step 4: Cost
control report C.

which is a copy of Figure 7. Then a die or dice are thrown to determine the actual results of the first period of operation.

Results are then recorded on Figure 7 and Figure 8. Variance data are computed on Control Report A (Figure 7) and indicated on Cost Control Report C (Figure 9). Percentage overruns or underruns are recorded on Report C. Technical systems performance information (as in Figure 6) is updated. Display data are computed based upon actual hours expended as indicated on Report B (Figure 8).

The operational cycle for the next period is started by placing the dollars and time target figures from Report B (Figure 8) onto Figure 7. The same cycle of operation is repeated for the number of time periods the project is expected to take. Then all output reports are updated with actual data and summary results of the simulation are indicated on Report G (Figure 10).

Table of Fees

			Actual
Target Cost	1455		1865
Target Fee	116	(8%)	–
Maximum Fee	204	(14%)	–
Minimum Fee	20	(2%)	–
Fee (Profit) Swing	175	(12%)	85 (4.4%)
Ceiling Cost	1746	(120%)	–
Value Engineering Share 50%			–
Total Program Cost-Ceiling—1950 (1746 + 204)			1865 + 85 = 1950

Basic Incentive Matrix Table

Incentive Element	Outcome for Max. Reward	Target	Outcome for Min. Reward	Actual
Syst. Performance (MPH)	50	30	25	50
Cost	1638	1455	1746	1865
Schedule (Time Units)	4	6	7	6
Fee (Profit)	204	116	29	85

Incentive Dollar Pool

Incentive Elements	Dollar Pool	Actual
Syst. Performance	87	85 (1950-1865)
Cost	73	0
Schedule	44	0
Total	204 (14%)	85 (4.4%)

Figure 10. Output report G.

The simulation exercise—with revisions of the model as required—is repeated over and over again until management not only understands the model's logic completely but also agrees that it presents a straightforward facsimile either of actual present operations or of a hoped-for idealized operation.

Conclusion

By thus simulating the information system, the systems designer can construct and walk through an information system cycle for management's benefit. From this trial run, he should obtain the following benefits:

1. A methodology for constructing an information system.

2. A simplified—but particular—pilot information system that contains the basic requirements for an expanded system.

3. The basic decision making logic that can be used to determine the essential data and their dependencies.

4. Clarification of the major decision making actions required and their interaction responses (alternatives), including resource trade-off alternatives.

5. An outline of essential data flow reflecting the operational controls required at the top management level—major actions, responses, and data feedback.

The information system that the company finally adopts may not bear much resemblance to the first model that is simulated. But, thanks to the simulation technique, it will probably be an information system that works.

Simulation in Financial Planning

E. N. Khoury
H. Wayne Nelson

Simulation, the mathematical representation of a system in order to see how a change in one of its elements will affect the others, is—at least potentially—one of the most powerful tools of operations research. It is finding increasing use in the solution of military and production problems.

In the financial area its application is less well known. Simulations of economic and financial processes have been employed mainly as research and teaching aids. Little has been done to develop simulation techniques to improve precision and response in the financial planning process within the corporate structure.

At Burroughs we have been experimenting with a simulation of the financial structure of the entire company. Our experience thus far has convinced us that this technique can provide management with an effective new planning tool.

This article, based on that experience, discusses the development of a financial simulation model structured around traditional accounting reporting practices. It emphasizes (1) the understanding of the business processes necessary to structure a useful model, (2) the model as a mirror of corporate policy, (3) the values and pitfalls in the use of a simulation model and (4) certain methodological issues involved.

Reprinted by permission of the authors and the publisher from *Management Services*, Vol. II, No. 2 (March–April, 1965), pp. 13–21.

Simulation

Whenever the logical relations between the elements in a structure or a system can be quantified or expressed in measurable terms, a mathematical representation of these relationships can be formulated. The set of all these formal statements is then a model of the system. When we manipulate this model, the technique is called simulation. (This definition lacks the precision that the professional operations researcher would require, but it is adequate for the needs of the financial executive.)

As a tool applied to management problems, simulation is comparatively new. Its development and application are closely tied to the development and application of computer technology. It has been used to study complex problems in military strategy, traffic control, machine loading and process control that do not lend themselves to solution by mathematical programming and other optimization techniques.

Because simulation has generally been applied to the nonfinancial aspects of business, many financial executives are as yet unaware of it. Yet simulation has proved to be a powerful tool when applied to the planning process.

In almost everything we do the ultimate test of the adequacy of our decisions is the test of reality. But today business can seldom afford the luxury of testing the consequences of major decisions in the real world. Rather than determining the flight characteristics of a proposed missile by building and launching it, we now first simulate its performance on the basis of its design characteristics. In this way we can experiment without incurring the full cost of failure.

Similarly, in his role as planner, the executive is well aware of the magnitude of his investment decisions and the difficulty (sometimes the impossibility) of systematically evaluating all alternatives available to the company. He is also aware that he has at his disposal finite resources that have to be allocated among competing demands. Simulation techniques allow the businessman to examine the probable consequences of his decisions without the risk of real-life experimentation. They allow him to test the effects of his decisions on the whole corporation before these decisions are implemented.

Computers shorten the computational time period and thus permit repetitive use of the simulation model. This ability of the computer to compress the time needed to test the results of decisions makes experimentation much easier.

Management Science

Simulation is, of course, only one of a number of new mathematical techniques whose use has been facilitated by the availability of computers. During the past decade we have seen a growing recognition by management of

its need for newer and more sophisticated planning tools. Operations research and other techniques now frequently referred to as management
science have emerged to help satisfy that need. They are contributing new
skills to aid management in meeting the complexities of the decision making
process.

Not too long ago it was unusual to find a mathematician or statistician
working in management. We had grown accustomed to his presence in the
engineering department or the research laboratory, but we were surprised
when we found him attacking such operational problems as production
scheduling or inventory control. Now we even see him contributing to the
financial planning function in such areas as capital budgeting, sales forecasting, and investment analysis. We see operations research and management science departments on the organization charts of many of our more
progressive companies.

These professions, like all others, have developed their own characteristic
approaches, methodology, tools and techniques—decision theory, information theory, linear and dynamic programming and network analysis as well
as simulation. These are now being applied to an increasing array of complex business problems.

Many of these techniques offer significant potential for use in financial
planning. Simulation is particularly useful in this area because it can be
applied to problems that are too complex and have too many variables to
be reduced to optimization formulas. That is the reason we chose the simulation approach at Burroughs. It seemed to us the only means by which we
could cope with the complexity of the financial planning process in the level
of detail deemed essential while retaining the inherent flexibility needed to
accommodate change.

Simulation Model

A financial simulation model can be defined as a formal statement of the
relationships among the elements of a company's financial structure. Figure
1 illustrates what we term the "accounting dependencies" within the corporate structure of Burroughs. It has some similarity to our organizational
pattern in that the elements on the chart represent units of management responsibility and managerial control, but they are not necessarily described in
their organizational hierarchy. The figure reflects one aspect of our accounting practice—the way we consolidate. As such, it defines the framework of
our financial model.

Two key points in our concept of financial simulation are illustrated by
this figure. The first is the concept of modular construction. The total Burroughs model is actually a set of sub-models, one for each of the manage-

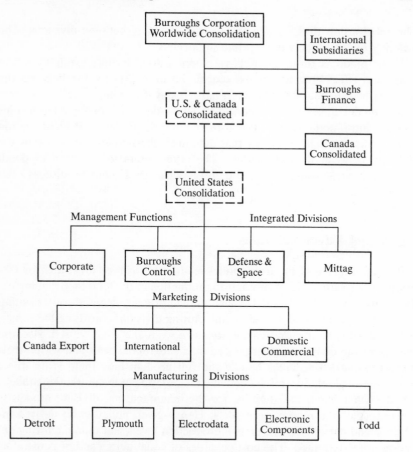

Figure 1. The "accounting dependencies" diagramed above define the framework of the model.

ment units shown. Specifically, we constructed individual models for each of these management units, expressing their output in accounting terms, and aggregated this output to produce the accounting consolidations indicated.

This design gives us the ability to identify and summarize the activities of each major corporate management unit. In addition, we can vary the form and level of detail between organizational units as a function of their inherent characteristics and their contribution to the planning process. Finally, the modular construction provides us with great model flexibility; it facilitates the introduction of worthwhile change to the program.

The second point we mean to illustrate in the figure is that there is a logical sequence that must be followed. This sequence depends on the structure of the business. The output of certain models forms the input for others.

The relationship thus created reflects the interplay between divisions. The ordering of the models is of prime importance.

If the model is to be an effective planning tool, it must explicitly reflect cause and effect both within the specific business process and between the business and the market in which it participates. In defining cause and effect in the model there are two considerations—the inter-model relationships and the intra-model detail. The former refers to the explicit identification of the cause and effect factors that determine the relationship and thus the ordering between the sub-models. The latter refers to the level of detail essential in structuring one of the sub-models per se. Let us discuss each of these factors.

Cause and Effect Relations

The importance of the inter-model relationship can be illustrated by discussing the relationship of demand to production in the total model complex. The marketing division models constitute the primary demand source within the total corporate model. The manufacturing divisions constitute the principal production source and capability since we make what we sell. Because the marketing divisions are organized on a geographic basis and within their respective marketing areas handle the full product line, there is no direct inter-divisional relationship influencing the ordering of the marketing models. On the other hand, the stimulus for the manufacturing division models is the output of the marketing models. Here—given policy as to desired inventory and capacity constraints—production levels and manufacturing expenses are determined. The cost penalties of constraints (and of constraints masquerading as policies) can also, often, be determined. This creates opportunity to assess the value of making changes. The models must specifically describe the form in which marketing demands are translated into production requirements both as a direct functional relationship, acknowledging the explicit interplay of company policy, and in terms of the time transformation represented in this relationship. The output of both the marketing models and the manufacturing models provides input to the "management" model where we determine financial capacity, taxes, etc.

A complex interaction exists among our various manufacturing facilities. While they are each primarily identified with a specific product, each acts as a sub-contractor for assemblies, sub-assemblies, or parts to the other manufacturing facilities. Obviously, with this type of interaction any decisions made by the marketing organizations which affect demand rate will influence in varying degrees each of the manufacturing divisions, even though the decision might affect only one product in a wide product line. In order to create a useful planning tool, the development of the sub-models must explicitly include a formal statement of this inter-model cause-effect relationship.

In the Burroughs Financial Simulation Model the manufacturing inter-divisional relation is accomplished by having the demand for all product lines carried to each manufacturing unit, even though they are primarily product organized, in order to acknowledge this inter-divisional relationship. The model itself does not allocate total capacity among products so as to maximize production efficiency. In other words, the production sites for the various products have been predetermined for any simulation run. If capacity of a given producing unit will not satisfy the generated demand, both primary and secondary, we do not automatically adjust the demand. Rather we determine the imbalance and generate a report which states the deficiency in terms of demand lost or added capacity required to satisfy the demand input.

During the development of our model we found it expedient to view the cause-effect relationship we have just illustrated in a serial fashion. A better understanding is obtained by viewing the process as continuous rather than as sequential. The marketing demand interacts in the manufacturing sectors with capacity constraints and inventory policy to generate a production requirement. When this production requirement is accepted and met, goods are provided to marketing to satisfy the demand. Pricing and other marketing policies then determine revenue potential. This, in turn, affects the capital position and debt level of the firm. The capital position in turn defines the limits for the marketing activity. The financial simulation model must reflect this feedback relationship explicitly or have some check and balance features incorporated to assure reasonable constraint.

Effects of Input Change

To illustrate the level of detail which we felt necessary to reflect in the simulation structure, we will trace the impact of a hypothetical change in input to our simulation model. Assume that we desire to evaluate the aggregate impact of a change in sales manpower in one of our marketing divisions. We have structured our demand forecast to be a function of the amount of direct sales manpower and a productivity function. In addition to evaluating the impact of the proposed manpower change through the relationship just identified, we explicitly evaluate the impact of the demand change on equipment and services revenue, cost of sales, and finished goods inventory. The impact of the demand change together with an inventory policy allows us to determine the resultant production requirement. This production requirement is an input in determining the in-process inventory. The determination of the production in-process activity provides the necessary stimulus for the determination of the sub-assembly and part manufacturing requirements, which in our model interact throughout the whole manufacturing sector. We must further relate this activity to its effect on variable, semi-variable, and fixed costs of manufacturing, which collectively affect the burden absorption functions. Marketing expenses and commissions, freight and shipping costs, and interest expense will be affected. The change will affect the tax provision, after-tax profits, accounts receivable, and liabilities. It will affect the equity section since dividends and retained earnings are both functions of net income. Indeed, it will be essential to evaluate the magnitude of funds required to carry out the suggested program which in itself has a feedback to marketing, where we began the illustration.

Process vs. Policy

Two categories of causative action are involved—one a function of the physical process, the other a matter of corporate policy. The establishment of an appropriate training pipeline to support a desired sales force represents a cause-effect relationship that is related to the "physical process" of the operation of the corporation; it also illustrates the introduction of a balancing and control mechanism on the marketing assumption. On the other hand, the inventory policy, which affects production requirements, is a reflection of corporate policy.

There is no pat answer to the choice of level of detail which must or should be represented within the simulation model. Nevertheless it is important that those specific considerations to which system performance is sensitive be separately identified and treated within the models. Certainly, all aspects of policy should be separately identified. The aggregation of details not only masks their individual impact but makes it difficult to use the results of the simulation; through lack of detail, precise responsibility for a change is unknown. Either condition makes it difficult to interpret an output of a simulation run for planning purposes. In creating a useful planning model, prudence cautions against presenting too much detail, but an excess of detail is preferable to over-aggregation.

We have discussed the kinds of effects on the corporate plan caused by introducing a single change of input to the marketing division sub-model. We have mentioned the complex functional relationships that are affected throughout the system. It is important to reemphasize that the complexity of this relationship is not only a functional interaction but is also compounded by a time dimension; the nature of the relationship explicitly changes as time passes. For example, expenditures for research and development are not expected to produce revenue in the same period. These expenditures are investments in future revenue. We could term R&D a "lead" factor. It is important that we know, or make assumptions about and test the sensitivity to, the exact form of this time translation. On the other hand, administrative expenses may follow changes in revenue and thus, in certain instances, could be classed as a "lag" function. In many situations the semi-variable costs in the manufacturing sector show "asymmetric" properties relative to changes in production volume. That is, changes in semi-variable costs may lead changes in production volume when they are increasing but lag changes in production volume in a down trend. These relationships must be derived. Their specific form is in most instances unique to a particular firm. It is essential that the relationships used in the model be adequately representative of the corporation's own processes.

A financial simulation model must not only reflect cause and effect within the firm and between the firm and its market. It must also be logically consistent with the financial practices of the firm and be a true representation of management policies and plans. These relationships are not simple—they are not God-given. To establish an adequate representation that will assure an effective planning tool requires a rigorous and continuous study program within the firm.

So far in our discussion we have used some language that may be peculiar to Burroughs' operations. It is not our intent, however, to emphasize our unique operating characteristics. The most important point is this: Since we have unique characteristics in our operations, our model must be structured to acknowledge and represent them. Furthermore, we are not unlike any other dynamic organization. The interactions within our corporate structure are complex. The relationships are varied. The importance of the planning process to our operations forced us to seek new tools. In order to use simulation techniques effectively, we had to establish a program which would result in a better understanding of our business in order that we could identify and quantify the essential cause-effect relationships and assure a realistic representation of management policies and their effect on the firm.

Uses of the Model

Because of the complexity of the interactions that take place within the firm, it is difficult if not impossible for a human to think through all of the ramifications in the systematic form demanded for proper planning. Without the assistance of the simulation technique, we would have an overwhelming computational task and a very nasty communications problem in trying to respond to today's demands for planning information. The simulation model lessens the communications problem through the definition and quantification of the relationships within the system. We cannot emphasize too strongly that you must be honest with yourself; you must learn about yourself and the way you do business; you must explicitly define and quantify the relationships applicable to your operation and your business. Otherwise a simulation model will produce uninteresting irrelevant or erroneous information.

Our experience has verified that financial simulation can add a new dimension to the planning process. Simulation provides flexibility by making is possible to generate a number of different plans quickly, easily and cheaply. By forcing management to define and to quantify the relationships existing within the system and the interactions among its elements, it brings into clearer focus the hidden determinants of policy and practice. By making automatic the process of tracing the effects of decisions throughout the system, it solves the problems of communication that exist within any dynamic and diversified organization. By integration with management information systems, it provides the potential for the development of feedback control systems. The following are some examples of the uses we have made of our financial simulation model:

At the Division Level

1. To learn the combined influence of independent decisions.
2. To improve decision making ability:
    a. To enforce discipline through formal relationships;
    b. To allow the testing of independent decisions;
    c. To point out problem areas;
    d. To point out some inconsistent areas in decision making.
3. To allow divisions to make several test runs before preparing their detailed forecasts.

At the Corporate Level

1. To learn the effect on the corporation of a proposed divisional plan.
2. To evaluate divisional "profit plans" and study alternative plans with respect to:
    a. Growth objectives;
    b. Asset management;
    c. Profit maximization;
    d. Cash flow.
3. To evaluate corporate decision alternatives.
4. To prepare long-range financial and debt management plans.

Clearly, financial simulation increases the effectiveness of the financial analyst. The responsible analyst has, of course, always been aware of the interactions among elements in the system and has considered these in the development of his projections. At the same time, however, he has been hampered by the restrictions placed on him by computational limitations.

He has had to ignore variables and relationships that he knew were important, simply because they could not be considered with the time and manpower resources he had available. He has been curious about the effects of altering certain basic assumptions but has never been able to test more than a few alternatives.

Today, burdened by increasing demands from top management, faced with more complex systems to analyze, and operating within the complex organizational and communications structure of a diversified corporation, the financial analyst needs the assistance that the technique of simulation can give him. Through the use of simulation, he acquires the potential for doing his job the way he has always wanted to do it.

Dos and Don'ts

Now that we have examined the concepts of a financial model and seen how financial simulation contributes to the planning process, it may be helpful to summarize what we have learned about setting up a simulation program and the steps that must be taken in its implementation.

Construction of a model is an expensive, time-consuming process and requires the cooperation of middle and some lower management across the organization. Without the active interest and participation of top management, the project is doomed to failure from the start. This fact is of primary importance.

A second ingredient essential to the success of the project is the joint participation of the operations research or management science staff and the corporate financial analysis group in the development of the model. This inter-disciplinary approach is necessary to provide a balance between simulation technique on the one hand and financial logic and knowledgeability on the other. In our case the operations research man acted as the hub of the simulation team. At the same time, participation by financial analysis guaranteed that the operations research techniques were not applied in a vacuum but were kept within the bounds of logical and meaningful financial relationships.

A fine measure of success of a financial simulation program is its actual use by management in the planning process. If executives' participation has been enlisted in the development of the model, they will become knowledgeable concerning the nature and use of the approach. They will understand how the model works, how to use the model to simulate various policies and plans, and how to interpret its output. This understanding on the part of managers and their willingness to participate adds realism to the model and facilitates its acceptance as an official corporate planning tool.

In developing a model, it is necessary to examine a multitude of data.

Sound research and financial logic are required in order to extract from the total information stream those data that reflect cause and effect. Initial efforts should be directed toward examining past research and making use of relationships previously developed and tested. Where previous research has not provided an adequate base for model design a research program must be initiated. If historical data are inadequate or judged not to be indicative of the future, one is forced to depend upon estimated relationships. Here the judgment of the informed manager is of great value in developing the necessary estimates.

After this approach has created an initial model, the model should be tested with actual data to measure the reasonability of its results. It is then modified and re-tested in a process continued until a simulation close enough to reality is obtained. No generalized criteria can be provided. What we are in fact doing is engaging in a formal validation procedure, to ensure that the model actually mirrors the corporate financial structure and that it truly reflects the effects of policies, plans and actions.

A financial model must be dynamic in nature. It must be periodically reworked in order to improve the precision with which functional relationships are stated, to incorporate the organizational changes that occur in any dynamic organization, and to reflect changes in accounting practice which could lead either to changes in established relationships or changes in the accounting structure of the model.

A simulation model, like anything else in life, can always be improved. We can simulate, test, modify and simulate again, until we get as close to reality as we wish. However, in expending this effort, we should try to strike a happy and acceptable balance between realism on the one hand and cost, time and complexity of the model on the other.

In guarding against over-simulation, however, we should not go to the other extreme of oversimplification. For then the accuracy and the realism of the model are destroyed, and the effort expended becomes a costly exercise in futility.

The Planning Problem

The effort is worthwhile, for corporate planning—in particular, long-range planning—is a complex and difficult task. It requires sophistication and know-how on the part of the corporate executive who must formulate the corporate policies and plans that determine the future course of his organization.

The planning function is, first of all, a complex process. The executive is seeking to identify the alternatives available and assess their relative worth. The identification of reasonable alternatives is in itself a time consuming task, requiring the executive to sift through and analyze volumes of information. The determination of the relative desirability of these alternatives is made more difficult because of the element of uncertainty about the future within which each has been cast.

Uncertainty and change must be acknowledged as paramount forces to be coped with in the planning process. The balance between the need to make decisions and take action and the need for flexibility to permit adaptation to change remains a matter of judgment.

Changes are not only external. The organization, through expansion and diversification, may become more complicated as well. The economic environment, the acceptance of the company's product in the market place, and the company's cost of doing business are all affected in subtle but powerful ways by the complex interactions taking place between the enterprise on the one hand and government, labor, competition and consumer demand on the other.

In addition to being complex, the planning process is a difficult one, increasingly so because of the shrinkage of time allowed the executive for response. As he attempts to cope with the complexities of his environment, the executive finds that his traditional patterns of decision making are breaking down in the face of ever increasing demands for faster reaction times. He recognizes the need for new planning tools to assist him in his planning role.

Traditionally, management has relied upon the financial segment of the organization for counsel in formulating plans. All activities have cost consequences. Hence, regardless of who else takes part in planning, the financial staff is an essential participant.

Top executives recognize the importance of the financial ramifications of planning. They are aware that decisions on budgets, appropriations, new product development, plant acquisition and resource allocations made anywhere within the corporate structure have a far-reaching effect on the total fabric of the organization. They realize that policies and plans to achieve desired corporate objectives are embodied in these decisions.

Today we find the role of the financial manager in a corporation to be of primary importance. The financial manager is being asked to share the increased planning burden, to produce more planning exercises, to explore more alternatives, to provide information in greater detail and most significantly, to respond more rapidly.

The financial manager enjoys the confidence of top management because of his contribution to the planning process. The financial people have dedicated themselves to the development of technical competence and the accumulation of the experience necessary to act as consultants and advisors to top management. They have evolved accounting systems and analytical tools to aid them in performing this function.

The pressures under which the financial manager must now operate are obviously not due to any decrease in his capability. Instead, they stem from the increased demands now being put upon him by top management. The problem facing the financial manager, then, is only in relatively small part that of developing new theory, for the existing body of theory has proved generally adequate. Instead, he must acquire new tools, tools that are appropriate to his changing planning environment, tools that permit him to respond more quickly, more flexibly and with greater accuracy and precision to requests from top management.

An attempt to use the traditional management structure of the corporation for financial planning creates significant communications problems that do not satisfy the executive response requirements. If management finds it necessary to communicate with all echelons and activities in order to determine the ramifications of a single "I wonder what would happen if" condition, the planning potential of the organization is limited. Yet relying solely on the experience of executives around the board room table does not satisfy today's need for explicit and systematic testing of the impact of change.

In financial simulation we have the potential for an effective solution to this problem. If a sound program—based upon top management participation, an interdisciplinary approach, and a thorough preliminary study phase —is established, this potential can be realized.

The structuring of a financial model is a difficult and sensitive task. We must learn and understand a great deal about the behavior of our organizations before we can produce workable and meaningful models. There is no cheap way to buy the tool. There is no such thing as a general financial simulation model that will act as an effective planning tool for a specific organization. There are no general equations applicable to every organization. While some equations in functional form can be expressed so as to be universal, their real value is in providing a guide for study and development. Even if our study provides a validation of their applicability we have, in fact, developed our own.

Thus, Burroughs' experience and Burroughs' model are hardly to be taken as universal. Indeed, our experience may not even provide an adequate sample from which to state a set of hard and fast rules. However, our experience has been sufficient to identify some important dos and don'ts. And this description of the relationships and circumstances that have produced an effective planning model may be useful as a general guide to those interested in applying the technique.

Additional Selected Readings

EDP and The Accountant

Boyle, Edwin T., "What the Computer Means to the Accounting Profession," *The Journal of Accountancy,* Vol. CXXI, No. 1, January, 1966, pp. 56–67.

Burrill, John C., "Training Accounting Personnel for EDP Systems," *Management Accounting,* Vol. XLVIII, No. 1, Sec. 1, September, 1966, pp. 12–16.

Carey, John L., "CPA's: Leaders or Losers in ADP?" *CPA* (American Institute of CPA's) Vol. XLIV, September, 1964, p. 4.

d'Agapeyeff, A., "The Accountant's Attitude to Computers," *The Journal of Accountancy,* Vol. CIXX, No. 3, March, 1965, pp. 64–66.

Editorial, "The Computer Revolution," *The Journal of Accountancy,* Vol. CIXX, No. 4, April, 1965, pp. 31–32.

Golding, Jordan L., "Accountant and the EDP Installation Responsibilities Apart from Audit Considerations," *Massachusetts CPA Review,* Vol. XXXVII, April-May, 1964, pp. 184–190.

Jasper, Harold W., "Future Role of the Accountant," *Management Services,* Vol. III, No. 1, January-February, 1966, pp. 51–56.

Johnson, John E., "Electronic Data Processing as it Affects the Accountant," *NAA Bulletin,* Vol. XLV, No. 4, Sec. 1, December, 1963, pp. 41–48.

Joplin, Bruce, "Can the Accountant Manage EDP?," *Management Accounting,* Vol. XLIX, No. 3, Sec. 1, November, 1967, pp. 3–7.

Rice, L. W., "Computers: the Challenge to Industrial Accountants," *Cost Accountant* (Eng.) Vol. XLII, October, 1964, pp. 357–69.

Stonier, K. Brian, "Influence of Electronic Data Processing Upon the Accountant, Accounting Thought and Practice," *Australian Accountant,* Vol. XXXII, December, 1962, pp. 653–60.

Toan, Arthur B., Jr., "Data Processing, Accounting, and Business Administration," *The Journal of Accountancy,* Vol. CIV, No. 5, November, 1962, pp. 43–49.

Tufer, Armin C., "Accounting Implications of Non-accounting Computer Applications," (In Haskins and Sells. *Selected Papers,* 1962, pp. 374–79).

Wright, M. G., "Accountant's Part in Computer Developments," *Accountants Journal* (Eng.) Vol. LVI, January, 1964, pp. 26–29.

Basic Computer Concepts

American Standards Association, "Standard Vocabulary for Information Processing," *Journal of Data Management,* Vol. II, November, 1964, pp. 22–38.

Boutell, W. S., "Business-Oriented Computers: A Frame of Reference," *The Accounting Review,* Vol. XXXIX, April, 1964, pp. 305–11.

————, "Problem-Oriented Languages: FORTRAN vs. COBOL," *Management Services,* Vol. III, No. 3, May-June, 1966, pp. 41–48.

Auditing

Arkin, Herbert, "Computers and the Audit Test," *The Journal of Accounting,* Vol. CXX, No. 4, October, 1965, pp. 44–48.

Baurle, F. C., "Case Study of a Computer Audit Program; a Description of the Use of a Magnetic Tape Computer System to Perform Certain Time-Consuming Audit Procedures," *Price Waterhouse Review,* Vol. VIII, Spring 1963, pp. 46–49.

Boni, Gregory M., "Impact of Electronic Data Processing on Auditing," *The Journal of Accountancy,* Vol. CXIV, No. 3, September, 1963, pp. 39–44.

Boutell, Wayne S., "Auditing Through the Computer," *The Journal of Accountancy,* Vol. CXX, No. 5, November, 1965, pp. 41–47.

Broncek, Gerald R., "An Automated System for Internal Audit and Control," *Management Services,* Vol. IV, No. 3, May-June, 1967, pp. 20–29.

Connolly, James J., "Case Study of a Computer Audit Program; An Application of a Computer to a Traditional Audit Procedure in a Steamship Company," *Price Waterhouse Review,* Vol. VIII, Winter, 1963, pp. 42–46.

Danehower, G. N., "Automation, EDP, and the Internal Auditor," *Internal Auditor,* Summer, 1964, pp. 43–54.

Davis, Gordon B., "The Auditor and the Computer," *The Journal of Accountancy,* Vol. CXXV, No. 3, March, 1968, pp. 44–47.

Denz, Ronald F., "Auditing the Data Processing Department," *DPMA Quarterly,* April, 1967, pp. 24–44.

Dill, Leland S. and Donald P. Adams, "Automated Auditing," *The Journal of Accountancy,* Vol. CXVII, No. 5, May, 1964, pp. 54–59.

Golding, Jordan L., "The Nonauditing Aspects of EDP Installations," *The Journal of Accountancy,* Vol. CXVIII, No. 1, July, 1964, pp. 43–46.

Hamman, Paul E., "The Audit of Machine Records," *The Journal of Accountancy,* Vol. CI, No. 3, March, 1956, pp. 56–61.

Harvey, J. H., and P. M. McCollum, "Automated Internal Auditing Tools," *Management Accounting,* Vol. XLVII, No. 2, Sec. 1, October, 1965, pp. 44–50.

Kanter, Jerome, "Can Systems Men and Auditors Work Together?," *Financial Executive*, Vol. XXXI, August, 1963, pp. 26–28.

Kaufman, Felix, "Using EDP as an Audit Tool," (In Institute of Internal Auditors. *Proceedings 22nd International Conference 1963*, pp. 68–72).

Pain, George R., "A Case Study in Auditing A Medium Scale Computer Installation," *Management Accounting*, Vol. XLVII, No. 12, Sec. 1, August, 1966, pp. 55–63.

Pelej, Joseph, "How Will Business Electronics Affect the Auditor's Work?," *The Journal of Accountancy*, Vol. XCVIII, No. 1, July, 1954, pp. 36–44.

Seitz, Philip, "Auditing Electronic Data Processing Systems," *Illinois Certified Public Accountant*, Vol. XVII, June, 1955, pp. 42–48.

Shontig, Daniel M., and Leo D. Stone, "Audit Techniques for Electronic Systems," *The Journal of Accountancy*, Vol. CVI, No. 4, October, 1958, pp. 54–61.

Toan, Arthur B., Jr., "Auditing, Control, and Electronics," *The Journal of Accountancy*, Vol. XCIX, No. 5, May, 1955, pp. 40–45.

———, "The Auditor and EDP," *The Journal of Accountancy*, Vol. CIX, No. 6, June, 1960, pp. 42–46.

Internal Control

Joplin, H. Bruce, "Internal Control Checklist for EDP," *Management Services*, Vol. I, No. 4, July-August, 1964, pp. 32–37.

Kaufman, Felix, "Effects of EDP on Internal Control," *The Journal of Accountancy*, Vol. CXI, No. 6, June, 1961, pp. 47–59.

Lueth, Wesley A., "Organizing EDP for Internal Control," *NAA Bulletin*, Vol. XXXXIV, No. 5, Sec. 1, January, 1963, pp. 39–40.

Porter, W. Thomas, Jr., "A Control Framework for Electronic Systems," *The Journal of Accountancy*, Vol. CXX, No. 4, October, 1965, pp. 56–63.

———, "Evaluating Internal Controls in EDP Systems," *The Journal of Accountancy*, Vol. CXVIII, No. 2, August, 1964, pp. 34–40.

Schlosser, Robert E. and Donald C. Bruegman, "Effect of EDP on Internal Control," *Management Services*, Vol. I, No. 2, March-April, 1964, pp. 44–51.

Schrey, Jack W., "Internal Control and EDP—A Company's Experience," *NAA Bulletin*, Vol. XLVI, No. 3, Sec. 1, November, 1964, pp. 49–53.

Systems and Systems Planning

Bower, James B., and J. Bruce Sefert, "Human Factors in Systems Design," *Management Services*, Vol. II, No. 6, November-December, 1965, pp. 39–50.

Christoph, T. G., "Organization of Systems Work: Review and Preview," *Management Services*, Vol. III, No. 3, May-June, 1966, pp. 32–35.

Doherty, Philip A. and Justin G. F. Wollaston, "Effective Management of a Systems Project," *Management Services*, Vol. II, No. 2, March-April, 1965, pp. 22–31.

Dykeman, Frank C., "New Techniques for a Management Information System," *Financial Executive*, Vol. XXXIV, No. 3, March, 1966, pp. 46–52.

Gargiulo, Granville R., "Use of CPM in Systems Installation," *Management Accounting*, Vol. IV, No. 3, May-June, 1967, pp. 30–38.

Goddard, V. K., "Three Steps to Systems Analysis," *Journal of Data Management*, Vol. II, No. 9, September, 1964, pp. 38–41.

Greco, Joseph A., "Comments on the Structural Check of Input Data in a Computer System," *The Journal of Accountancy*, Vol. CXXV, No. 6, June 1968, pp. 46–52.

Guest, L. C., Jr., "Meeting the Challenge of 'Information Systems'," *Financial Executive*, Vol. XXXIV, No. 8, August, 1966, pp. 44–51.

Harrelson, Fred A., Jr., "Document Your Data Processing Systems," *Management Accounting*, Vol. XLIX, No. 1, Sec. 1, September, 1967. pp. 43–49.

Kozik, Eugene, "Computer Augmentation of Managerial Reasoning," *Management Accounting*, Vol. XLVIII, No. 4, Sec. 1, December, 1966, pp. 35–43.

Krafft, J. Edward, "A Payback Approach to an Integrated Business System," *Management Accounting*, Vol. XLIX, No. 1, Sec. 1, September, 1967, pp. 50–54.

Li, David H., "A Structural Check of Accounting Input Data in a Computer System," *The Journal of Accountancy*, Vol. CXXIII, No. 6, June, 1967, pp. 54–57.

McRae, T. W., "Self-Checking Number Codes: An Aid to Accurate Accounting Reports," *The Journal of Accountancy*, Vol. CXVIII, No. 2, August, 1964. pp. 60–62.

Moravec, A. F., "Basic Concepts for Planning Advanced EDP Systems," *Management Services*, Vol. II, No. 3, May-June, 1965, pp. 52–60.

———, "Basic Concepts for Designing a Fundamental Information System," *Management Services*, Vol. II, No. 4, July-August, 1965, pp. 37–45.

Peirce, Richard F., "Functional vs. Multifunctional Data Processing Systems," *Management Accounting*, Vol. XLVI, No. 10, Sec. 1, June, 1965, pp. 9–13.

Rowe, Alan J., "Coming to Terms with Computer Management Systems," *Financial Executive*, Vol. XXXVI, No. 4, April, 1968, pp. 64–73.

Rudolph, Harley K., Jr., "Flow Charting—A Systems and Control Technique," *Management Service*, Vol. III, No. 5, September-October, 1966, pp. 24–30.

Schorr, Saadia, M., "Influence of the Computer on Business Information Systems," *Canadian Chartered Accountant*, Vol. LXXXIV, No. 2, February, 1964, pp. 125–9.

Schroeder, William J., Jr., "Toward A Documentless System of Inventory Control and Material Accounting," *Management Accounting*, Vol. XLVII, No. 4, Sec. 1, December, 1965, pp. 41–52.

Schubert, Richard F., "Systems Documentation," *Management Accounting*, Vol. XLIX, No. 1, Sec. 1, September, 1967, pp. 29–42.

Shultis, Robert L., "Are There Real-Time Financial Statements in Your Future?," *Management Accounting*, Vol. XLVIII, No. 12, Sec. 1, August, 1967, pp. 13–22.

Staats, Elmer B., "Information Systems in an Era of Change," *Financial Executive*, Vol. XXXV, No. 12, December, 1967, pp. 37–41.

Feasibility Studies

Boyce, L. Fred, Jr., "Installing a Medium-Sized Computer," *The Journal of Accountancy,* Vol. CX, No. 1, July, 1960, pp. 48–53.

Campise, J. A., "Using PERT to Plan a Computer Installation," *Journal of Data Management,* Vol. I, No. 7, December, 1963, pp. 12–16.

Kelley, Thomas J., and John R. Nolan, "EDP Feasibility Study," *Management Services,* Vol. I, July-August, 1964, pp. 48–54.

Sherwood, Peter W., "Is It Best to Buy, Lease, or Hire Your Computer?," *Office,* Vol. LIX, April, 1964, pp. 102–3, 192, et seq.

Wolf, E. D., "Rent or Buy?," *Management Services,* Vol. I, November-December, 1964, pp. 44–51.

Wright, Robert G., "Changing Concepts in EDP Feasibility Studies," *The Journal of Accountancy,* Vol. CXIII, No. 6, June, 1962, pp. 47–51.

EDP Systems and Management Concepts

Blank, Virgil F., "The Management Concept in Electronic Computers," *The Journal of Accountancy,* Vol. CXI, No. 1, January 1, 1961, pp. 59–66.

Brown, F. Harry, and Alfred H. Lovell, "Electronic Computer as a Management Tool," *New York Certified Public Accountant,* Vol. XXXIV, July, 1964, pp. 502–11.

Buge, Edward W., "Computers, Electronics, and Budgeting—A Challenge," *Budgeting,* Vol. XII, No. 5, May, 1964, pp. 2–3, 32.

Burstein, Herman, and Daniel V. Goodstein, "Using Statistical Sampling and Computers in Financial Analysis," *Management Services,* Vol. III, No. 1, January-February, 1966, pp. 23–28.

Hurni, M. L., "Some Implications of the Use of Computers in Industry," *The Accounting Review,* Vol. XXIX, No. 3, July, 1954, pp. 447–55.

Huskey, H. D., and V. R. Huskey, "New Frontiers in Business Management Control Are Being Established by Electronic Computers," *The Journal of Accountancy,* Vol. LXXXXIII, No. 1, January, 1952, pp. 69–75.

McLaughlin, William J., "EDP Contribution to a Manufacturing Operation," *Financial Executive,* Vol. XXXIV, No. 4, April, 1966, pp. 14–26.

O'Toole, Edward F., "Long-Range Planning and Top Management's Role in EDP," *Financial Executive,* Vol. XXXIV, No. 2, February, 1966, pp. 22–31.

Protzel, Harvey W., "What Top Management Should Expect from an Integrated Data Processing System," *Computers and Automation,* Vol. XIII, No. 9, September, 1964, pp. 12–15.

Shays, E. Michael, "The Feasibility of Real Time Data Processing," *Management Services,* Vol. II, No. 4, July-August, 1965, pp. 19–29.

Zimmer, Robert K., "On-Line Real Time Systems for Customer Service Operations," *Management Services,* Vol. IV, No. 5, September-October, 1967, pp. 25–32.

EDP and Business Organization

Brabb, George J., and Earl B. Hutchins, "Electronic Computers and Management Organization," *California Management Review,* Vol. VI, Fall, 1963, pp. 33–42.

Goodman, Edith Harwith, "Effects of Computers on Corporate Management," *Data Processing for Management,* Vol. V, January, 1963, pp. 11–22; February, 1963, pp. 19–26.

Grant, H. C., "Impact of Computers on Corporate Organization," *Canadian Chartered Accountant,* Vol. LXXXII, April, 1963, pp. 276–9.

Porter, W. Thomas, Jr., "Organization for Effective Information Flow," *Management Services,* Vol. II, No. 6, November-December, 1965, pp. 13–20.

Schwartz, M. H., "Organization and Administration of Electronic Data Processing Operations," *DPMA Quarterly,* Vol. I, No. 1, October, 1964, pp. 2–15.

Smith, W. Boyd, "Data Processing Management: Defining the Job," *Journal of Data Management,* Vol. I, No. 9, September, 1963, pp. 36–39.

Tuthill, Oliver W., "The Thrust of Information Technology on Management," *Financial Executive,* Vol. XXXIV, No. 1, January, 1966, pp. 18–29.

Whisler, Thomas L., "The Manager and the Computer," *The Journal of Accountancy,* Vol. CXIX, No. 1, January, 1965, pp. 27–32.

Ziessow, Bernard W., "Managing the Data Processing Operations," *Data Processing for Management,* Vol. V, No. 3, March, 1964, pp. 9–14.

Applications

Aiken, T. E., "Processing Our Payroll on the Univac," *N.A.C.A. Bulletin,* Vol. XXXVIII, No. 3, Sec. 1, May, 1957, pp. 1167–78.

Bean, Alan M., "Portfolio Analysis and Stock Selection by Computer," *Financial Executive,* Vol. XXXV, No. 2, February, 1967, pp. 26–37.

Bergwerk, "Data Processing for Small Business," *The Journal of Accountancy,* Vol. CXVI, No. 6, December, 1963, pp. 51–54.

Berkeley, Edmund C., "Uses of Automatic Computers in Financial and Accounting Operations," *Journal of Accountancy,* Vol. LXXXX, October, 1950, pp. 306–11.

———, "Uses of Automatic Computers in Financial and Accounting Operations," *The Journal of Accountancy,* Vol. LXXXX, No. 5, October, 1950, p. 306.

Besler, E. L., "Use of a Computer in Inventory Control—A Case Study," *Canadian Chartered Accountant,* Vol. LXXXIII, July, 1963, pp. 27–31.

Bill, Robert W., James K. Harrison, and Harry R. Maly, "An EDP System for Stores Inventory Control," *Management Accounting,* Vol. XLVIII, No. 12, Sec. 1, August, 1967, pp. 35–42.

Brown, Arthur A. and Leslie G. Peck, "How Electronic Machines Handle Clerical Work," *The Journal of Accountancy,* Vol. LXXXXIX, No. 1, January, 1955, pp. 31–37.

Deidrich, Andrew J., and Dale A. Denker, "Flexible Budgeting—A Proven Computer Application," *Management Accounting,* Vol. XLVII, No. 12, Sec. 1, August, 1966, pp. 18–24.

Graham, H. L., and D. C. Johnson, "An EDP System for Integrated Payroll," *Management Accounting,* Vol. XLVII, No. 12, Sec. 1, August, 1966, pp. 36–43.

Humbert, Harry O., "The Computer and Hospital Management," *Financial Executive*, Vol. XXXV, No. 1, January, 1967, pp. 43–49.

Jewett, Grandjean G., "The Distribution of Overhead with Electronic Calculators," *The Journal of Accountancy*, Vol. LXXXXVII, No. 6, June, 1954, pp. 698–701.

Kelley, William T., "Advertising Control: A Computer Application," *Management Services*, Vol. IV, No. 5, September-October, 1967, pp. 41–48.

Kircher, Paul, "Study of a Successful Computer System," *The Journal of Accountancy*, Vol. CIV, No. 4, October, 1957, pp. 59–65.

Kramer, Arthur M. and Lewis M. Weinstein, "How Computers Can Help the Retail Merchandiser," *Management Services*, Vol. III, No. 3, May-June, 1966, pp. 26–31.

McIlwain, Arnold P., "Utilizing EDP for Stock Material Inventory Transactions," *Management Accounting*, Vol. XLVIII, No. 12, Sec. 1, August, 1967, pp. 28–34.

McLaughlin, William J., "Data Processing in a Manufacturing Industry—A Case Study," *Management Accounting,* Vol. XLVII, No. 11, Sec. 1, July, 1966, pp. 41–51.

McNahoe, Eugene J., "Flexible Budgeting Through Electronic Data Processing," *Management Accounting*, Vol. XLVII, No. 7, Sec. 1, March, 1966, pp. 9–16.

Manes, Rene Pierre, "Using Computers to Improve Distribution of Service Costs," *The Journal of Accountancy*, Vol. CXIV, No. 3, March, 1963, pp. 57–60.

Nichols, John R., "An Accounts Payable Application of EDP," *Management Accounting*, Vol. XLVII, No. 7, Sec. 1, March, 1966, pp. 17–33.

Parks, William H., "Simplified Inventory Control for Computer," *Financial Executive*, Vol. XXXVI, No. 5, May, 1968, pp. 86–93.

Rubinfien, David, "Automation of Bank-check Accounting," *The Journal of Accountancy*, Vol. CIII, No. 3, March, 1957, pp. 41–47.

Sasanecki, L. James, "Introduction to EDP—Controlled Inventory," *Management Services*, Vol. IV, No. 6, November-December, 1967, pp. 34–39.

Smith, Robert M., "Automated Inventory—Production Control," *Management Services*, Vol. II, No. 4, September-October, 1965, pp. 18–25.

_____, "How to Automate a Hospital," *Management Services*, Vol. III, No. 4, July-August, 1966, pp. 48–53.

Solomon, Sid J., "Making Accounts Receivable Processing More Automatic," *Management Services*, Vol. III, No. 5, September-October, 1966, pp. 48–51.

Swearingen, J. K., "Financial Systems on Univac 1," *Journal of Machine Accounting Systems and Management*, Vol. IX, March, 1958, pp. 4–7, 36–37, 39.

Swyers, William E., "A Computerized Approach to Timekeeping," *Management Accounting*, Vol. XLVII, No. 2, Sec. 1, October, 1965, pp. 25–31.

_____, "Employee Compensation Accounting in a Total Information System," *Management Accounting*, Vol. XLVII, No. 11, Sec. 1, July, 1966, pp. 11–19.

Vallario, Anthony A., "An Inventory Control System With Profitable By-Products," *Management Services*, Vol. IV, No. 1, January-February, 1967, pp. 31–36.

Weinberg, Seymour, "Order Handling—A Computer Application for Small Companies," *Management Accounting,* Vol. XLVII, No. 12, Sec. 1, August, 1966, pp. 44–48.

Service Bureaus

Broucek, Gerald R., "Computer Operation by a CPA Firm," *The Journal of Accountancy,"* Vol. CIX, No .6, June, 1960, pp. 47–50.

Coleman, David, and Theodore Cohn, "Some Specialized Uses of Data Processing Centers," *Management Services,* Vol. II, No. 5, September-October, 1965, pp. 40–46.

Crovatto, Raymond A., "Data Processing for Small Clients," *The Journal of Accountancy,* Vol. CX, No. 6, December, 1960, pp. 57–62.

Lennox, John E., "The Accounting Service Bureau: One CPA's Experience," *The Journal of Accountancy,* Vol. CXVIII, No. 5, November, 1964, pp. 49–54.

Lewis, Rolf F., "Data Processing Centers and the CPA," *The Journal of Accountancy,* Vol. CXII, No. 1, July, 1961, pp. 45–51.

Lundy, Todd S., "The Use of Data Processing in the Accountant's Office," *The Journal of Accountancy,* Vol. CXXI, No. 3, March, 1966, pp. 33–42.

Puder, Richard K., "Local Practitioners Can Use Computers," *The Journal of Accountancy,* Vol. CXIV, No. 1, July, 1962, pp. 47–52.

Robertson, Wilson A., "Make Friends With Your Computer," *Management Accounting,* Vol. XLVII, No. 3, Sec. 1, November, 1965, pp. 30–34.

Shein, Stanley, "A Practical Data Processing Application for a Small Business," *Management Services,* Vol. III, No. 6, November-December, 1966, pp. 40–44.

Smith, Robert M., "Accounting–EDP Center," *Management Services,* Vol. II, No. 3, May-June, 1965, pp. 34–44.

Vannais, Leon E., "Service Centers and the CPA," *The Journal of Accountancy,* Vol. CVII, No. 2, February, 1959, pp. 47–59.

Simulation

Harty, James D., and George W. Plossl, "Inventory Management Simulation," *DPMA Quarterly,* Vol. II, No. 2, January, 1966, pp. 16–35.